Weathering the Psalms

Weathering the Psalms

A Meteorotheological Survey

STEVE A. WIGGINS

CASCADE *Books* • Eugene, Oregon

WEATHERING THE PSALMS
A Meteorotheological Survey

Copyright © 2014 Steve A. Wiggins. All rights reserved. Except for brief quotations in critical publications or reviews, no part of this book may be reproduced in any manner without prior written permission from the publisher. Write: Permissions. Wipf and Stock Publishers, 199 W. 8th Ave., Suite 3, Eugene, OR 97401.

Cascade Books
An Imprint of Wipf and Stock Publishers
199 W. 8th Ave., Suite 3
Eugene, OR 97401

www.wipfandstock.com

ISBN 13: 978-1-62564-777-1

Cataloguing-in-Publication Data

Wiggins, Steve A.

    Weathering the Psalms : a meteorotheological survey

    xiv + 188 p. ; 23 cm. Includes bibliographical references.

    ISBN 13: 978-1-62564-777-1

    1. Bible. Psalms—Criticism, interpretations, etc. 2. Weather—Bible. 3. Theophanies in the Bible. I. Title.

BS1430.52 W54 2014

Manufactured in the U.S.A.   12/02/2014

Parts of chapter 3, The Wind, appeared as "Tempestuous Wind Doing Yhwh's Will: Perceptions of the Wind in the Psalms," *Scandinavian Journal of the Old Testament* 13/1 (1999) 3–23. Used with the permission of *SJOT*.

To Kietra
The harbinger of sunny skies

Contents

Preface | *ix*
Acknowledgments | *xi*
List of Abbreviations | *xiii*

Introduction | 1

CHAPTER ONE
Ancient Weather, Ancient Poetry: Parameters and Possibilities | 11

CHAPTER TWO
The Thunderstorm | 22

CHAPTER THREE
The Wind | 62

CHAPTER FOUR
Rain and Clouds | 82

CHAPTER FIVE
Hail, Snow, Frost, Rime, and Dew | 120

CHAPTER SIX
Temperature | 140

CHAPTER SEVEN
Synthesis and Development | 151

Afterword | 160
Bibliography | 163
Ancient Documents Index | 183

Preface

No author likes to admit his or her work is out-of-date. I have worked in the publishing industry long enough now, however, to realize that few books are not dated by the time they appear; it is only a matter of degree. This book was completed in 2002. I was an associate professor and academic dean at Nashotah House Theological Seminary at the time. The seminary is framed around a monastic model that included required attendance at daily prayers, those medieval vehicles for reciting the Psalter. During a spate of severe weather in that context, the present book was conceived and written.

Then the wheel of misfortune turned. I lost the first, and to date only, full-time academic job I ever held. The book was complete but unpublished. I very much wished to revisit it, but as any of my fellow full-time adjunct instructors know, research time is limited when you are teaching eleven courses a year. Once I moved into publishing, the research was even more difficult with no access to a research library and even less time than an adjunct for actually conducting research. So the book manuscript languished as my career came to look and feel like the radical turbulence inside a thundercloud. Colleagues, however, continued to encourage me to publish the work. I held out, believing a teaching post would once again materialize and I would be able to make all the changes from what I had subsequently learned. This never happened. Meanwhile, no other book appeared that attempted to do what I had set out to accomplish, however, meagerly.

No doubt the book would be very different if I had written it today. As I formatted it for publication, however, the temptation to rewrite what seemed like overly general and timid assertions—the marks of the young scholar who wrote it—had to be resisted. Although works directly on this topic have not appeared, enough new material had been churned out of the ever-turning academic presses, that I knew a revision here and an updating there would consequently lead to the book languishing away yet again for several more years. I chose to seek a publisher because there is much useful information included in this study. Not the most elegant or eloquent, but if I did not publish it, it was certain to be lost. Several readers of the material offered suggestions for substantial changes since it was not clear what my objective had been. In different circumstances I may have heeded them.

What was I trying to do? In a word, meteorotheology. I have never considered myself a theologian, but the weather terminology of the Bible has such a striking theological presence that I felt it merited its own nomenclature. I wished to clarify infelicities in translations of Psalms I read. Although "hurricane" is a poetic word, for example, Israel has never experienced one. What exactly is a tempest? How did the weather function? To my mind at the time, side-by-side comparison seemed the best way to bring this out. I divided the weather into component phenomena, translated every verse where they appeared, and summarized the functions. During the course of this investigation it became clear that some difficulties in translating some of the Psalms could be resolved, or at least enlightened, by proper attention to the weather terms, in short, meteorotheology.

This was meant to be the start of a larger research agenda—the agenda that is the luxury of only those who have managed to find full-time teaching or research positions. Since I had been excluded from those professions, I wanted to give back the results of several years of research so that others, if so inclined, might take it further. There is a thesis, certainly stronger than I was able to present it in this kind of survey, underlying the work. That thesis will not be articulated fully until this kind of exercise is expanded to other parts of the Hebrew Bible. The occasional article or very rare monograph on a similar topic that have appeared since this study was written demonstrated that others had noticed there was something here as well. I could not incorporate these new studies without beginning the work all over again. Although it may be dated, the data are sound. When I wrote this book internet research was in its infancy and some of the statements made below will reflect that. The web has become a vast resource for information on the weather, but the sun still shines on the wicked and good alike. Some aspects of life will never change.

The Psalms continue to be among the most read and recited parts of the Bible. We owe it to ourselves to delve into their original contexts and let them speak.

Acknowledgments

A book such as this requires much assistance, especially when undertaken at a seminary that does not have the benefit of a meteorology department! My wife Kay and daughter Kietra never ceased believing in my ability to complete this task and kept me firmly footed in reality while undertaking it. Kay was unstinting with her time in assisting me with French translation and proofreading. Kietra, now a computer engineering student at Binghamton University, resolved a vexing technical issue regarding Hebrew fonts that would soon have left me hairless and in deep despair. It would be impossible for me to conceive a more deserving person for the dedication of this book.

Professor Joseph Kucharski, a fellow faculty member in my time at Nashotah House and fellow weather enthusiast, has from the beginning encouraged me to press on with this idea, and always discussed it with animation when my zeal flagged. The entire project was initially undertaken at his suggestion. Mention should also be made of Neal Stephenson, my brother-in-law. Neal took an active interest in the larger picture of the implications of this study, and in a couple of conversations (often punctuated by the pressing concerns of our respective children) helped me to clarify my thinking on some of the points I was making. That was so long ago, I'm sure he has forgotten.

Four very able library assistants at Nashotah House, Leigh Ann Barnett, Amy Townsend, Emily Rowe, and Vicki Terry, skillfully and with good humor sought out rare sources of a kind never before requested by interlibrary loan at the seminary. Dr. Reid Bryson of the Center for Climatic Research at the University of Wisconsin, Madison, kindly supplied me with offprints of sources of which I would have been otherwise ignorant. Amos Porat and Avner Furshpan of the Climatology Branch of the Israel Meteorological Service mailed me relevant data and pointed me to further sources for the climate of modern-day Israel. Dr. Alexander Jones of the University of Toronto corresponded with me concerning the state of studies on Ptolemy's *Geography*, a document intimidating in its complexity to a non-specialist, but vital to Psalm 68.

Professor Nicolas Wyatt, my doctoral advisor and true friend, has been the steady source of support through all of my career and encouraged me in this project, even though I never sent it to him for review, as I probably should have.

Dr. Mark S. Smith of New York University pointed out two important bibliographic items and offered me his feedback in the early stages of this project.

Dr. Mayer Gruber of Ben-Gurion University of the Negev encouraged me at several points, and supplied me with contacts and references to establish current understanding of the climate of Israel.

Dr. David Stephenson, retired from Iowa State University (and also my father-in-law), discussed some of the scientific aspects of this study with me during the writing up of my research, enhancing my understanding.

Dr. Thomas Guback, retired from the University of Illinois, a longtime friend and one-time student, raised with me the related issue of nature in the Psalms, which led me in a direction necessary to lay some of the basic groundwork for this study.

The members of the Milwaukee area Hebrew Bible reading group were encouraging in my academic development, unfortunately cut short, and Drs. Bruce Malchow and Lawrence Sinclair suggested some further sources for my consideration of this project.

Dr. Brent Strawn, of Candler School of Theology, effectively resurrected my interest in this project after it had lain dormant for a decade. He encouraged to me continue seeking a publisher. Dr. Andrew Mein of Westcott House, the University of Cambridge, graciously read the manuscript and made suggestions, which, in a perfect—or at least better—world, I should have been glad to integrate. Time, although relative, is also non-negotiable. If time were different, my friend! Dr. Robin Parry of Wipf and Stock was encouraging from the beginning of this renewed interest in publication. I am grateful for his help and support in seeing the book to fruition.

Professor Niels Peter Lemche recognized the worth of this project early by accepting a preliminary version of chapter three for publication in the *Scandinavian Journal for the Study of the Old Testament*. He also was instrumental in acquiring permission to reuse some of that material in this study.

To each of these people I express my profound gratitude, and I hope that their encouragement will have proved fruitful in the production of a worthwhile resource for future students of the topic. Any errors or infelicities, of course, remain my own.

Abbreviations

ABD   *Anchor Bible Dictionary*, 6 vols. D. N. Freedman, ed.
AJBA   *Australian Journal of Biblical Archaeology*
AnOr   Analecta Orientalia
ATR   *Anglican Theological Review*
BAMS   *Bulletin of the American Meteorological Society*
BDB   Brown Driver Briggs Hebrew-English Lexicon
BHS   Biblia Hebraica Stuttgartensia
BN   Biblische Notizen
BTB   Biblical Theology Bulletin
CB   Coniectanea Biblica
CRB   Cahiers de la Revue Biblique
DCH   *Dictionary of Classical Hebrew*, D. J. A. Clines, ed.
DDD   *Dictionary of Deities and Demons in the Bible*, K. van der Toorn, B. Becking and P. W. van der Horst, eds. 2nd ed.
ECW   *Encyclopedia of Climate and Weather*, S. H. Schneider, ed.
ETR   Études Théologiques et Religieuses
GKC   Gesenius, Kautzsch. Cowley, *Gesenius' Hebrew Grammar*
HB   Hebrew Bible
ICA   *International Cloud Atlas*, 2 vols. (World Meteorological Organization, Geneva)
JSJ   *Journal for the Study of Judaism*
JTS   *Journal of Theological Studies*

KBS	*The Hebrew and Aramaic Lexicon of the Old Testament*, 5 vols., L. Koehler, W. Baumgartner, J. J. Stamm, eds.
KTU	*Keilschrift Texte aus Ugarit*
LXX	Septuagint
MT	Masoretic Text (Hebrew text of the Hebrew Bible)
OTS	Oudtestamentische Studiën
SJT	*Scottish Journal of Theology*
StTh	*Studia Theologica*
TZ	*Theologische Zeitschrift*
UBL	Ugaritisch-Biblische Literatur
VTS	Vetus Testamentum Supplement

Introduction

From the moment an atmosphere enveloped the nascent earth four billion years ago there has been weather. From the moment that the ancestors of *Homo sapiens* first took shelter from the rain, there has been weather observation. Weather is an unavoidable and important part of life. Weather is so deeply rooted in human experience that it has from the earliest times been associated with divinity.

Perhaps because of a general lack of comprehension of atmospheric dynamics in pre-scientific eras, the weather was frequently relegated to the realm of God or the gods. This "God of the gaps" thinking often persists even today in matters concerning the weather.[1] Why is it that the weather and the divine are brought together by ancients and moderns alike? While this question must remain rhetorical, there can be no doubt that the Bible presents evidence for one of the steps along the path of this cognitive journey.

As a pedestrian on this path, I found that my own experience brought me into this cognitive journey as well. This study was undertaken while my teaching position required worship twice daily, morning and evening prayer, in which the repetition of Psalms played a major role. This discipline brought into relief how the motif of the weather was omnipresent in the Psalms. During this time I discovered a book on the perception of the weather in American life which also became a generative element for this project.[2] Together these interests coalesced into a systematic study of how weather terminology was used by the psalmists. After an exploratory article was published,[3] it became obvious that this study was more than a series

---

1. A priest of my acquaintance routinely attributed fair weather to the direct intervention of saints on their calendrical dates. When I once asked him if he really believed this, he answered that he did. This was as recent as the year 2000.

2. Laskin, *Braving the Elements*. A similar book, concerned with British perceptions, is Janković, *Reading the Skies*.

3 Wiggins, "Tempestuous Wind Doing Yhwh's Will," 3–23.

of articles, and that it required the cohesion of a survey monograph. Like the atmosphere itself this topic could not be seen in one glance: a more comprehensive view was required.

PREMISES

The atmosphere above and around us is constantly changing; it is so fluid that it has become symbolic of the chaos theory of science in what is often called "the butterfly effect."[4] Chaos theory is relevant to the discussion of biblical weather as well, a subject that will be explored presently. Initially, however, some of the other premises underlying this monograph must be brought to the surface. A most basic premise of this study is that we are able to understand something about the weather. In this regard, this book relies heavily on recent studies in the field of meteorology.

Another basic premise is that there is some continuity of present weather with the weather of the Israel of the Bible. To discern what the weather of ancient Israel might have been will require some consideration of palaeoclimatology. This aspect will be considered briefly in chapter one. A further premise is that God-consciousness is related to the weather. Early West Asian cultures clearly attributed weather phenomena to divinities. Far from demythologizing this relationship, the ancient Israelites participated in a celebration of Yahweh's ability to control the weather. This study will examine this perception in depth in the context of the Psalms.

Being primarily a student of ancient sacred texts, I tend to eschew the designation of "theologian." Yet, as an advocate of the "history of religions" hermeneutic, I see a clear connection between these sacred texts, the weather, and an ancient theology. This connection might whimsically be termed "meteorotheology"—the theological understanding of the weather by the ancients. This study is not, however, an exercise in natural theology; rather, it demonstrates how nature was perceived by the psalmists and related by them to their religious worldview. I am not the first to try to explain the weather or meteorological phenomena in the Hebrew Bible,[5] nor am I the first to notice the weather as a motif in the Psalms.[6] This book is, however,

---

4. Gleick, *Chaos*, 9–31.

5. Dalman, *Arbeit und Sitte in Palästina*; Scott, "Meteorological Phenomena," 11–25; Stadelmann, *Hebrew Conception of the World*, 97–127; Orni and Efrat, *Geography of Israel*; Baly, *Geography of the Bible*, are some of the major sources.

6. Futato, *Meteorological Analysis*; I thank Mark S. Smith for pointing out this important source to me; Klingbeil, *Yahweh Fighting from Heaven*. See also Fitzgerald, *Lord of the East Wind*, published after this study was written.

a first attempt to treat the motif of the weather in the Psalms systematically and comprehensively, and to consider the scope of interpretations offered for the weather in the Psalms.

This study is more than a catalogue of weather terms as they appear in the Psalms. It may appear a strange hybrid: part hermeneutical and part lexical, part scientific and part textual, but it quickly becomes evident that the weather was a favorite metaphor with the psalmists and there is no single way to treat it. This powerful metaphor requires the application of both lexical groundwork and interpretive principles in order to be truly appreciated. The unavoidable conclusion that the weather had strong links to the ancient perception of the divine makes this a most fascinating field of exploration. As a survey, no strong thesis pervades this study. The responsibility of bringing what is known of science into the study of Scripture is a fraught, but necessary, enterprise.

One of the less obvious premises of this exploration is that biblical study has much to learn from science. Empirical method is how humans learn about the world, and throughout the history of religion science and the Bible have been uncomfortable together at best. Part of this is no doubt due to the ever-expanding horizons of science: people have a tremendous capacity to increase their knowledge by applying reason and empirical method. This expanding horizon has often clashed with the idea of realms of nature relegated to God's direct control. The Bible represents a fairly stable text; such texts, and especially their attendant faith systems, tend to be resistant to change. The issue is much larger than the present project, yet one of the premises assumed here is that biblical study benefits from the insights of science. The premise will be revisited in the conclusions to this monograph.

PURPOSE

The purpose of this study is to explore the meteorological language of the Psalms in the light of the current knowledge of and interest in the weather. As a student of the Hebrew Bible and the history of ancient religions with a persistent interest in meteorology, I have long noticed that these fields are related. This study arises out of the conviction that weather touches the very heart of ancient perceptions of the divine. Whether reflected in a crude idea of God in heaven, in the sky, or in an acknowledgment that weather is beyond human control, God is still often viewed as the ghost in the machine.[7] To understand the weather is somehow to glimpse the divine.

7 In the modern scientific worldview nature is often viewed as a machine. For the ancients, divine activity was ghostly in that it was unseen—they recognized the ghost

This monograph attempts to interpret how the weather was perceived by the psalmists. To fulfill this purpose, lexicographical issues must be considered. Biblical weather terms are often translated in inconsistent ways in modern translations, sometimes without regard to whether or not the meteorological phenomenon represented by a chosen term was known in ancient Israel. I have attempted to apply weather terminology which is as accurate as possible to the weather references in the Psalms. Another primary purpose of this book, however, is hermeneutical and exegetical. The contexts of weather terminology in the Psalms lead to a more precise understanding of how these terms are being used. The weather is never a neutral phenomenon in the Hebrew Bible, as will be demonstrated throughout this work. The interpretation of weather remains an important element which has never been systematically explored in the entire book of Psalms. Both of these biblical foci taken together shed some light on the history of religions aspect in which Yahweh and the weather interact.

This book is thus a cross-disciplinary study juxtaposing weather perception and the Psalms. It has been demonstrated by past and current scholarship that these fields are related.[8] Scholars have long recognized that the weather plays an important role in the Hebrew Bible, but it has seldom been the focus of a study specifically dedicated to it. To comprehend how the weather was perceived in the Hebrew Bible the evidence itself must be considered. At the risk of being accused of being Baconian in my method, the most obvious way to consider the evidence is simply to list and compare it. To this humble starting point, a theory of how the weather functions in the Bible must be added. This theory will be presented in the course of this introduction. In this book I have attempted to offer the results that such a theory can bring.

WHY SUCH A STUDY IS NECESSARY

What makes a study such as this necessary? The answer to this question lies rooted in the purposes for this study noted above. One of the objectives is in the service of translation. As guardians of the ancient Hebrew idiom who attempt to make sense of the text in a modern context, translators must attempt to be precise as possible. Vast strides have been made in meteorology

without the machine. The truly remarkable facet here is that scientifically inclined moderns continue to associate God with weather in an otherwise mechanized universe.

8. Most obviously in Futato, *Meteorological Analysis*, and Klingbeil *Yahweh Fighting from Heaven*. The royal psalms are explicitly connected to the weather in Gammie, "A New Setting for Psalm 110," 4–17.

since the advent of the computer. It has become obvious to me, even as an amateur meteorologist, that if weather language is used to represent the presence of God in some sense in the Bible, translators are obligated to be as precise as possible when translating that language. Since more precise terminology is available for describing the weather, and since climatological studies may help present-day students of the Bible better understand the weather in ancient Palestine, a study of the weather and the Bible suggests itself. New evidence is available in both Psalm studies and meteorological studies; together the Psalms and the weather present a compelling juxtaposition.

Climate, as the long-term pattern of weather, changes over time. This study is not properly an exercise in climatology; however, climatology informs our understanding of past settings and warns against the easy equation of how weather is today and how it was millennia ago.[9] What we are now able to determine about the weather of ancient Israel should allow us to discern how rare certain phenomena were in biblical times, and therefore we may assess their particular impact to a more precise degree.

With the entire known universe available to poets of the temple hymnary for rich imagery, the weather featured prominently among their motifs. It had an enduring quality as it appeared in both early and late psalms. With well over a hundred references to weather, it is evident that it was a favored literary image among psalmists. Awareness of the plenitude of meteorological references itself invites the exploration of how this imagery was used.

This study fills a void in the various cross-disciplinary approaches to the Bible which attempt to apply current scientific understandings to an ancient text. In the context of one of the many weather references in Ps 18, Kraus notes in his commentary: "We can no longer penetrate the great variety of the symbols of antiquity."[10] It is my contention that a great many of the weather symbols in the Psalms *can* be penetrated when placed in their larger context and compared with one another. A systematic survey such as this one allows the full weight of comparison to be applied to otherwise disparate references.

---

9. While not specifically climatology, a nevertheless dramatic example of how geological changes may have affected ancient religious ideas may be seen in the work of two oceanographers, Ryan and Pitman (*Noah's Flood*), who believe that they have discovered in Black Sea core samples, the antecedent to "Noah's flood"! For an example of a study which presupposes a constancy of weather in ancient Syria, see deMoor, *The Seasonal Pattern in the Ugaritic Myth of Baʻlu*.

10. Kraus, *Psalms 1–59*, 260.

A WORD ON SOURCES

An unusual dichotomy arose during the course of this study. While little was found in the area of biblical studies concerned with the climate and weather of ancient Israel, an ever-increasing volume of material was available in the field of meteorology. Meteorology, as science in general, has been constantly reevaluating and reinvestigating the world in which we live. Advances in science have made incredible amounts of information available to the interested layperson as well as to the specialist. The world-wide web has become the storehouse of so much raw data that an embarrassment of riches exists. Daily weather reports from Israel's major cities may be perused by reading the *Jerusalem Post* online, or by downloading the latest satellite loop from the Weather Channel pages. Resources from the World Meteorological Organization and the Israel Meteorological Service may be ordered from the web. Each passing day adds to climatic summaries and statistics. This is even more the case now that a number of years have passed since this text was originally written.

With such a wealth of information comes the prospect of being swiftly and absolutely proven wrong because of new developments. Such a risk, however, must be undertaken in order to describe adequately how the biblical writers perceived the weather. It appears to have been largely unexplored how the ancients were fascinated with and affected by the weather, just as current populations continue to be. As a mundane example, there were several days when work on this monograph had to be halted because of the danger that electric storms posed to costly computer components. Likewise, the ancients often found themselves the victims of natural phenomena from the skies. They, however, had a very different conception of what was happening. Often it is simply assumed by commentators that a deity had control of the weather, and little more needs to be said concerning it. From the amount of material I discovered in the course of this project, I believe that the biblical perception was more complex than it is sometimes believed to have been. This complexity bears investigation.

In the course of my research I often found myself resorting to "purely" biblical or "purely" meteorological sources, since the two have seldom coalesced in the past.[11] I admit at the outset that this monograph makes

---

11. One obvious exception is Futato, *Meteorological Analysis*, unfortunately never published. Scott's "Meteorological Phenomena" fills a gap in our knowledge, but it is nearly half of a century out-of-date. More recent, but still over forty years old, is Stadelmann's *Hebrew Conception of the World*, 97–126. Even the more recent Houtman, *Der Himmel im Alten Testament*, is a updated translation of a work dating to 1974 (see the preface, ix).

no pretense of being a comprehensive survey of everything written on the Psalms; far too much has been published for any one person to find or to read it all.[12] I did, however, seek out sources that discussed in any depth the phenomena under consideration in relationship to the Psalms. Such sources frequently based their translations of phenomena on out-dated meteorological observations or on biblical texts utilized as scientifically accurate. Nevertheless, these sources, which will be cited throughout this study, have been attempts to bring these two fields together. Such sources receive the lion's share of attention regarding the terminology since they were the most relevant among the vast resources on both disciplines of meteorology and the Psalms.

One source was somewhat misleadingly entitled *Weather and the Bible: 100 Questions and Answers*.[13] Although the title indicates its popular appeal, the source turned out to be a creationist apologetic for science. Although no information was found there for this study, it stands as a further illustration of how the modern mind still associates God with the weather. Much more useful was the dated but still relevant meteorological section of Philippe Reymond's monograph *L'eau, sa vie, et sa signification dans l'Ancient Testament*. Of a similar utility were R. B. Y. Scott's "Meteorological Phenomena and Terminology in the Old Testament," and the relevant pages of Luis Stadelmann's *The Hebrew Conception of the World*. Mark Futato's dissertation, "A Meteorological Analysis of Psalms 104, 65, and 29," began this kind of study with only three psalms. Futato, however, was interested in using the weather as an interpretative device for the whole of Psalms 104, 65, and 29, rather than examining how weather functioned in the Psalms as a whole. His dissertation attempts to demonstrate how the entirety of these three psalms is meteorologically significant, often finding interesting connections. His study thus leaves the majority of references unexplored. What I am presenting, however, is an analysis of all the actual, obvious references to weather in the Psalms.

Another, published, dissertation directly related to this topic is Martin Klingbeil's *Yahweh Fighting from Heaven*. As his sub-title (*God as Warrior and as God of Heaven in the Hebrew Psalter and Ancient Near Eastern Iconography*) indicates, Klingbeil also addresses the connection between weather and the divine. As with Futato, however, his purpose and results are quite different from those which I am presenting. Klingbeil is interested in

---

12. The honest scholar has to admit the dilemma posed by the necessity of publication. Each new generation has added an entire new layer of secondary literature to the primary sources. Familiarity with it all requires more than a lifetime of study, and, by definition, will soon be impossible.

13. Donald DeYoung.

correlating the metaphor of the "God of Heaven" in the Psalms with ancient West Asian iconography. His book shares some common ground with my study, but Klingbeil chooses portions of only eight psalms (18, 21, 29, 46, 65, 68, 83, and 144) and limits his meteorological discussion to its metaphorical usage. My approach is to treat the weather motif as a whole throughout the entire book of Psalms.

Another avenue which appeared promising at the outset was the "green" literature generated by the ecological movement from the 1960s onward. Perhaps the flagship of this approach was Richard Austin's *Hope for the Land: Nature in the Bible*.[14] This kind of approach, however, was also something very different from what I am attempting. The ecological method was an attempt to fit Scripture into a theological model. As much as I support the ecological cause, that is not my method here. A comprehensive study of how "natural phenomena" (as we would call them) were perceived and understood in the entire Hebrew Bible remains a desideratum. This book is a first, tentative step in such a comprehensive study. Hopefully this experimental method used on weather terminology in the Psalms will lead to other similar studies throughout the Bible.

A desideratum of anyone concerned with a precise understanding of the lexicography and perception of the physical world in ancient Palestine is an updated work in the parameters of Gustav Dalman's classic series *Arbeit und Sitte in Palästina*.[15] Dalman has rightly been cited as an authority ever since the production of his work, but books published as early as his series (prior to 1930 for the seasonal information) cannot be regarded as being abreast of continued scientific understanding of the land and climate of Palestine.[16] Also, his particular observations of terminology currently used, while helpful, are sometimes anecdotal in nature and are in some sense period pieces. Dalman was not attempting a scientific rendering of the climate of Palestine, and cannot be faulted for not producing one. The fact that his important work has not been superseded illustrates the need to attempt an understanding of the climate of the biblical period (discussed in chapter one of this study).

An observational account of the land in its broadest sense, a source to supplement and complement the work of Dalman, would greatly assist the student of the Bible who is interested in the details of such phenomena. Dalman's accurate observations were produced before the advent of either radar

14. Other examples of this kind of approach are represented in such diverse sources as Barr, "Man [sic] and Nature," 9–32 and Malchow, "Nature from God's Perspective," 130–33.

15. In seven volumes, 1928–42.

16. Healey, "Ancient Agriculture and the Old Testament," 110.

or the supercomputer, both of which are the standard tools of the trade for modern understanding of meteorology.[17] As a period piece, however, Dalman's work has limited application to what I am attempting here.

Commentaries also have a limited role in a study such as this. The vast number of the commentaries on the Psalms I reduced to the most textually useful. Some readers may be surprised to find little reference to the giants of the Psalms, Gunkel and Mowinckel. Their landmark works, however, had a very different purpose than this present project. The commentaries, in any case, were consulted, especially in the cases of difficult words, in order to demonstrate the range of interpretations available. For assistance in determining the actual meaning of the words I have relied primarily on contexts and meteorological glossaries, used in connection with the standard lexica and comparative philology where it was relevant.

It quickly became clear that this kind of study is interrelated with many other fields, both in biblical and scientific disciplines. Theophany studies, warfare and royal ideologies, pre-biblical theology, exodus theology, comparative philology, and the study of the many areas of the Psalms, on the biblical side; geography, geology, climatology (particularly palaeoclimatology), hydrology, and botany, on the scientific side, immediately suggest themselves. The tendency is to try to treat each of these areas with an expert hand, although the task outstrips the abilities of even multiple authors and becomes unwieldy. I have attempted, therefore, to limit myself to the discussion of immediate concern: weather in the Psalms. Where these other fields have pertinent material to add to the discussion, they will be considered, but they will not be pursued beyond that.

TRANSLATION ISSUES

All of the translations in this study are mine, unless otherwise noted. I have translated the Hebrew with special concern to emphasize the "meteorologically correct" rendering of weather terms, sometimes at the expense of aesthetic sensitivities. For the purposes of a study such as this, that is a necessary evil: to make the point clear, some over-emphasis on a neglected topic is required. I have attempted to avoid overly using technical language regarding translation issues, since this study is offered to several different

17. The science of meteorology, coincidentally and ironically, has been closely tied to warfare. The early history of meteorology in America was tied to the United States Army Signal Corp (Fleming, *Meteorology in America*, throughout). The "quantum leap" into radar and many weather observational practices resulted from World War II and the need to understand the weather for tactical purposes. Supercomputers were also developed for military purposes. This will be discussed in the conclusions to this book.

levels of reader. Nevertheless, at various points the discussions of weather terms could not take place without setting out the principles by which the translation was achieved. It is my hope that these necessary lapses into technical jargon will not hamper the reading of those unfamiliar with Hebrew.

When the Hebrew demands a masculine pronoun for Yahweh, I will translate it literally for the sake of precision in translation. When I refer to the divinity in my own comments I will maintain gender neutrality.

A further necessary point to be addressed concerning translation is the omnipresent issue of textual emendation. Being a believer in the principle of *lectio difficilior probabilior* (a more difficult reading is more likely original), my perspective on emending the text is that it should be an option of final resort only. The Psalms, being imperfectly understood ancient poetry, are frequently subjected to the criticism of textual corruption. It is my distinct sense that the problem here often lies with the modern reader and not with the ancient text: poorly understood texts are *our* problem. To change the text is often not playing by the rules. Most of my translations, therefore, are based on the received MT, as reflect in *BHS*. I will discuss relevant suggestions of textual error, but in general I do not accept them unless there is a case of complete incomprehensibility in the original. Ironically, the psalms which are often regarded as the most difficult to decipher frequently employ the language of meteorology.

As some readers are no doubt aware, the verse numbers in English translations of many of the psalms are off by one or two from the Hebrew verse numbers.[18] For the sake of those who wish to compare the Hebrew to the translations offered here, all verse numbers are those of the MT. Where these numbers differ from standard English numeration, I have provided the English verse number in square brackets.

In order to understand what this study is intended to do, and not to do, I urge the reader to read the preface, above.

---

18. See Holladay, *The Psalms through Three Thousand Years*, 4–5, for a helpful discussion of the difficulties in numbering the psalms and their verses.

CHAPTER ONE

Ancient Weather, Ancient Poetry

Parameters and Possibilities

The weather, as an integral aspect of nature, has theological implications.[1] Such implications led to the pursuit of a theology of nature, which was popular a couple of decades ago. As Terence Fretheim noted in 1988, the theme of nature in the Bible is one that has been studied only minimally.[2] Taking his observation a step further, it is important to note that to date, no full-length study of the weather in the Psalms has yet appeared.[3] Even in books concerning nature in the Bible, the weather is an aspect of the natural world often overlooked, although its presence is noteworthy in several biblical books.[4]

---

1. The implication of nature and theology have been admirably explored in one context by Hiebert's *The Yahwist's Landscape*.

2. Fretheim, "Nature's Praise of God in the Psalms," 16.

3. An unpublished dissertation considered the weather as an interpretative device in three psalms—104, 65, and 29 (Futato, "Meteorological Analysis," PhD diss., Catholic University of America), but the remainder of the psalms have not been studied in a systematic way. Additionally, Futato's study sought a considerably different outcome than does the current study. Likewise, Klingbeil (*Yahweh Fighting from Heaven*) considers the "God of Heaven" metaphor in selected psalms and compares them to the iconographic material of ancient West Asia. His purpose and outcome are also quite different from what is here presented.

4. For example, Nash, *Palestinian Agricultural Year*, has drawn out the implications of the weather for the book of Joel.

The science of meteorology is a relative newcomer among the physical sciences, but it is a field of immense importance, as well as of popular interest. It is also a field that humanity is only beginning to understand. "In the last thirty years and especially during the war of 1939–45," R. B. Y. Scott began his article on weather terminology in the Bible in the early 1950s, "immense advances have been made in the scientific observation of weather and climate."[5] The same basic sentiment may be echoed today, and doubtless will be echoed again in the future. Any study concerning weather terminology must admit that it cannot be the final word, since new techniques of studying the atmosphere continue to develop and the precision with which the general principles are understood is constantly increasing. At the same time, a strong urge persists to find the common level which the weather shares with religious language—a phenomenon especially evident in the religious language of the Psalms. The many biblical weather citations provide fixed points of reference to which new meteorological understanding may be applied with fruitful results for the student of the Bible.

M. D. Futato wrote in his 1984 dissertation on the subject that "OT poets knew the weather of Palestine well and took it seriously."[6] This led him to ask: "How is it that they [i.e., the conclusions based on a meteorological analysis of Psalms 104, 65, and 29] have been missed for so long? I would suggest that the problem is the different ways in which the ancient and the modern worlds talk about weather."[7] Futato here makes explicit the relationship between the weather and the Psalms. The gauntlet he tossed down, however, has not been picked up; no full treatment of how the psalmists, as representatives of the ancient worldview, perceived the weather has yet appeared.

Although ancients, and some moderns, attribute the weather to God (or the gods), the language used to discuss this connection has, as Futato suggests, changed over time. Such a change makes a study like this one necessary. In important ways there is a continuity of thought, while in other ways, worldviews have changed radically. In the context of this change, it is important to keep tradents of theology and the Bible in communication with scientific developments.[8] Twenty-first-century people still take the weather seriously, and the Psalms continue to hold a special place in the religious language of many in this same era. There seems to be an implicit awareness

---

5. Scott, "Meteorological Phenomena and Terminology," 1 1.

6. Futato, "Meteorological Analysis," 245.

7. Ibid., 246.

8. An important work that demonstrates the importance of a proper perspective on theology and science is Pennock's *Tower of Babel*.

Ancient Weather, Ancient Poetry 13

of the relationship between perceptions of God and the weather. It is this implicit awareness that will be brought to the surface in this monograph.

As the title of this chapter suggests, both of the disciplines brought together in this study involve ancient contexts. The Psalms are an ancient book of liturgical poetry.[9] The weather scenarios utilized in the Psalms are ancient, unrecoverable meteorological events, or metaphors. Each subject requires careful handling, lest modern constructions read current agendas into the text. This chapter brings together the two separate disciplines of Psalms study and meteorology to set the groundwork for the chapters that follow.

THE PSALMS: ANCIENT POETRY

The Psalms are an unusual collection of ancient literature. They are unusual in a number of aspects,[10] not least of which is the sheer number of ways in which they have been utilized. This current work is a further example of the wide usage to which the text has been put.

The Psalms were chosen to compare with meteorology for several reasons. Prolonged familiarity with the Psalms, in either academic or liturgical settings, leads to the recognition of the large number of meteorological references within the corpus. Having been written over many centuries and by many different authors, the Psalms represent a cross-section of ancient thought rather than a monotypic view. This cross-section demonstrates a remarkable convergence on the importance of weather in relationship to God. Within the parameters of this study such a cross-section also reveals different perceptions of the same weather phenomena. This convergence and divergence begs for exploration.

Study of the Psalms, however, has considerable limitations, both ancient and modern. These parameters must be kept in mind for any literary exploration of the Psalms, especially one that attempts to relate this literature to both science and theology. Dating the Psalms, with rare exceptions, involves considerable guesswork, and this robs the researcher of one of the most basic literary analytical devices. Despite the advances in Psalms studies, the history of the development of the book and the history its ancient liturgical use remain uncertain. The titles added to many of the Psalms cloud the issues of authorship, provenance, and date. In modern times, the issue is complicated by an ever-increasing number of publications on the Psalms for

---

9. I use this word guardedly, yet intentionally. For the issue of poetry in the Bible, see Kugel, *The Idea of Biblical Poetry* and Watson, *Classical Hebrew Poetry*.

10. Holladay, *The Psalms through Three Thousand Years*, 1–5.

any number of uses: popular piety, academic study, literary value, modern liturgical renewal. Among these, the academic aspect itself is crowded with commentaries, monographs, and periodical articles.

For the purposes of this study, which is specific as to the material to be gleaned from the Psalms, some parameters are necessary. Many major commentaries have agendas that do not inform the specific concern of weather imagery in the Psalms. Commentaries remain useful tools for illuminating specific words and issues of prosody, but their value for a thematic study is often limited.

Nearly every imaginable aspect of the Psalms has been probed by various periodical articles, as a survey of the recent indices demonstrates. Not all of these sources have any significant impact on the theological use of weather terminology in the Psalms, and these articles clarify only specific, mostly unrelated, issues. These issues tend to be mostly structural studies or individual lexical issues. Fuller bibliographic resources on the Psalms can be found in many of the monographs and a few of the commentaries cited below.

While the issues of authorship, and particularly date, are often essential elements for interpreting an individual psalm, these issues are largely unaddressed in this work. It is sufficient to note that time of composition of a particular psalm has little to do with how the weather was perceived, suggesting a considerable stability of the issue in antiquity.

As a working hypothesis, the composition of the Psalms dates very roughly to the period 1200 to 500 B.C.E. This dating scheme is based on the parameters provided by the historical environment which gives a context to ancient Israel, namely, from the collapse of many Late Bronze Age civilizations to the relative stability of the Persian administration. This dating scheme is intended to be a rough guide only. Some individual psalms may fall into a later time period, but that does not affect the approach taken here, for reasons which will soon become clear. The climate during this period seems to have been relatively stable (as will be discussed below), and most of the Psalms were likely composed within this period.

It must be admitted from the outset that the Psalms were not written to provide the modern reader with a scientific outlook on the weather.[11] Indeed, the purpose of including weather observations in the Psalms was often metaphorical and theological, and not empirical study.[12] Several of the Psalms, however, do provide the modern reader with a *theological* outlook on the weather. As this study will clearly demonstrate, the weather is never

---

11. This is a point also made by Janecko, "Ecology, Nature, Psalms," 97.
12. This point is stressed by Gammie, "A New Setting for Psalm 110," 4–8.

a neutral, or even a "natural" phenomenon in the Psalms.[13] Always, in some way, it is indicative of Yahweh's relationship with humanity. The book of Psalms, as a collection which reflects on the divine from the perspective of the human authors, is especially valuable in demonstrating the perceptions of how Yahweh utilizes the weather.

METEOROLOGY

Weather is essentially aeolian and hydrological activity in the troposphere, or lowest layer of the earth's atmosphere. The weather elements considered in this study generally involve either the water cycle or the air movements of the troposphere. In a climate such as that of ancient Israel, long stretches of the year pass without precipitation (although dew sometimes occurs in these periods). This weather is what is now often called "fair weather." In a climate such as that of Palestine and Israel, calling this "fair" weather is perhaps a misnomer, since rain was often an eagerly-awaited aspect of the water cycle.

The question is therefore raised: whose weather is this study about? There is no Hebrew word for "weather." As will become clear throughout this book, the current perception of what weather is was not shared by the psalmists. Their "meteorology" did not include "natural" phenomena. They did not understand the processes of condensation which leads to precipitation. Dew was thought to have fallen from the sky. The psalmists did not label the effects of solar radiation as weather, any more than they did rain.

The answer to the question must be, therefore, that this study is about weather as we understand it, but as it was interpreted by the psalmists who experienced it. One of the parameters in the area of meteorology is the limitation of the discussion to what actually constitutes weather. A working definition of weather is "the state of the atmosphere, with special emphasis on the local and short-term variations of temperature, wind, cloudiness, precipitation, and humidity."[14] Each of these aspects is addressed in the following chapters.

A further parameter concerning weather concerns the kinds of weather that would possibly have been experienced in ancient Palestine during

---

13. The situation is well-summarized by Nash, in the context of the book of Joel: "As will become evident from the following discussion of 4:14b–16, *details of meteorology and geography in Joel 3–4 . . . are very much under the control of theology rather than of nature*" (*Palestinian Agricultural Year*, 192, my emphasis). The same may clearly be stated for the Psalms.

14. Somerville, "Climate and Weather," 127.

the period of the composition of the Psalms. In other words, what would the ancient weather have been? This is the question of climatology.

CLIMATES ANCIENT AND MODERN

Climate is the average of the parameters of temperature, precipitation, and humidity over a period of time.[15] The constancy of weather patterns is an essential concern for any study which includes weather-related phenomena in antiquity. Climates and weather patterns change over time and from region to region. This change in climate must be considered for any study of the weather.

Climate is a global phenomenon, and each local weather event is related to all others as the atmosphere constantly seeks homeostasis. Many studies exist that explore the global climate throughout history. These studies are readily available, although it must be kept in mind that even these explorations are subject to change as new data become available. Climate does affect all life on our planet, and the relationship between religion and climate is striking.[16] Climate influences all areas of life. Setting some basic climatic parameters for ancient Israel, however, is necessary.

In geological time, our current age is designated the Holocene Epoch of the Quaternary Period. The Holocene Epoch begins about 11,000 years before present, at the cessation of the last ice age. Studies within the Holocene Epoch indicate a great difficulty in precise scientific determination of climate change from about 2,000 B.C.E. onward.[17] Advances have been made in computer modeling and archaeoclimatology to the point that small scale reconstructions may be both century-specific and site-specific.[18] The architects of this method, however, caution that such computer reconstructions must be supported by field evidence, in this case, provided by archaeology.[19] Further, the reconstruction of ancient climates also relies on

---

15. Tsonis, "Climate," 123.

16. See the somewhat ambitious study on this subject by McCown, "Climate and Religion in Palestine," 520–39.

17. Crown, "Climatic Change, Ecology and Migration," 9; Crown, "Toward a Reconstruction of the Climate of Palestine," 327; Street-Perrott and Perrott, "Abrupt Climate Fluctuations in the Tropics," 611; Raikes, *Water, Weather and Prehistory*.

18. Bryson and Bryson, "High Resolution Simulations of Regional Holocene Climate," 565–93. The Brysons have named this discipline "archaeoclimatology." I would like to thank the Brysons for supplying me with climatological material which would have otherwise been beyond my ability to find.

19. Bryson and Bryson, "High Resolution Simulations," 579.

accurate records in the modern period.[20] For the area under study (ancient Palestine) records have historically, until the 1940s, been of poor quality, thus making any reconstruction based on meteorological models tenuous.[21]

A debate over the consistency of the climate of ancient Israel has persisted for many years. The basic question is whether the climate has changed substantially since biblical times, and, if so, how it has changed. Many separate disciplines are marshaled for evidence in the debate: palynology (pollen studies), zoology, weathering patterns of stone, eustatic (lake level) studies, geochemical methods, analysis of sediment cores. Historical records are commonly read through the lens of climate change.[22]

About fifty years ago, Robert Raikes, a hydrologist, argued that if substantial climate change had occurred in the Holocene Epoch, all of the available evidence should point in that direction. His reasoning was straightforward: the water cycle encompasses nearly every aspect of life, including the weather. If something as dramatic as a significant climatic change had occurred, the evidence should agree on this point. Raikes concluded that substantial climatic change in antiquity was unlikely.[23]

Since Raikes published his work, others have continued the quest for certainty regarding ancient climates. One important facet is often noted, namely, that human activity affects the environment in ways that distort the data necessary to reconstruct ancient climates. This means that the period under study (c.1200–500 BCE) involves an environment intricately interlocking human activity and natural processes. The researcher must rely on the texts to determine what the weather elements were, but what these elements were depends on the ancient climate. A consensus of sorts exists among those who explore the various sources: major climate changes have not occurred between the period covered in this book and the present.[24] Further study may dislodge this tentative consensus; however, even should that happen the effect on the specifics of this study would be minimal.[25] The fact remains that the various psalm writers referred to lightning, hail, rain,

---

20. Wigley and Farmer, "Climate of the Eastern Mediterranean," 25.

21. Ibid., 31.

22. See, for example, Cullen et al., "Climate Change and the Collapse of the Akkadian Empire," 379–82; Stiebing, "Did the Weather Make Israel's Emergence Possible?" 18–27, 54.

23. Raikes, *Water, Weather and Prehistory*, 110.

24. For support of this statement, see the sources listed below in footnote 30.

25. Climate change is now being understood as more sudden and profound than previously thought. See Weiss and Bradley, "What Drives Societal Collapse?" 609–10.

and thunder. Even if some of these weather events were rare, they were known, and may have even inspired greater awe in the light of their rarity.[26]

In this state of current understanding, a full rehearsal of the climate of ancient or modern Israel by a non-specialist, such as the current author, would be of limited value. Rather more helpful might be a statement of Israel's climate in very general terms, and what climatic changes have been substantiated to some degree. This should allow the reader to decide whether or not the interpretations put forward in this work are probable or not.

The modern climate of Israel is easily ascertained in several studies of the land and weather of Palestine and Israel.[27] The climate of Israel and Palestine is classified as sub-tropical. There are two major seasons, often labeled summer and winter, although spring and autumn are sometimes referred to as the "interchange" periods.[28] Because of the prevailing motion of the major climatic belts which follow the apparent latitudinal movement of the sun, the weather in summer and winter is largely constant and predictable. The summers are hot and dry while cyclonic storms follow the Mediterranean trough in the winter, bringing rain. The beginning and ending points of the rain, however, are largely unpredictable and cause anxiety for farmers. Within this weather milieu, rain and dew commonly occur. Snow, frost, and rime also occur, but more rarely, and mostly in higher elevations. Thunderstorms, with their attendant thunder, lightning, and occasional hail, while not frequent are also not unusual. Severe weather can occur, often in the form of siroccos and occasionally as tornadic storms. In short, all of the weather forms discussed in the Psalms are meteorologically attested for the region.

As Crown has pointed out, the study of palaeoclimatology requires that both the region and the era must be specified.[29] A very detailed focus on regional or local weather events, however, is unnecessary here. Even in a country as relatively small as ancient Israel, weather differed in different regions, as it does today. Microclimates can be studied, but such information is of dubious value to such a study as this—precisely where or when a particular psalm was written is unknown.

---

26. Cressey, *Crossroads*, 107.

27. For climatic studies of the late Holocene period, see Ashbel, *Bio-climatic Atlas of Israel*; Baly, *Geographical Companion to the Bible*; Baly and Tushingham, *Atlas of the Biblical World*; Cressey, *Crossroads*; and Orni and Efrat, *Geography of Israel*.

28. This terminology is used by Nash throughout *Palestinian Agricultural Year*. Much of the information on the weather here is gleaned from Baly, *Geography of the Bible*, 43–68.

29. Crown, "Climatic Change, Ecology and Migration," 6–8.

Some climate change is evident in ancient Israel; however, the climate appears to have remained roughly the same in Palestine from the Chalcolithic period until the present.[30] As pollen studies of Kinnereth Sea core samples and the accretion of sand dunes over loess soils indicate, there have been episodes of higher humidity and cooler temperatures in Israel in the historical period.[31] These episodes, however, have been of limited duration and therefore fall outside of the concern of this study. Current evidence also indicates that sudden climatic change may have led to the collapse of the Akkadian Empire, but this climatic episode ended before the period under consideration in this book began.[32] As Raikes has demonstrated, climate is a phenomenon intimately linked with hydrology, geology, and human activity.[33] Along with Raikes, this study considers the "big picture" as an indicator that climate has not significantly changed over the past 9,000 years,[34] at least not in any way that directly affects the phenomena examined here. Although it may not be definitively stated that the climate has been stable, until evidence arises to counter this assessment, it may be used as a working hypothesis.

WEATHER AND POETRY: POSSIBILITIES

In three of the years that it took to write the main body of this book, the state of Wisconsin experienced its three warmest consecutive winters on record. History will have to decide whether this reflects a climatic change, but a poetic record written by a casual observer during this time would likely reflect current conditions, without a concern for overall climate. Such a source might well ponder what God is doing with the weather. The all-too-human focus on weather and God is evident throughout the Bible, but the attempt to categorize this focus in the Psalms requires an adequate method.

In a sense this book is akin to Erik Haglund's 1984 study, which attempted to place the historical themes of the Psalms into a systematic format.[35] The meteorological themes of the Psalms may likewise be placed

---

30. Butzer, *Quaternary Stratigraphy and Climate*, 104–10; Horowitz, "Climatic and Vegetational Developments," 274; Ben-Yoseph, "The Climate in Eretz Israel," 225–39; Danin, "Palaeoclimates in Israel," 33–43; Henry, Turnbull, Emery-Barbier, and Leroi-Gourhan, "Archaeological and Faunal Evidence," 61.

31. Issar, Tsoar, and Levin, "Climatic Changes in Israel," 525–41.

32. Cullen et al., "Climate Change," 379–82.

33. Raikes, *Water, Weather and Prehistory*, throughout.

34. Ibid., 131.

35. Haglund, *Historical Motifs in the Psalms*. A closer example in kind to this current study is Klingbeil's *Yahweh Fighting from Heaven*. It is not, however, as comprehensive

into a systematic format. By examining how each weather reference is used, it is possible to establish an aggregation of a certain number of usages of the weather language in the Psalms. Weather is not used for the setting of a mood or just any random purpose; boundaries may be established for the use of meteorological terms. These boundaries will be presented below under each separate weather category in the aspect of their individual functions.

Within these boundaries, the precise weather phenomena being referenced have been determined as closely as possible. Current meteorological understanding makes this difficult task somewhat easier, but it must always be borne in mind that the references are ancient and reflect ancient perspectives. Once the phenomenon has been identified, how the weather functions in each category will be examined. Weather terms are often used in different ways among the aggregations presented in this monograph. Storms, for example, are sometimes a positive phenomenon, sometimes a negative one.

Any division of meteorological phenomena into categories will be somewhat arbitrary since all weather events are in some way related.[36] Nevertheless, an organizational scheme is required to cover the material adequately.

Each meteorological phenomenon mentioned in the Psalms is treated in the following chapters. Phenomena with obvious connections will be considered in the same chapter. Chapter two will consider phenomena exclusive to storm terminology (including lightning and thunder references). Chapter three explores wind terminology. Rain and cloud terminology, as specifically associated with liquid precipitation, are classified together in chapter four. Chapter five combines various phenomena which involve ice, snow, and "ground weather," thus the references to hail, snow, frost, rime, and dew will be considered together. Chapter six addresses the final weather-related terms concerning temperature in the Psalms. As I have noted, there is some arbitrariness to this scheme, but there is a kind of internal logic as well.

The method employed throughout the main body of this monograph is the introduction of the phenomena (storm, lightning, thunder, wind, whirlwind, etc.), followed by an analysis of the Hebrew words used for the particular phenomenon. Words are treated in the order in which they are initially listed, the order of the verses follows the order of their appearance in the Psalms. This layout is intended to be logical as well as intuitive. The

---

as Haglund's study.

36. This is the basic tenet of the "butterfly effect." See Gleick, *Chaos*, 9–31.

reader may look up an individual verse or phenomenon without having to read the entire book or an entire chapter.

As a further organizing principle, when a verse contains multiple meteorological terms, it will be presented in each relevant chapter or each relevant section of a chapter. This may appear to make the reading somewhat repetitious, but it saves the reader from the necessity of flipping back through the pages to find the previous translation of the verse. For the purposes of making this a useful reference tool as well as a monograph, the reader will hopefully treat this detail with patience. Additionally, several re-readings of a passage which contains multiple meteorological images will help to highlight the interaction of the phenomena and their importance.

Although each Hebrew term is examined in canonical order, occasionally a parallel is so striking that it may be taken out of order to demonstrate the comparison. When this is done, a cross reference is placed at the appropriate place. Following the exploration of each of the phenomena, a summary is given encapsulating the function of the imagery. After each category has been examined, some conclusions will be presented.

One of the possibilities here presented is the definition of meteorological terms on the basis of textual comparison within the Hebrew Bible, comparative philology, and current meteorological understanding. Often the words are so well-established that no new meaning has to be explored. For words of lesser certainty, context and, secondarily, comparative philology frequently offer potential parameters. The reason for this priority is that, in general terms, the basic meaning of most weather-related words is already known. What is frequently lacking is knowledge of their specific meaning or function within the context of a given verse or a given psalm. In attempting to determine how such terms function and what they mean, the context provides the most information. If it can be established that the psalm tends to use meteorological imagery when referring, for example, to a theophany, then comparison of this imagery in the psalm with a more obscure reference may very well clarify it.

When this method does not work, comparative philology is used. Comparative philology necessarily forces the translator to utilize meteorological evidence from a different geographical context. The experience of weather in a different geographical context may reflect different nuances of what the weather meant and how it functioned. "Ancient Israel" is the limit for this exploration. This term is ambiguous enough to cover all the material discussed below, but specific enough that it does not run the danger of using Mesopotamian or Egyptian weather experience as normative for the Hebrew Bible.

CHAPTER TWO

The Thunderstorm

Of all weather phenomena, the thunderstorm is among the most dramatic. Entailing, as it does, rain, thunder, lightning, gusty winds, and sometimes hail and tornadic winds, the thunderstorm remains, even with advanced meteorological study, an awe-inspiring event. Partially this is because such storms affect people in many ways. "Every society in a climate that spawns thunderstorms makes some adaptations to those events."[1] These words apply to ancient societies as well as the modern communities with which they are primarily concerned. Whether it is moving animals out of harm's way or seeking personal shelter during a storm, people react to the weather in a thunderstorm situation.

This chapter is limited to words that denote either a storm proper, lightning, or thunder. These three elements are necessarily collateral. There will be frequent interchange with chapters three (on the wind) and four (concerning rain) since wind and rain are also essential parts of a thunderstorm, but both may exist independently from a storm. Rain, although a common storm element, also occurs in other contexts, both in nature and in the Psalms. Its unique role requires a separate chapter. The same may be stated regarding clouds—although they are necessary for a thunderstorm, they are not necessarily indicative of one. Hail, although usually a product of the thunderstorm, has close associations with other frozen forms of hydrometeors, such as frost, rime and snow. Rather than enlarging the current chapter with just one of these elements, the frozen forms of weather will be

---

1. Kessler and White, "Thunderstorms in a Social Context," 5.

considered in chapter five. As earth scientists know, all aspects of nature are interconnected: this study will inevitably reflect this truth in the weather.

The Psalms reflect the awe that accompanies the thunderstorm, especially emphasizing its destructive potential. It is thus appropriate to begin this study of meteorological terms in the Psalms with the storm terminology. Specifically this terminology will be divided into three sections, each focusing on a different aspect of the storm: storms generally, lightning, and thunder.

STORMS

The first of the three sections in this chapter concerns words actually used to describe a storm itself. Four different roots are apparently used to denote a storms in the Psalms: שַׂעַר/סַעַר, סוּף, גלגל, and הוה. Implied descriptions also occur without using the word "storm" in any of its variant forms.

סַעַר / סְעָרָה / שַׂעַר

The basic sphere of meaning for the root סער entails intensity of action, whether its subject is the weather or human emotion. It is the word used to describe the cause of the state of the sea in Jonah (1:4), and the passions of the unnamed Aramean king in 2 Kings 6:11. Whenever it occurs in a meteorological context, it is generally understood to denote the "stormy" or "tempestuous"—an intense state of weather.[2] Both BDB and KBS suggest a connection with שׂער, which is in turn associated with Akkadian *šâra*, "windy."[3] A word of caution, however, is necessary on the latter association. While comparative philology will be helpful in establishing meanings, the recognition must be kept in the forefront that the weather varies in different terrain. The Mesopotamian river valleys would experience somewhat different weather than the Mediterranean coast. Even different regions of Palestine have different weathers.[4] Differing cultures, more importantly, may have perceived the same weather phenomenon somewhat differently.

The word "tempest," often used to translate the word סער, has fallen out of meteorological usage as imprecise and archaic. The very vagueness and poetic connotations of this word, however, may make it appropriate in

---

2. The word סערה is thoroughly discussed in Lugt, "Wirbelstürme im Alten Testament," 202–3.

3. BDB, 704a; KBS, 762a.

4. Baly, *Geography of the Bible*, 43; Frick, "Palestine, Climate of," 121–22.

a biblical context which does not present enough detail to provide a more precise meteorological term such as "severe thunderstorm."[5]

When the related root שׁער is used, it is generally found in verbal form.[6] In the Psalms, both references to שׁער utilize its verbal form, creating challenging translation issues.

Meteorological words based on the root סער occur in Pss 55:9 [8]; 83:16 [15]; 107:25, 29; 148:8. There is no apparent difference in meaning between the masculine and feminine nominal forms. Meteorological references based on שׁער occur in Pss 50:3 and 58:10.

Psalm 50:3

> Our God enters and is not silent,
> fire consumes before him,
> and around him it storms severely.

A theophanic element accompanies this reference to a storm. The verbal form "storms" utilizes the root שׁער. שׁער is modified with the adverb מאד, indicating greater intensity. The usual meteorological terminology for an intense thunderstorm is "severe." Since severe thunderstorms indicate danger and unapproachability, the storm in this verse serves to conceal the deity who is revealed in the very same event. This diametrically opposite function of weather is found elsewhere in the Psalms, and it becomes obvious that this ambivalence is characteristic of how the psalmists perceived the weather. From this dramatic yet obscure appearance, the psalm moves into a celebration of God's function as the judge of Israel.

The fire consuming before God is likely a reference to lightning, since אשׁ frequently carries that connotation in the Psalms (see below, under Lightning).

Psalm 55:9 [8]

> Let me quickly come to my escape
> from dashing wind and from storm.

---

5. The characteristics of a severe thunderstorm are "a thunderstorm which produces tornadoes, hail 0.75 inches or more in diameter, or winds of 50 knots (58 mph) or more" (Branick, *A Comprehensive Glossary of Weather Terms*, http://server.maxdiamonds.com/images/GLOSSARY_NWS-SR145.pdf, accessed 2/22/2014). See also Geer, *Glossary of Weather and Climate*, 199.

6. There is one exception to this: Isa 28:2 uses a nominal form.

There is some question whether the two lines belong together as a bicolon here. Many modern translations take lines of this verse as the two cola of a bicolon,[7] a division that I follow as well. There is no need to find a textual error here,[8] as the utilization of parallel meteorological terms serves to intensify the psalmist's perception of the unspecified problem.

The context for this verse is a psalm of lament. It is clear that the meteorological terms in this verse are being used as metaphors for the troubles of the psalmist, but it is not clear what the specific troubles are. The psalmist expresses a wish to escape these difficulties by utilizing two similar meteorological phenomena as symbolic of the problem. The reference to the psalmist's enemies in v. 3 [2] and the personal pronoun "their" in the immediately following verse (10 [9]) support the idea that the storm language is a metaphor in the context of trouble with human foes.

The use of meteorological language in this verse reflects its symbolic value in representing human difficulty. The Briggses suggest that these meteorological terms should actually be placed with the next verse where they would be used as Yahweh's instruments to discomfit the enemy.[9] This would match the use of meteorological language elsewhere in the Psalms, but it is not necessary here since the anticipated escape and the celerity of the wind also suggest a unified idea; the psalmist hopes for a swift escape as the wind quickly rises and more quickly than the enemies arrive.

The connotation of the storm in this verse is that of a destructive agent. Yahweh is able to deliver from this destructive power, and this is the basis of the psalmist's appeal. The storm is understood as a destructive element vis-à-vis Yahweh's ability to prevent its harm.

The translation "dashing wind" will be further explored below in chapter three.

Psalm 58:10 [9]

> Before your pots discern brambles,
> living and burning alike,
> let him storm him.

---

7. This monograph does not include a full discussion of poetic terms, as this can be found elsewhere. Throughout I have utilized the terms as clearly spelled out by Watson's *Classical Hebrew Poetry*.

8. Briggs and Briggs, *Book of Psalms*, 2:22. Manuscript evidence for a textual error is minimal.

9. Ibid.

This verse suffers from textual complexities. The term "your pots" has a decidedly colloquial air to it, and it is followed by an imprecation in the third person "storm *him*." This naturally leads to suggestions of textual corruption, as the apparatus in *BHS* suggests.[10] Regardless of corruption, the basic idea of this imprecatory psalm is evident: before too long, Yahweh should smite the evil-doer. The term utilized for the divine smiting is the second and final appearance of שׂער in the Psalms. שׂער again appears in verbal form, making for somewhat awkward translation into English. The use of "storm" as an intransitive verb is probably the most accurate way to translate the sense of the verse, especially within the context of how storm language is used in the Psalms. The wish of the writer is that Yahweh would violently burst upon—that is, "storm"—the enemy. The function of the storm language is, therefore, that of divine aggression against God's enemies.

Psalm 83:16 [15]

Thus you pursue them with your storm,
and with your storm-wind terrify them.

There are two meteorological terms used in a parallel position in this verse:[11] בְּסַעֲרֶךָ and סוּפָתְךָ. They occur in the context of the mildly imprecatory Ps 83. The *Gattung* of this psalm is difficult to identify precisely, although lament elements are present, particularly on a national level.[12] This would suggest perhaps a communal lament;[13] the psalm, however, does not follow standard lament form. The main thrust of the psalm is to implore Yahweh to take vengeance on the surfeit of national enemies.

The root סער "storm" (as found in Ps 55:9 [8]) occurs in the first colon: בְּסַעֲרֶךָ "with your storm." The wish being expressed in this verse is that Yahweh will drive away the enemies of the psalmist with a storm. In the most basic sense, this is an indication of the destructive nature of the storm—it is a phenomenon from which the foe must flee. This understanding of the storm categorizes it with the classification posited for the previous psalm; both psalms see the storm as a threat to human life. In Ps 55:9 [8] there is

---

10. Dahood, *Psalms*, 2:62, confesses "The Hebrew of this verse is unintelligible to me." Kraus, *Psalms 1–59*, 534, concurs "The text is disordered and meaningless." See also Briggs and Briggs, *Book of Psalms*, 2:45, 48.

11. See also the discussion of this verse in chapter three below.

12. Dahood, *Psalms*, 2:273.

13. A. A. Anderson, *Book of Psalms*, 2:595; Weiser, *The Psalms*, 562.

no direct attribution of the storm to Yahweh as there is in this verse. That the storm is an agent of Yahweh is made clear in this psalm by the use of the pronominal suffix in "*your* storm."

The second weather term סוף "storm wind," will be discussed below in chapter three where other wind terms are discussed.

Psalm 107:25

> And he commanded
> and raised a stormy wind,
> and lifted up its waves.

Psalm 107 is a hymn of thanksgiving which praises Yahweh for the deliverance of four types of people in distress: those in the desert, in prison, afflicted with illness, and those who went down to the sea in ships. Each deliverance is announced with a common refrain. The weather-related language occurs in the context of the final group, the seafarers. Verse 25 recounts the onset of a storm on the sea, which is described in terms of its affect on the sailors down to verse 27. The refrain occurs in verse 28, and the resolution of the storm occupies verse 29 (see below).

The description in this verse introduces the peril with which seafarers are faced in order that their deliverance may glorify Yahweh. רוח, "wind,"[14] is here qualified with סערה, "stormy," and thus its destructive potential to ships is obvious. The storm builds until v. 29 where it is calmed. The perception of the storm aspect of this verse might be classified as a potentially destructive divine agent or as a reference to the storm causing awe of Yahweh's control over the forces of nature.

Psalm 107:29

> He reduced[15] the storm to a whisper,
> and its waves were stilled.

This verse represents the cessation of the storm (סערה). The meteorological implications are that Yahweh was able to create the storm, and Yahweh is

---

14. This aspect of the verse will be considered in chapter three.

15. For this "particular" use of the Hiphil of קום, see KBS, 1088b. Beyerlin (*Werden und Wesen des 107. Psalms*) appeals to the mythological background (56) and the wider context (60) to secure the meaning of this verse.

able to dissipate it. The attribution to Yahweh is clear in the subject of the verb, which refers back to the auditor of the supplication given in verse 28.

The weather terminology in this psalm reveals that life-threatening, destructive storms give glory to Yahweh by virtue of the divine control over the elements. The storm, in other words, is not a chance occurrence but an instrument to magnify God's awe.

Psalm 148:8

> Fire and hail, snow and dark cloud,
> stormy wind doing his command.

In this hymn, all created orders are invited to praise Yahweh, regardless of their animate state. The storm wind is commanded to praise Yahweh along with the other elements. Its function, therefore, is to be an agent of praise. How this is to happen is not detailed in the psalm, but it is a commission given to every created thing.

Meteorologically, this verse also combines the nouns "storm" (סערה) and "wind" (רוח), as did 107:25. Further consideration of this verse will be given in chapters three, four, and five below, under the various meteorological elements mentioned in it.

To summarize the use of סער in the psalms, in all citations except one (Ps 148:8), the destructive nature of the storm is its main point of reference. This destructive nature may be invoked to terrify the enemy (83:16 [15]), to plead for the deliverance of the psalmist or other parties in distress (Ps 55:9 [8]; 107:25), or to demonstrate Yahweh's power over this most violent element (Ps 107:29). When the destructive nature is not foremost (Ps 148:8), the storm is simply a subordinate phenomenon called upon to praise Yahweh.

גַּלְגַּל

This word occurs in two psalms, 77:19 [18]; 83:14 [13], where it is often translated "whirlwind"; the NRSV, REB, NASB, and NJB all translate at least one of these verses with "whirlwind." The meaning of the word is disputed, as will be discussed in the next chapter. It is important to clarify at this point that, although whirlwinds are often associated with severe thunderstorms in the form of tornadoes, a number of alternate "whirls" exist in nature. In dry climates dust devils are classified as whirlwinds, as are waterspouts over the sea in any climate. Given the possibility that these whirls may not necessarily be tornadic, they will be considered in chapter three under wind, their constituent element. Their mention here, however, is a necessary cross-reference since the term "whirlwind" is connected with thunderstorms by many.

הַוּוֹת (√הוה)

Psalm 57:2 [1]

Be gracious to me, God,
be gracious to me!
For in you my soul seeks refuge,
and in the shadow of your wings I seek refuge,
until הַוּוֹת pass by.

Translations differ on whether the word "storm" is denoted or even implied by the word הוות in this verse. The lexica also differ in their construal of the word.[16] Commentaries are equally perplexed.[17] Elsewhere in Psalms this word is not associated with weather.

Psalm 5:10 [9] parallels הוות with "open graves." In Ps 38:13 [12] speaking הוות is paralleled with striking or taking aim at the psalmist. Ps 52:4 [2] presents the psalmist's enemy as plotting (חשׁב) הוות, while v. 9 [7] sees the foe seeking refuge in "his" הוות. Ps 55:12 [11] speaks of הוות in the midst of a wicked city. הוות is placed in parallel with a bird snare in Ps 91:3. Ps 94:20 uses הוות to describe the authorities (כסא). Is there something in the context of Ps 57:2 [1] that requires a meteorological allusion other than the intrinsic *Sturm und Drang* of life?

DCH posits an hypothetical root הַוָּה III, "wind," which includes as examples Pss 5:10 [9]; 38:13 [12]; 52:9 [7]; 55:12 [11]; 91:3; and 94:20, as well as the current verse under discussion.[18] Since no cognate evidence is offered, presumably the context has led to this suggestion. Cheyne's early commentary on the Psalms, cited by BDB for their suggestion "storm of ruin,"[19] offers an impressionist explanation for the use of storm language: "the choice of the verb suggests that a storm is more present to the writer's

---

16. For example, the NRSV and REB use the word "storm" in translating Ps 57:2 [1], while the NAB and NJB do not.

17. BDB, 217b ("desire; . . . chasm, fig. destruction"); KBS 242a ("destruction" as a separate root from "desire").

18. *DCH* 2:503a. Ps 52:9 is actually cited as 52:11, probably in error.

19. BDB, 217b.

imagination [than a yawning gulf]."[20] A more substantial explanation would be more compelling.

The evidence for a tempestuous meaning of הַוָּה is not especially strong. As *DCH* indicates, it may not be ruled out on the basis of context, on the other hand, the contexts do not necessitate a meteorological meaning. "The substantive *hawwōt*, usually rendered 'ruin, destruction,' carries the nuance 'poisonous, pernicious' when describing 'tongue' or 'speech,'" according to Dahood.[21] An association between wind and speech may be cogent, but it does not readily suggest a stormy connotation.

The suggestion of "destroying 'storms'" appears in the NRSV, attributable to G. R. Driver.[22]

If the word does designate stormy phenomena here, its function is a destructive force from which the psalmist appeals to Yahweh for deliverance.

SUMMARY OF STORM TERM FUNCTIONS

The storm terminology in the Psalms is utilized for two basic functions. Primarily the storm is noted for its destructive potential (Pss 55:9 [8]; 58:10 [9]; 83:16 [15]; 107:25) or kinetic destruction (especially if 57:2 [1] refers to storms, otherwise this aspect will be considered under "wind" in the next chapter). A second function of the storm is to glorify Yahweh for the divine control of such a powerful force (Pss 107:25, 29; 148:8). The storm is understood to be, at the least, under the control of Yahweh, at the most advanced, it is Yahweh's agent doing the divine bidding. While the storm glorifies Yahweh, it also serves to conceal the divine presence (Ps 50:3). Theophanic appearances reveal God, yet also hide the divine figure. This ambivalence is present in many weather references in the Psalms.

LIGHTNING

Although lightning may be divided into different types (for example: cloud-to-ground, cloud-to-cloud, ball lightning)[23] this does not seem to have been central to the psalmists' purposes when they described lightning or utilized it for a metaphor. Their concern was not to classify lightnings, but to tell

---

20. Cheyne, *The Book of Psalms*, 160.
21. Dahood, *Psalms*, 2:13.
22. *Journal of the Royal Asiatic Society* (1943) 8, unavailable to me.
23. See Geer, *Glossary of Weather and Climate*, for definitions. For more detail, consult Uman, *All About Lightning*.

how Yahweh used it. Lightning, like other weather-based phenomena, was mentioned by virtue of its relation to the divine sphere, never because of its inherent interest.

The task of this section, therefore, will not be to classify the references into different types of lightning. Rather it will be to determine the various uses of lightning terminology in the book of Psalms and to discern the metaphors used of it. Because of its fiery aspect, lightning could be referenced by several metaphors: Yahweh's arrows, burning ones, fire, and perhaps flame and glowing coals. Additionally, it may be directly named. The words potentially utilized for lightning in the Psalms are: ברק, חצים, אש, and גחלים, and possibly להב, להט, נגה, and רשפים. In this section an attempt will be made to substantiate whether or not these various images necessarily or potentially refer to lightning.

בָּרָק

The standard poetic word for "lightning," ברק, occurs in Pss 18:15 [14]; 77:19 [18]; 97:4; 135:7; and 144:6. It occurs in both nominal and verbal forms, the latter in Ps 144:6 alone. The basic meaning of the root is related to brightness, one of the essential attributes of lightning. From a modern perspective it is perhaps unusual that lightning is not often paired with thunder in the psalms. The causality between lightning and thunder, it must be remembered, had not yet been discovered, although their juxtaposition is occasionally noted.

Psalm 18:15 [14]

> And he shot his arrows and scattered them,
> even many[24] lightnings and discomfited them.

The peculiar circumstances that this hymn describes involve a theophany.[25] The psalm as a whole is a celebration of Yahweh's deliverance of the psalm-

---

24. This word (רָב) is missing from the parallel version in 2 Sam 22 and its meaning is disputed in this context. I have chosen to follow the best-attested meaning of this form "many," particularly since the 2 Samuel version has lightning in the singular (ברק) as opposed the the plural utilized in this psalm.

25. In addition to the commentaries, see Cross and Freedman, "A Royal Song of Thanksgiving," 15–34; Schmitz, "World and Word in Theophany," 50–70. For the theophanic aspect of this psalm, see Jeremias, *Theophanie*, 34–38; Miller, *Divine Warrior*, 121–23.

ist, possibly a king (see vv. 44 [43], 51 [50]). Within this context, the first six verses of the psalm proper lament the straits of the supplicant. This is followed by a vivid description of a theophany which includes much meteorological imagery (vv. 8–16 [7–15]).

As will become clear whenever this psalm is discussed, a comparison with 2 Sam 22 is cogent. The differences between these two versions of the same hymn are sometimes instructive, although they will not be utilized here to attempt to discern which is the earlier of the two.

Psalm 18:15 [14] juxtaposes two words for lightning in the specific context of the routing of Yahweh's enemies: "his arrows" (חציו) and "lightnings" (ברקים). These words appear in a context of a synonymous parallelism, both being objects of the verb ישלח ("he shot").[26] The implications of this parallelism are at least two-fold: "arrows" are a metaphor for lightning, and lightning is considered to be a divine weapon. The association of arrows with lightning is self-evident to those who observe both: they both fly swiftly, both can be deadly, and may appear to have sharp points.[27]

Since חץ is clearly a metaphor for lightning here, it opens the possibility that in other instances in the Psalms where arrows occur, particularly when they are cited as Yahweh's weaponry, they may also analogize lightning. These verses will be considered following those citing lightning directly.

The function of lightning in this verse is to be a divine weapon that scatters and discomfits the enemies of the psalmist, who are therefore enemies of Yahweh. As with storms, the destructive potential, or fear of that destructive potential, is highlighted.

Psalm 77:19 [18]

> The voice of your thunder was in the whirlwind,
> lightnings lit the world,
> the earth quaked and shook.

This psalm is similar to the previous one in form and in the way in which it uses the lightning imagery. It begins as a lament, then turns to a plea for deliverance with the remembrance of a theophany. The theophanic language,

---

26. Literally it could be translated "he sent." In the context of weapons such as arrows, "shot" is a better reflection of the meaning. See Kraus, *Psalms 1–59*, 253.

27. This idea has a long pedigree. As early as the eighteenth century BCE the image of lightning as a tree appears in the Levant (Williams-Forte, "Symbols of Rain, Lightning, and Thunder," 185–90). It continues into the famous Baal Stela found at Ugarit, and continues on into the Hebrew Bible in contexts like the present verse.

which begins in v. 17 [16], includes several meteorological references. The thunder and whirlwind aspects of this verse will be considered below, in this chapter and in the next, respectively.

The enemy to be impressed by God's lightning display in this psalm is the sea. In classic *Chaoskampf* language,[28] the waters (v. 17 [16]) see Israel's God and are afraid. The language that follows is martial: Yahweh is marshaling the divine arsenal against the sea. The sea that is defeated is revealed in the final two verses of the psalm to be the Red Sea,[29] bringing the *Chaoskampf* imagery to the account of the exodus. The book of Exodus cites a divine wind which drove back the waters (Exod 14:21), but the even more mythological Song of the Sea (Exod 15) does not portray Yahweh's use of lightning. The theophany in Ps 77 has moved further into the mythological realm and has made God's struggle with the sea a dramatic reminder to the psalmist of Yahweh's ability to control adversity.

Lightning functions in a similar way in this psalm as it did in Ps 18:15 [14]. It is a weapon of God, here apparently brandished, but not necessarily utilized, to inspire terror in the enemy. In broad terms it is an agent of divine destruction, although its precise function in this verse is to cause light—a light which terrifies the sea.

Psalm 97:4

> His lightnings lit the world,
> the earth saw and trembled.

The context for this fulgurous reference is an enthronement psalm, celebrating the kingship of Yahweh. Verses 2–5 utilize several meteorological terms to describe the theophanic appearance of Yahweh enthroned.

The function of the lightning in this verse appears to be the glorification of God. Its destructive potential is emphasized by the response of the earth, seeing and trembling.[30] More precisely, however, the lightning here does not destroy, but illuminates. It is not clear from the stichometry whether the earth trembles because of the lightning or because it discerns

---

28. For a useful compendium of creation essays, including helpful discussions of the *Chaoskampf* theme, see Anderson, *Creation in the Old Testament*. For more focused studies on *Chaoskampf*, see Kloos, *Yahweh's Combat with the Sea*, and Day, *God's Conflict with the Dragon*.

29. The deciphering of the geographical name ים סוף is fraught with difficulty. I follow the lead of Batto, "The Reed Sea," 27–35 and "Red Sea or Reed Sea?" 57–63.

30. The root of this word may have connotations of whirling. See Gruber, "Ten Dance-Derived Expressions," 341–45.

the hand of Yahweh in the lightning. The possessive suffix on ברק ("*his* lightnings") points to the possibility that the lightning is construed as a divine weapon. This would account for the trembling of the earth at the sight of lightning, Yahweh's armament. This verse is yet another description of the divine employing the language of storms, especially lightning, to enhance the portrayal of Yahweh.

Psalm 135:7

> He elevates rising clouds from the end of the earth,
> he makes lightnings with the rain,
> the source of the wind from its storehouses.

This literal rendering of the Hebrew, although not a pristine translation, does emphasize the meteorological elements for which Yahweh is praised. In the purely hymnic context of this psalm, Yahweh is being praised for various aspects of the divine puissance over nature. The effusion of praise for Yahweh's power in vv. 5–7 is sandwiched between an inclusion of Yahweh's historical acts with Israel. The initial act of divine grace was the selection of Israel celebrated in v. 4. The subsequent action is again the exodus (vv. 8–12).

The function of lightning, in the midst of other meteorological phenomena (to be discussed below), in this verse appears to be a display of divine majesty. In other words, the lightning serves no specific utilitarian purpose in this verse. It may be a divine weapon, but if it is, it is only on display in this verse, it is not being brandished or directed at any enemies.

The Tanach, RSV, NASB, NRSV, and REB render the phrase ברקים למטר עשה as making "lightning for the rain," implying a "benefactive" use of the preposition ל (the lamed of interest),[31] whereas I have taken the ל in a comitative sense.[32] The choice of the preposition to be used here is important, since it may imply how the lightning functions in the psalm.[33] Perhaps this is best illustrated by Anderson's attempted justification of the RSV's "lightnings for the rain" by noting "this is rather an odd expression, but it is usually suggested in Canaan there was seldom rain without lightnings; as a

---

31. Waltke and O'Connor, *Introduction to Biblical Hebrew Syntax*, 207–8.
32. Gibson, *Davidson's Introductory Hebrew Grammar: Syntax*, 146.
33. While Weiser's "changes lightnings into rain" (*The Psalms*, 787) is an interesting suggestion, it is meteorologically untenable and without support elsewhere within lightning or rain references.

generalization this may be acceptable."³⁴ First it would need to be established that most Syro-Palestinian rains accompanied thunderstorms, and then the generalization would have to be found acceptable in a meteorological sense. Neither tenet has yet been established.

The sense of this verse is that Yahweh creates both the lightning and the rain (as in the NAB and NJB), and, although these phenomena are related, there is no inherent connection implied. The translation "for the rain" carries the implication that the lightning functions as an instrument of the rain. Since the verse offers a list of the divine meteorological wonders, I find no causality implied, but rather a rendering of the several aspects of the weather for which Yahweh is to be praised. Primarily I take this view based on the other uses of the lightning in the Psalms, where it is seldom taken as an agent of the rain, and frequently it is taken as the weapon of Yahweh. The other meteorological elements, "rising clouds," rain, and wind, will be discussed in the appropriate chapters below.

Psalm 144:6

Blaze lightning and scatter them,
shoot your arrows and discomfit them.

This prayer for deliverance from enemies in battle naturally makes use of much martial imagery. Together with Ps 18:15 [14] it brings together two of the most common words for lightning in the Psalms: ברק and חץ. This verse is a close parallel to Ps 18:15 [14]: even the royal aspect is shared between them.

This lament-like prayer pictures lightning as a divine weapon. The psalmist implores Yahweh to "blaze"³⁵ (בְּרוֹק) the lightning (ברק) at the enemies. The use of this strong imagery implies that both the destructive, fiery element of lightning and its celerity are being invoked by the psalmist as fit punishment to the yet-to-be-mentioned foes. In addition to being martial, the imagery is also theophanic. The wish is for Yahweh to appear, in the face of human frailty, and display the awesome majesty of the divine, as evident in lightning and volcano (v. 5). This general awe is conflated with the idea of the enemies of the psalmist, cited in v. 7 as aliens and in v. 8 as liars.

---

34. A. A. Anderson, *Book of Psalms* 2, 891.

35. Although normally an intransitive verb in English, "blaze" adequately captures both the fiery aspect and swiftness of the lightning that the psalmist implores.

חִצִּים

The most frequent parallel to ברק is חצים, "arrows." It occurs as the parallel to ברק in Pss 18:15 [14] and 144:6, explored above, as well as in the previous verse to Ps 77:19 [18], also examined above. These parallels raise the question concerning the intent behind the use of חצים: when it appears without "lightning" as a parallel, does it still denote lightning? The means of determining an answer to this question is to examine each occurrence with possible meteorological allusion in its context in order to determine how it is being used. Aside from the two verses already examined, potentially meteorological reference is made to arrows in Pss 7:14 [13]; 38:3 [2]; and 77:18 [17]. Other references to arrows occur in the psalms (for example Ps 91:5), but nothing in these further references, no matter how slight, suggests an allusion to lightning.

Psalms 18:15 [14] and 144:6 (above) clearly use חצים as a parallel to lightning, and there is no reason to doubt that in these two verses it is a metaphor for lightning.[36]

Psalm 7:14 [13]

> He has furnished himself with implements of death,
> he makes his arrows burning ones.[37]

The description of Yahweh's war preparations in this lament is part of a longer poetic unit that encompasses v. 13 [12], in which God readies the divine sword (חרב) and bow (קשת). The expected accessory to the bow in v. 13 [12] is arrows. These armaments function in the context of this lament as the psalmist's assurance that Yahweh will punish the wicked. There is no other meteorological imagery presented in the course of the divine preparations.

Given this information, is there any reason to suspect that arrows in this verse denote lightning? The only hint that this may be the case, in context, is the word דלקים ("burning ones") used to describe the arrows. The basic meaning of the root דלק seems to be "heat,"[38] an apt concept to describe lightning, but not necessarily reflecting lightning. The concept of flaming

---

36. Greenstein, "Yahweh's Lightning," 54.

37. The construction with an active participle prefixed with a preposition (לְדֹלְקָם) is unusual. It is not described in Waltke and O'Connor, *Introduction to Biblical Hebrew Syntax*, 612–31 (the section on participles).

38. BDB 196a, KBS 223b.

arrows, used to set cities on fire, does not seem to be attested in the warfare of pre-exilic Israel.[39] Why would arrows be denoted as "burning ones"?

To understand the metaphor, it is necessary to find the point of comparison between arrows and heat. Specifically, the rather rare word דלק appears in contexts that suggest different varieties of heat.[40] In Gen 31:36 Jacob refers to the heat of Laban's chase by use of the verb דלק, a usage similar to that of the chase of the Babylonians in Lam 4:19 and the Israelites' pursuit of the Philistines in 1 Sam 17:53. Obad 18, after describing Israel (house of Jacob, house of Joseph) as flame, indicates that Edom (house of Esau) will be burned (verbal form of דלק) by them. The heat of intoxication is mentioned in Isa 5:11. Most instructive for the current verse are the references in Ezek 24:10 and Deut 28:22.

Ezekiel 24:10 is part of the allegory of the boiling pot. The prophet is warning those who deny Jerusalem's vulnerability that the city will become like a rusted pot under which a fire is kindled. A hiphil form of דלק is used to describe the building of a fire beneath the pot. Deut 28:22 is part of the litany of curses Israel is to pronounce upon themselves if they do not keep the commandments of the rest of the book. The punishments to be meted out in this verse revolve around heat: consumption (שחף), fever (קדח), inflammation (דלק), fiery heat (חרחר), drought (חרב), blight (שדף), and mildew (ירק). All of these ailments involve heat in some way (a little less obvious in the case of mildew, but present nevertheless). These two final verses establish the offensive use of calefaction, and tie the meaning in these verses back to Ps 7:14 [13].

Obviously דלק denotes the generation of heat, and occasionally it is used in an offensive manner. Nowhere else than Ps 7:14 [13] is it used to describe arrows, and nowhere else does it describe lightning. The case for Ps 7:14 [13] bearing a reference to lightning must remain a possibility, but if so, it is a reference that cannot be established with certainty. If lightning is referenced, it occurs here as a divine weapon, as in previous usages.

---

39. Yadin (*The Art of Warfare in Biblical Lands*) does not mention the flaming arrow as a tactic of warfare. He does note that flaming torches were dropped on the Assyrians at the siege of Lachish (plates and text on pp. 434–37), but does not mention flaming arrows. Weiser simply makes the equation "What is meant here are incendiary arrows" (*The Psalms*, 135), as does Kraus "the fiery arrows (used in sieges) are mentioned" (*Psalms 1–59*, 174). Craigie (*Psalms 1–50*, 99) is much more cautious: "the reference may be to arrows dipped in a kind of oil or pitch and set alight before shooting." Drews (*The End of the Bronze Age*, 186, n. 53) notes that a catalogue of Near Eastern arrowheads does not yet exist, making these assertions difficult to substantiate.

40. The heat element is more obscure in Ps 10:2 where the verb דלק indicates the persecution of the poor at the hands of the wicked, and Prov 26:23 where it is used to describe the lips of the wicked.

Psalm 38:3 [2]

> For your arrows descended into me,
> and your hand descended upon me.

In the context of this individual lament, the penetration of Yahweh's arrows into the psalmist may offer a description with a meteorological referent. Being struck by lightning could possibly be compared to being shot by God's arrows, particularly since the divine arrows elsewhere were understood to denote lightning. In this case the connection is extremely tenuous. The main evidence for the possible use of lightning language here is the verb associated with the arrows—נחת "descend." Lightning appears to descend from the sky, and the natural association of coming down from God suggests itself. It should be noted, however, that any perceived punishment could equally be understood as coming down from on high.[41] Furthermore, the ailments the psalmist goes on to present in vv. 4–9 [3–8] (including tumult of the heart and burning in the loins) do not correspond to the effects of having been struck by lightning.[42]

Like 7:14 [13], this verse may refer to lightning, but such an assertion is far from certain. Such a dramatic event in the life of the psalmist would likely have been described in more explicit terms if lightning were involved. If lightning lies behind this image, it is yet again a divine weapon, this time it would be for the cure of the psalmist.

Psalm 77:18 [17]

> Waters poured forth from cumulus,
> clouds gave out voice,
> indeed your arrows scudded.

By virtue of the context and the continuation of meteorological imagery into the next verse (see above), the reference to divine arrows in Ps 77:18 [17] is the only certain reference to arrows as lightning beyond Pss 18:15 [14] and 144:6. The arrows (lightning) are concomitant with clouds, rain, and thunder as part of a theophanic display to disconcert the sea. Parallels with the Enuma Elish[43] may suggest the arrows are God's weapons di-

---

41. Weiser (*The Psalms*, 608–9) presents a useful discussion of divine arrows as other troubles in the context of Ps 91.
42. Uman, *All About Lightning*, 22–23. The heart stops, it does not tremble.
43. For a recent translation see Foster, *Before the Muses*, 1:351–402, especially 375.

rected against the sea, although in this verse they are not shot at the sea, but scudded⁴⁴ (Dahood: "shot back and forth;"⁴⁵ Kraus: "darted about").⁴⁶ The function of such a fulgurous display is to terrify, not to destroy, the sea, according to v. 17 [16]. The end result, however, is the division of the sea for the safe exodus of Israel.

Not surprisingly, whenever חצים, "arrows," is used to describe lightning, it has a martial connotation. This corresponds to a common function of the word ברק, "lightning," discussed above.

אֵשׁ and גֶּחָלִים

The common word for "fire," אש, is possibly used to refer to lightning in ten verses of the Psalms: 11:6; 18:9 [8], 13 [12], 14 [13]; 50:3; 97:3; 104:4; 105:32, 39; 148:8. The Psalms contain many other references to fire, but these are the citations that possibly have a meteorological referent. The association of lightning to fire is natural enough to anyone who observes a lightning strike starting a fire, presumably a very ancient observation. The associations of the main sources of light, the sun and fire,⁴⁷ with lightning would also lead a casual observer to suspect lightning as a source of heat, even without a personal experience of feeling it.

The word גחלים, "coals," has no empirical connection to lightning, but it may be used occasionally in connection with אש to represent lightning. When גחלים does appear to have that meaning, it is only in verses in a construct relationship with or in parallelism to אש: 8:9 [8], 13 [12], and 14 [13] (a less likely verse is 140:11 [10]). Given this juxtaposition, these two metaphors will be considered together.

Psalm 11:6

> He will rain coals (of)⁴⁸ fire and sulphur upon the wicked,
> and a raging wind will be the portion of their cup.

---

44. Although an uncommon verb, "scud" is especially appropriate both for the variety of motion it indicates as well as its meteorological double entendre.
45. Dahood, *Psalms*, 2:224.
46. Kraus, *Psalms 60–150*, 113.
47. See chapter six below for further discussion of the heat of the sun. Like lightning, the sun's primary characteristic in the Psalms seems to have been light rather than heat.
48. Understood, if not actually to be read, as the apparatus of *BHS* suggests.

This mildly imprecatory psalm of confidence utilizes at least two, possibly three, meteorological images. After asserting Yahweh's control of humanity, the psalmist addresses the fate of the wicked. The instrument of "raging wind," treated in the next chapter, is certainly a weather-based image. It is paralleled by "coals (of) fire" (פחים אש), and this parallel with a meteorological image suggests the possibility that "coals (of) fire" might be a reference to lightning. The verb used to describe these coals is מטר, "rain"—another weather-related term. To rain something on someone implies that the object is coming from the sky, which again supports a lightning interpretation.

The further parallel with sulphur (גפרית), on the other hand, suggests a reference to the destruction of the cities of the plain in Gen 19:24 (in which at least three of the elements of this verse recur: המטיר ... גפרית ואש) where supernatural phenomena, not the natural phenomenon of lightning, is the focus.[49] The word "coals" (פחים) does not occur in the construct state in this verse, instead it is a plural absolute; however, the sense of the verse appears to require a genitival translation. If this translation is accepted as a working hypothesis, then it is difficult to discern why a physical object, coal, would be used to describe lightning, which has no physical form or residue.

In the end, this verse must remain ambiguous. A meteorological reference to lightning is possible, but not certain. If lightning is intended, it is used in the way that lightning has been used elsewhere in the Psalms—as a divine weapon to be used against the wicked.

Psalm 18:9 [8]

> Smoke ascended from his nostrils,
> and devouring fire from his mouth,
> coals blazed out from him.

Psalm 18 contains a plethora of weather terms, especially when describing the theophanic appearance of Yahweh coming to the aid of the psalmist. This context lends credibility to some of the meteorological implications of weather-neutral words, as in the case of this verse.[50] Upon first glance "fire" in this verse is simply a parallel to "smoke" in the first line of the tricolon and "coals" (גחלים) in the final line of this verse. This assessment may

---

49. Sarna, *Genesis*, 138, makes this clear despite the common attempt to find an historical antecedent (Speiser, *Genesis*, 142; von Rad, *Genesis*, 220–21; Vawter, *On Genesis*, 240–41).

50. A. A. Anderson (*Book of Psalms*, 1:157) suggested that the reference to fire here "may be to the lightning-flashes since a number of the following metaphors are derived from the experience of thunderstorms."

indeed be accurate since the verse itself does not require a meteorological interpretation. The reason for suggesting a weather aspect to fire here is its larger context. Theophanic descriptions frequently use severe weather terms to describe the awesomeness of the coming of Yahweh.

In this particular verse it is very difficult to determine whether or not weather lies behind the referents. The immediate cause of the calefactory elements (fire, smoke, coals) appears to be the anger of Yahweh mentioned in the previous verse (v. 8 [7]). The natural phenomena mentioned in that verse correspond to an earthquake, and that is followed by these aspects of a conflagration. The verb associated with smoke and fire, עלה ("ascend"), does not inherently suggest weather.

The reason for listing this verse as a possible weather reference is its context. In several of the following verses, beginning with v. 11 [10], undisputed meteorological imagery is used. This verse may be a precursor to that usage, but it cannot be considered certain. If fire refers to lightning here its function is to demonstrate the anger of Yahweh. Its destructive potential is not far from mind, but it does not actively participate in any devastation in this verse.

The word which may more likely resemble lightning in this verse, by virtue of its verb, is "coals" (גחלים). This word, however, has a straightforward referent in physical coals, according to the lexica.[51] There is not enough contextual force for either fire or coals necessarily to represent lightning in this verse.

Psalm 18:13–14 [12–13]

13 [12] From brightness before him,
through his cumulonimbus traversed
hail and coals of fire,

14 [13] Yahweh even caused thunder in the heavens,
and Elyon gave his voice,
hail and coals of fire.

The context here is much more certain. The theophany has moved from the initial description of the awe of Yahweh's appearance to the action Yahweh takes, portrayed in the language of a severe thunderstorm. Kraus suggests that this is actually "the activities of a mighty thunderstorm and a volcanic eruption ... telescoped into each other."[52] Be that as it may, the weather

---

51. BDB, 160b–161a; KBS, 188a; *DCH* 2, 342.
52. Kraus, *Psalms 1–59*, 260.

images will each be discussed in their relevant chapters, but here our focus will be on lightning terminology.

The word "brightness" (נגה) in this context may refer to the brilliance of lightning, which is the brightest form of natural light visible on the earth. The word itself does not denote lightning, but the context here supports the possibility of its metaphorical use to describe a fulgurous display.

The phrase, however, to which we should pay special attention in these verses is גחלי־אש, "coals of fire," which is undoubtedly lightning in this context.[53] This construct chain, along with the noun "hail," is used as a refrain at the termination of both verses.[54] The listing of "coals of fire" along with hail, cumulonimbus clouds, and thunder in these two verses, and followed in the next verse by direct reference to lightning, the context demands the interpretation of lightning for the phrase. The obvious use of גחלים, or lightning, lends credence to the interpretation of "coals" as lightning elsewhere as well.

The lightning is used in these two verses to describe the majesty of the divine appearance. It may be construed as Yahweh's weaponry, as in the next verse, but if so, it is only a potential weapon in vv. 13–14 [12–13] since it is not used against any foe. This is the function of lightning noted for Pss 97:4 and 135:7, above.

Psalm 50:3

> Our God enters and is not silent,
> fire consumes before him,
> and around him it storms severely.

As noted above, this verse contains storm language (שער). A verse utilizing storm terminology which also mentions fire (אש) is a good candidate for a lightning reference. The psalm as a whole celebrates Yahweh's ownership of and judgment over the world. This verse in particular describes a theophanic appearance of Yahweh, with attendant storms, and perhaps lightning. The "fire" is said to "consume" (אכל) before the divine appearance. The function

---

53. Brown, "Yahweh, Zeus, Jupiter," 186.

54. There is no reason that this must be a case of dittography, for which see Kraus, *Psalms 1–59*, 253, 255; Dahood, *Psalms, 1:1–50*, 108–9; Weiser, *The Psalms*, 183, 185. Its lack at the end of 2 Sam 22:14 does not indicate whether it is an error or an elaboration here. I prefer to understand it as the latter and to treat the text as received. On this point I concur with Craigie, *Psalms 1–50*, 169: "the variations between Ps 18 and 2 Sam 22 are considerable at this point, and Ps 18 has effective poetry through the duplication of the line. As repetition is a distinctive feature of some early Hebrew poetry . . . it is better to retain the phrase in both verses."

of such an awe-inspiring display is that it prevents too close an approach to the God of Israel. The consuming fire warns humans to keep their distance and adds to the awe generated by the divine manifestation. A second function of the consuming action of the divine fire is that it acts as weaponry. It appears here as a potential tool used by God to display divine power. If this is a fulgurous reference, it does not explicitly cite lightning as divine weaponry, but such a possibility remains open.

Psalm 97:3

> Fire goes forth from his presence,
> and incinerates his enemies around about.

This enthronement psalm celebrates Yahweh's victories over God's enemies. The suggestion that "fire" means "lightning" here is supported by the surrounding verses, which provide a strong meteorological context. Verse 2 mentions the clouds around Yahweh, and v. 4 cites lightning directly (see above). Furthermore, the function of the fire in this verse is the incineration (להט) of God's enemies. This function corresponds to the main function of lightning as a divine weapon, as it appears elsewhere in the Psalms. The secondary function, as gleaned from the hymnic nature of the psalm as a whole, is to magnify the awe of Yahweh.

These two factors, context and function, do not prove that אש should necessarily be interpreted as lightning in this verse; fire incinerates as well as lightning. Nowhere else in the Psalms is להט used with lightning terms. These aspects neither confirm or deny the connection, but they call for caution when using this verse for meteorological metaphors.

Psalm 104:4

> Making winds your messengers,
> fire (and) flame your servants.

Psalm 104 is noted as a hymn celebrating the created world and its attendant phenomena. It is also recognized as having some connection with the ancient Egyptian Hymn to the Aton, or solar disc.[55] The concern for this

---

55. The literature on this psalm is immense. For purposes of this study, the following sources are highlighted: Craigie, "The Comparison of Hebrew Poetry," 10–21; and Dion, "Yahweh as Storm-god," 43–71. For a translation of the Hymn to the Aton, see, conveniently, Pritchard, ed. *Ancient Near Eastern Texts*, 369–71; and Hallo, ed., *The*

study, however, is to determine if the terms "fire" (אש) and "flame" (להט) refer to lightning.

There is undoubtedly a mythological scenario behind the naming of the two elements fire and flame as divine servants,[56] as shown in *KTU* 1.2 i 32, where the two messengers of the deity Yammu are designated *išt ištm* "a fire, two fires." The reference to Ugaritic mythological messengers, however, does not clarify whether or not they are perceived as lightning in this verse.

Fire and flame occur in parallel with winds. As messengers, the celerity of the wind would be an asset, and is likely the reason for this designation of winds as messengers. Wind is a meteorological phenomenon. Is a similar dynamic at work in the choice of fire and flame? Once again the apparent swiftness of fire and flame could account for their status as servants, and this is a trait that they would share with lightning, which travels at speeds up to 60,000 miles per second on the return stroke.[57]

The meteorological context which this verse may implicate mostly occurs in vv. 3 and 6–9. Verse 3 clearly portrays Yahweh riding the wings of the wind (see the next chapter for further discussion), and vv. 6–9 may describe the coming of a rain storm (see chapter four). With this surrounding meteorological imagery, the possibility that lightning is intended should be left open. The calefactory connotation of fire and flame could also apply to lightning.

If lightning is intended in this verse, it has an entirely new function to those previously noted. Here it would serve as a servant of Yahweh, nearly a personified phenomenon. Lightning would be an agent of the divine, its particular mission, however, is not specified.

Psalm 105:32

> He gave (for) their winter rains hail,
> fire of flames in their land.

Psalm 105 is a lengthy recitation of Israel's checkered history, with hymnic and didactic intent.[58] The event alluded to is narrated in Exod 9:22–26, specifically v. 24. The story of the exodus relates how, as Moses was negotiating with Pharaoh, the plagues were sent upon Egypt. The seventh plague was hail that killed the cattle and crops. Verses 23b–24 read:

Context of Scripture, 1:44–46.

56. Dahood, *Psalms*, 3:35; Allen, *Psalms 101–150*, 26.
57. Uman, *All About Lightning*, 76.
58. Haglund, *Historical Motifs in the Psalms*, 22.

Yahweh gave voices (קלת) and hail, and fire went earthward and Yahweh rained hail upon the land of Egypt. (24) And there was hail and fire (אש) taking ahold of itself (מִתְלַקַּחַת) throughout; the like of the very heavy hail in all the land of Egypt has not been from the time that Egypt became a nation.

This plague is described more verbosely than previous plagues,[59] and the reference to the fire is ambiguous. It has been assumed that the fire refers to lightning—not an unreasonable conjecture since hail normally accompanies severe thunderstorms with their attendant lightning. The fit is even more likely if קלת, "voices," refers to thunder. The point of the Exodus narrative is, however, precisely how unusual this occurrence was. The verb used with fire (מִתְלַקַּחַת), a hithpael form of לקח, is attested only here and in Ezekiel's description of a theophany in Ezek 1:4 (where it is associated with clouds). The exact meaning of this verb is debated, and this information is necessary to ascertain how the fire was perceived. The description of the plague, particularly in Exod 9:23b–24 corresponds to a typical severe thunderstorm, if thunder and lightning are referenced.

The word אש, "fire," is used of lightning elsewhere in the Psalms (see above), and the word קול "voice" is likewise used of thunder in the Psalms (see below). Hail, discussed in chapter five, nearly always falls from thunderclouds. Given this concurrence of meteorological phenomena, despite the unusual nature of the plague,[60] it appears likely that the fire of Exod 9:24 refers to lightning.

If this is the case, then Ps 105:32 refers to lightning as well. In this particular verse "fire of flames" is paralleled by the meteorological phenomenon of hail given for rain. The wider context, therefore, suggests that the preternatural lightning is the concomitant of the hail. The lightning in such a case is referred to by a new phrase, אש להבות, "fire of flames," probably to account for the intensity of the fulgurous display. The function of the probable lightning is the same as the general function of lightning in the Psalms: it is used by Yahweh as an instrument of punishment, here for the recalcitrant Pharaoh.

---

59. Childs, *The Book of Exodus*, 158.

60. A standard explanation of oddity of such a storm is its timing (the flax was in bud and the barley in the ear, according to v. 31) and not necessarily the meteorological phenomena themselves. Even the event of a severe thunderstorm, that is, its very intensity, may render it unusual. This is true even in lands where thunderstorms are common.

Psalm 105:39

> He spread a cloud for a covering,
> and fire to light up the night.

Still in the context of the historically oriented Ps 105, weather terminology appears to explain the presence of Yahweh in the wilderness.[61] As with the previous citation, this verse hearkens back to the book of Exodus. First appearing as the Israelites journeyed into the wilderness, Yahweh demonstrated the divine presence in the form of a pillar of cloud by day and a pillar of cloud by night (Exod 13:21). There is nothing in the text to suggest that a meteorological phenomenon was occurring, but given the nomenclature, it is important to consider it here.

Slayton is certainly correct as he summarizes that the Exodus account "does not introduce the theophany by description. The title itself became the description. . . . Any natural explanation of these phenomena seems to be strained."[62] The parallel of fire with cloud might suggest lightning, if a natural phenomenon was being described.[63] The psalmist, however, is simply following the lead of the exodus tradition in using cultic experience to describe the divine presence.[64]

Psalm 140:11 [10]

> May coals from the fire drop upon them,
> may they fall into the watery pit, not to arise.

This reference is highly dubious as a possible meteorological citation of אש and גחלים, but it must be considered for the sake of thoroughness. Not only would a reference to lightning be out of context here, there may be a textual problem in this verse. The main reason for considering this personal lament as a potential weather reference is the motif of falling fire and coals (גחלים באש). These two nouns, when used together, frequently imply lightning, as

---

61. This is well summarized in Fox, *The Five Books of Moses*, 244–45.

62. Slayton, "Pillar of Fire and Cloud," 372, 373. The volcanic hypothesis (for example, Noth, *Exodus*, 109) tends also to reduce the blatant supernatural description to a modern historiographic concern.

63. For a helpful discussion of the meteorological imagery used with the Exodus account see Mann, "The Pillar of Cloud," 15–30.

64. For the cultic interpretation see Sarna, *Exploring Exodus*, 112–13. Perhaps the most popular interpretation is that the pillar is the Sinai theophany in miniature, see, for example, Haran, *Temples and Temple-Service*, 267; Noth, *Exodus*, 109.

noted in several cases above. In most of those instances either the context is decidedly meteorological or the verbs used with the flaming coals indicate that they are being thrown down from above, and therefore resemble lightning. Neither of these criteria apply here.

The verb used with fire/coals here is מוט, the root meaning of which is "to totter" or "shake."[65] The hiphil form takes on a meaning of "drop" only with a semantic twisting and stretching. KBS brackets the entire hiphil section for the verb, and *BHS* suggests that the root should possibly be מטר. Other than the wish of the psalmist that fiery coals be used as a divine weapon to punish the psalmist's foes, the use of these elements bears no resemblance to their connotation of lightning as seen elsewhere in Psalms.

Psalm 148:8

> Fire and hail, snow and dark cloud,
> stormy wind doing his command.

This psalm was initially introduced under storm terminology above. All of the elements represented as praising Yahweh in this verse are meteorological, and there is no reason to doubt that fire, here paired with its nearly constant companion hail, is intended to denote lightning. The function of lightning in this verse is to demonstrate the majesty of Yahweh, a function which was noted in Pss 97:4; 135:7 and 18:13–14 [12–13], discussed above.

לַחֲבוֹת

Psalm 29:7

> The voice of Yahweh cleaves flames of fire.

This psalm will be examined as a whole below, under thunder. At that point it will be considered whether or not "flames of fire" (להבות אש) represents lightning.[66]

---

65. BDB, 556b; KBS, 555.
66. See especially Greenstein, "Yahweh's Lightning," 49–57.

חֲנָמֵל and רְשָׁפִים

Two further words which may have been used to indicate lightning are רשפים and חנמל, which occur only in the following location in the Psalms.

Psalm 78:47–48

> 47 And he killed their vine with hail,
> and their sycamores with lightning (חנמל).[67]
> 48 And he delivered up their livestock to the hail,
> and their cattle to the flames (רשפים).

The context of these verses is a series of reminiscences of Yahweh's deliverance of Israel from Egypt in a lengthy didactic hymn of Israel's history. These verses commemorate the seventh plague, the same plague mentioned in Ps 105:32, above.

The first word for lightning, חנמל, will be fully discussed below in chapter five, since the context of hail clarifies the meaning of the term. It is sufficient here to note that context and intertextual comparison support the translation of this hapax legomenon as "lightning."

In v. 48 the word used for the fire, רשפים, is different from both Ps 105:32 and Exod 9:24 which mention אש as the agent of destruction. The connection of this word with the name of the deity Resheph has not gone unnoticed,[68] but the psalm clearly refers to the plagues prior to the exodus. Although the results of the plague resemble the works of Resheph,[69] here it appears as a common noun.

The analysis of these verses is complicated by the wide-spread suggestion of a textual error affecting both potential meteorological terms in the pericope. If, as Symmachus suggests, ברד should be read as דבר "pestilence," then the word רשפים could be translated as "the flame of fever,"[70] "epidemics,"[71] or "plague" or "disease."[72] This is an attractive suggestion since hail is mentioned in the previous verse,[73] and v. 48 would refer to another of the plagues (the fifth plague, death of the cattle). Metathesis could account

---

67. For a discussion of this term, see chapter five.
68. A. A. Anderson, *Book of Psalms* 2:572; Tate, *Psalms 51–100*, 283.
69. The standard work on Resheph is Fulco, *The Canaanite God Rešep*.
70. Briggs and Briggs, *Book of Psalms*, 2:88, 195.
71. Kraus, *Psalms 60–150*, 122.
72. Tate, *Psalms 51–100*, 283.
73. As pointed out by A. A. Anderson, *Book of Psalms* 2:572.

for the error, and there is manuscript support. Such a change, however, is more convenient than necessary. In keeping the MT, the meaning does not suffer, and the intensity of the hail is emphasized.

The function of the possible lightning, along with the hail, is to bring awe to Egypt's consideration of Yahweh. It functions as a divine weapon to punish the hard-heartedness of Pharaoh, and is thus little different than previous uses of the phenomenon.

SUMMARY OF LIGHTNING FUNCTIONS

Lightning, despite the several words used to denote it, has only two basic functions in the Psalms: to be divine weaponry and to show the glory of Yahweh. Lightning which shows the glory of Yahweh occurs in the following passages: Pss 18:13–14 [12–13]; 50:3; 97:4; 135:7; and 148:8. Lightning as a divine weapon may be divided into several categories. The divine weapons could plausibly be turned on the psalmist (possibly, Ps 38:3 [2]), the psalmist's enemies (Ps 18:15 [14]; 144:6, and possibly 7:14 [13]; 11:6; 97:3), or on the chaos of Sea (Ps 77:18–19 [17–18]). Specifically the enemies may be Egypt, as is the case in which the referent is the plagues of the exodus (Pss 78:48 and 105:32). It is possible that lightning is alluded to in order to demonstrate Yahweh's anger (Ps 18:9 [8]). In one place lightning may be intended to be Yahweh's agent or servant (Ps 104:4). In each of this cases lightning functions in relation to Yahweh's use of it or control over it. It is never described in purely naturalistic terms. Lightning may appear in both roles of weaponry and indicator of glory in Ps 50:3, where it consumes before the divine presence.

THUNDER

The final major component of a thunderstorm to be explored in this chapter is thunder.[74] Interestingly enough, thunder does not always accompany lightning, and it certainly does not occur paired with lightning as does hail. The causality between lightning and thunder has only recently, in historical terms, been understood.[75]

---

74. For a detailed exposition on the mechanism of thunder, see the chapter on thunder in Uman, *Lightning*, 181–201.

75. As noted in Uman, *All About Lightning*, 103–4, thunder was associated with the lightning channel by Benjamin Franklin, and only correctly understood in the twentieth century.

Thunder is represented both by nouns and verbs in the Psalms, and it is frequently considered, at least metaphorically, as the voice of Yahweh. Only two words are regularly used to refer to thunder: רעם and קול־יהוה (or its variants). Both of these will be considered together since they frequently occur in parallelism. When thunder is not directly mentioned, the verse will be analyzed for evidence of a meteorological connection for the word קול.

A word about "thunderbolts": as poetic as this word is, it is technically inaccurate.[76] Thunder consists of the sound waves caused by the rapidly expanding gases due to the heat of a lightning discharge. While pre-scientific societies frequently thought of thunder as a physical phenomenon, it is now understood to be primarily a form of sound energy. Nevertheless, since the Psalms fall under the category of pre-scientific writings, and since they participate in the mythological world of their surroundings, the translation "thunderbolt" may appropriately be used as an archaizing touch, but it will be avoided here.

Psalm 18:14 [13]

> Yahweh even caused thunder in[77] the heavens,
> and Elyon gave his voice,
> hail and coals of fire.

This verse was also considered in the context of lightning, above. Prior to the mention of lightning (coals of fire), two lines are addressed to thunder. This verse is part of an extended theophanic account of Yahweh coming to the rescue of the psalmist. Thunder is here cited by both the verb וירעם "and caused thunder" and the phrase נתן קלו "gave his voice." This verse, therefore, serves as a clear indication that God's voice is a direct parallel to thunder (supposing that Yahweh and Elyon are two separate names for the same deity used in proper congruence[78] or "synonymous parallelism"). The thunder is located in the sky in this verse, since it is from there that Yahweh appears to be descending in the larger pericope. This congruence of thunder and Yahweh's voice will be amply demonstrated elsewhere.

---

76. Geer, *Glossary of Weather and Climate*, 231, while noting its popular usage, ascribes the term to the realm of mythology.

77. This is an instance in which a constructive difference occurs between this psalm and 2 Samuel 22. As pointed out by A. A. Anderson (*Psalms*, 1:158), Craigie (*Psalms 1–50*, 169) and Dahood (*Psalms*, 1:108), 2 Sam 22:14 uses the preposition מן "from," which may well be the meaning in this verse, although expressed by the preposition ב.

78. Watson, *Classical Hebrew Poetry*, 118.

The function of the thunder here, in the theophanic context, is a war-shout. This tactic is the ancient art of intimidation; its inclusion in the account of Jericho (regardless of historical accuracy) demonstrates that it was an approved method of inspiring terror. This will become even clearer in Ps 29. Yahweh in Ps 18 is approaching to discomfit the enemies of the psalmist, and the thunderous shout helps to serve this purpose.

Psalm 29:3

Numerically the next reference to thunder is Ps 29:3. Since it is part of a paean to Yahweh's voice, probably intended to denote thunder, all of the references to Ps 29 will be considered together at the end of this section.

Psalm 42:8 [7]

> Deep calls to deep,
> with the voice of צִנּוֹרֶיךָ,
> all your breakers and your waves,
> they will pass over me.

This verse is more of an interpretative crux for the psalm than it appears from viewing standard translations. The noun צנור is uncertain in meaning, and, while not a hapax legomenon, its second HB occurrence does not enlighten its use in this verse.[79] The focus on this psalm of lament in the standard literature has tended to be an attempt to fix its provenance, which is suspected to have been the northern kingdom of Israel. The supposed northern origin of the psalm has become almost axiomatic in modern studies.[80] This northern origin then becomes a hermeneutic principle for interpreting v. 8 [7]. צנור becomes "cataract" or the like, referring specifically to Dan, at the head waters of the Jordan River, at Mount Hermon, with the added support of the LXX.[81]

---

79. The other HB occurrence is in 2 Sam 5:8 where David is attempting to take Jerusalem. This is ultimately accomplished by climbing the צנור, presumably part of the water system, into the city.

80. Goulder, *The Psalms of the Sons of Korah*, 25–28, 32; Rendsburg, *Linguistic Evidence*, 51–60; Holladay, *Psalms through Three Thousand Years*, 28–29; Briggs and Briggs, *Book of Psalms*, 1:370; Weiser, *The Psalms*, 348; and Kraus, *Psalms 1–59*, 438. This interpretation is, however, by no means universal; see Dahood, *Psalms*, 1:254–59; A. A. Anderson, *Book of Psalms*, 1:332–33; Craigie, *Psalms 1–50*, 325–26; and Reymond, *L'eau*, 170.

81. Goulder, *The Psalms of the Sons of Korah*, 27.

Many of the arguments for a northern origin of this specific psalm are geographical rather than linguistic. If the geographical identification is called into question then the northern evidence for Ps 42 is scant. The geographical reconstruction is bolstered by linguistic evidence, based on the fact that many of the Korahite psalms tend to show northern linguistic features. In Psalms studies in general the titles are not given much credence for establishing a provenance or setting since they are later additions. The question must be asked: are the Korahite psalms necessarily a homogeneous group? Even if the identification is correct, and even if the tradition predates the post-exilic period,[82] were the Korahites necessarily from one locale? Our knowledge of the Korahites is very slim.

Setting aside the geographical reconstruction for Ps 42, an examination of the linguistic evidence for this particular psalm shows some weakness. The only linguistic feature cited by Rendsburg for this psalm is that in v. 2 a third person, masculine singular verb occurs with a ת preformative (כְּאַיָּל תַּעֲרֹג).[83] The traditional explanation for this construction is that "[m]asculine nouns which either have a separate feminine form or might easily form one, are but seldom used as epicene [i.e., to indicate either sex]."[84] Dahood offers another explanation as well, namely, placing the ת on the end of כאיל, and considering the verb an infinitive absolute.[85] The end result of this ongoing discussion concerning this single grammatical feature is that the precise geographic location of the psalm is not assured.[86] Even pairing it with the following psalm, while traditionally taken as an original arrangement, does not prove that the psalms were written by the same author at the same location or time.

This, in turn, opens the possibilities for the meaning of צנור. Perhaps the best way to determine its meaning is to determine its textual context and see if that gives us any indications. The most basic textual context is that of a psalmist being separated from the temple and lamenting the fact. Nowhere is Jerusalem mentioned, a fact which has led some to suppose that the longing is for a rival sanctuary to the Jerusalem temple.[87] To be as objective as

---

82. Craigie, *Psalms 1–50*, 326.

83. Rendsburg, *Linguistic Evidence*, 53–54.

84. GKC§ 122f. Similarly, BDB, 788a.

85. Dahood, *Psalms*, 1:255.

86. A. A. Anderson, *Book of Psalms*, 1:329: "There are some doubts about the geographical terms in verse 6, and it is possible that they are metaphors rather than actual locations."

87. Goulder, *Psalms of the Sons of Korah*, 28, suggests the psalmist is wishing to worship at Dan.

possible, it is best not to commit the interpretation of the psalm to a specific sanctuary until further details can be deduced.

Being separated from the particular sanctuary, the psalmist possibly lists the features of his or her current location or of where he or she wishes to be. This is the immediate context of 7 [6]. The specific geographical location is speculative, although popularly accepted. The present verse is then followed by an assurance of divine help in v. 9 [8]. The remainder of the psalm continues in the vein of an individual lament. This textual context leads me to believe that v. 8 [7] is a fulcrum for the psalm; this verse is pivotal for the shift in mood in the following verse.

What is happening in v. 8 [7]? The "deep calls to deep" must reflect a cosmological circumstance. As has been noted already, cosmological events frequently accompany a theophany in the Psalms. I would suggest that this verse begins the assurance which is continued into the next verse by describing, in abbreviated terms, a theophany to the psalmist. After the deep calls to deep, this is further qualified in the next line: "with the voice of your צנורים. All of God's "breakers" and "waves" then pass over (עבר) the psalmist, in language reminiscent of "all of" God's "goodness" passing over (עבר) Moses in Exod 33:19. In that context as well as this, it is an individual's desire that is being fulfilled.[88]

Etymologically צנור is a mystery, its first root being unrelated to other languages by comparative philology, and being poorly attested in Hebrew. In such a case, the context must be the surest guide. Reymond, in his work on water in the Hebrew Bible, suggests that underwater currents would best fit this context.[89] Breakers and waves seem forced in a fluvial context, notwithstanding the certainty of the Briggses.[90] If these deeps, breakers, and waves are part of the mythological appurtenances of chaos, perhaps the צנורים are used to control that chaos as part of the theophany alluded to in this verse. "Thunder" may also be considered a potential candidate in the light of the psalmist's use of the word קול, "voice" or "sound." Since קול is sometimes utilized to designate thunder, it should remain an option here. Following Sukenik's explanation for this word, as ably utilized by Dahood, I believe "thunderbolts" to be the most adequate solution, since it retains the mythological essence of the image.[91]

If thunder is accepted in this verse, its function is to introduce a theophanic experience. In doing so, it announces God's presence to the

---

88. Sarna, *Exodus*, 214.
89. Reymond, *L'eau*, 170.
90. Briggs and Briggs, *Book of Psalms*, 1:370.
91. Sukenik, "The Account of David's Capture," 12–16; Dahood, *Psalms*, 1:254, 259.

Psalm 68:34 [33]

> To the rider in the heavens, ancient heavens,
> hark, he gives forth his voice, mighty voice,

Psalm 68 is notoriously difficult to translate and interpret.[92] This particular verse is thankfully straightforward, and it is a continuation of the thought of the previous verse that further qualifies the God who is being praised. God is being lauded in this hymn in both martial and liturgical phraseology. In this particular verse the deity is described as the rider in the heavens who gives out his voice—is the divine voice in this verse an analogue for thunder? Context must once again be the guiding principle for deciding the issue.

The last four verses (33–36 [32–35]) of this psalm form a sub-unit.[93] The universality of God is addressed in v. 33 [32], God's location in heaven is praised in vv. 34–35 [33–34]; and the final verse localizes God in the temple. Within this context, v. 34 [33] functions to praise God's activities in the heavens (the grammatically difficult בִּשְׁמֵי־קֶדֶם). Despite the grammatical difficulty, it is obvious that God is being considered in the role of sky-rider, first broached in v. 5 [4]. This places the locus of the activity in the meteorological realm and suggests that the voice of God in the context of the skies is an expression for thunder.

The function of thunder in this verse is to glorify God. This is shown in the context of v. 33 [32] which begins with the imperative to sing to God. This thought is directly continued into the verse under consideration with the addition of reasons for offering such praise: God rides in the heavens, God thunders. The following verse, 35 [34] returns to the bidding of praise to God "ascribe might to God," thus continuing the theme.

Psalm 77:18–19 [17–18]

> Waters poured forth from cumulus,
> clouds gave out voice,

---

92. See the commentaries, Mowinckel, *Der Achtundsechzigste Psalm*; and also Podechard, "Psaume LXVIII," 502–20; Caquot, "Le psaume LXVIII," 147–82.

93. A. A. Anderson, *Book of Psalms*, 1:498; Briggs and Briggs, *Book of Psalms*, 2:105; Goulder, *The Prayers of David*, 213; Kraus, *Psalms 60–150*, 56; Tate, *Psalms 51–100*, 184; Weiser, *The Psalms*, 490.

indeed your arrows scudded.
19 [18] The voice of your thunder was in the whirlwind,
lightnings lit the world,
the earth quaked and shook.

This reference to thunder appears in the context of a theophany. The lightning terminology was examined above; the question concerning the whirlwind will be considered in detail in the next chapter. In these verses thunder, רעם, and "voice" (or "sound," קול) occur together again. Each verse attributes thunder to a different locutor: the clouds provide thunder in v. 18 [17], while the thunder originates with God in v. 19 [18]. The attribution of thunder to the clouds, while close to technically correct, is unique to this verse. The voice God's thunder in the whirlwind may reflect the actual experience of a tornado, since besides the characteristic funnel, the most common element reported by tornado witnesses is the noise. This question will be explored more fully in the next chapter.

The pairing of "voice" (קול) and "your thunder" (רעמך) in a construct relationship in v. 19 [18] should dispel any doubt as to the relationship of God's voice and thunder.

The theophanic, meteorological elements cited in these two verses lead to an earthquake. Their function, as noted above, is to frighten the sea, chaos. This is done in the context of the deliverance from Egypt. Since the lightning in these verses represents a divine weapon, thunder, to continue the analogy, was probably intended to represent the divine war cry. This battle shout had the effect of intimidating an enemy before battle was actually engaged, as it does to the sea in this pericope.

Psalm 81:8 [7]

In trouble you cried out and I rescued you,
I answered you in the hiding place of thunder,
I tested you at the waters of Meribah (selah).

Psalm 81 is a song of praise. As with most songs of praise, reason is given for the adulation offered. The reason given in this psalm is historical—God's act of deliverance from Egypt. The theme of Egypt is introduced in v. 6 [5] and continues through the remainder of the psalm. In v. 8 [7] an explicit episode of divine care is singled out: the providing of water at Meribah (Exod 17:1–7), as a test.[94] Unlike the Exodus account, God here responds with

94. The "third theme" of the Meribah story, according to Sarna, *Exodus*, 93.

theophanic overtones (not to be confused with the appearance on Sinai, which has not yet been reached in the narrative).⁹⁵ Far more likely than the common suggestion that God is answering Israel from Sinai, the "hiding place (סתר) of thunder" likely refers to its "storehouse." The elemental aspects of theophanic displays were conceived of as hidden away in divine storehouses, as mentioned directly in Ps 135:7. Comparison should also be made with Job 38:22–24 where Yahweh directly confronts Job with the question of the hidden location of the storehouses of snow and hail and light. This storehouse aspect will be more fully discussed in the next chapter, but it is necessary to see it as the background for this verse since it occurs here.

As to the function of the thunder in this psalm, it again serves to glorify God. The Israelites required the sustaining power of water in the wilderness, and the God who controls thunder, known to be associated with storms and rain, provided them with water, yet withheld the storm. No thunder peals in this verse, but wonder is expressed at the God who controls that thunder in its hiding place.

Psalm 104:7

> From your rebuke they flee,
> from the voice of your thunder they hasten.

The subject to which the two verbs in this verse refer are the waters standing above the mountains mentioned in v. 6. To sharpen the focus on this frame of reference we must consider which waters these are. The entire context of Ps 104 is that of creation, and Yahweh's influence is seen on a cosmological scale. This is the frame of reference for the waters in v. 6: they are paralleled with "the deep" (תהום) and they stand above the mountains. These cosmological waters flee (נוס) and hasten (חפז) from Yahweh's voice in v. 7. Specifically they scurry away from קול רעמך "the voice of your thunder," raising the question of whether this verse contains a reference to rain—are these the waters that flee from the thunder during a rainstorm? This specific question will be addressed further in chapter four below. The reason for raising it here is to determine whether the thunder in this verse is meteorological or simply a reference to the roar of falling waters, as of perhaps a waterfall? Alternatively, it may be construed as a divine weapon in the *Chaoskampf* motif.⁹⁶

---

95. Kraus, *Psalms 60–150*, 151; Tate, *Psalms 51–100*, 323.
96. Allen, *Psalms 101–150*, 33; A. A. Anderson, *Book of Psalms*, 2:720; Briggs and

This latter sense of the scene is undoubtedly present as Yahweh is portrayed in this psalm as the creator who controls the unruly, chaotic waters with a thunderous voice. I would suggest, as will be argued further below, that there is a more naturalistic side to this cosmic action in that the thunder here accompanies a rainstorm in which the primeval waters fall to their assigned place from their locale above the mountains down to the valleys they occupied in biblical times.

What is the function of thunder in such a portrayal? Here it is a divine weapon to cause terror in the chaotic waters as they prepare to join battle with Yahweh. The battle, however, never takes place. The thunder is sufficient to cause the waters to flee.

Psalm 29

> Ascribe to Yahweh sons of gods,
> ascribe to Yahweh glory and might!
> 2 Ascribe to Yahweh the glory of his name,
> fall prostrate[97] before Yahweh in the splendor of holiness!
> 3 The voice of Yahweh is upon the waters,
> the God of glory makes thunder,
> Yahweh upon the mighty waters.
> 4 The voice of Yahweh has power,
> the voice of Yahweh has splendor.
> 5 The voice of Yahweh breaks cedars,
> and Yahweh splinters the cedars of Lebanon.
> 6 And he causes Lebanon to skip like a calf,
> and Sirion like wild ox calves.
> 7 The voice of Yahweh cleaves flames of fire.
> 8 The voice of Yahweh twists the wilderness,
> Yahweh twists the wilderness of Kadesh.
> 9 The voice of Yahweh makes deer writhe,[98]
> and strips bare the forests,
> and in his temple all say "Glory!"
> 10 Yahweh sits on the flood,
> and Yahweh is enthroned forever.

Briggs, *Book of Psalms*, 2:332–33; Dahood, *Psalms*, 3:36; Kraus, *Psalms 60–150*, 300; Weiser, *The Psalms*, 667.

97. On the root of הִשְׁתַּחֲווּ see Emerton, "The Etymology of *hištaḥᵃwāh*," 41–55; Kreuzer, "Zur Bedeutung und Etymologie," 39–60.

98. See the discussion below.

11 Yahweh gives might to his people,
Yahweh blesses his people with peace.

It is appropriate to translate this entire psalm since it is a paean to the God who issues thunder, Yahweh.[99] The focus of my observations, however, will be those verses that mention thunder specifically. The first reference to the divine voice comes in v. 3 where the initial identification between Yahweh's voice and thunder is explicitly made: the voice of Yahweh is congruent with thunder in the second of the three cola. This interpretation has been challenged,[100] however, and it must be asked if the context truly supports such an interpretation.

Initially it should be noted that the coincidence of Yahweh's voice and thunder elsewhere in the Psalms demonstrates a connection on a conceptual level. These two concepts were related in the minds of the psalmists who mention this aspect of the weather. Are they coincident enough that this meaning may be considered for this psalm?

The best approach to this question is to examine the effects of Yahweh's voice and ask if they correspond to thunder, not in our modern understanding of thunder, but in a biblical perspective.

The first mention of Yahweh's voice in v. 3 does not attribute any action to it; there is no verb used with קול in that verse. However, the parallel with thunder is explicitly present. This appears to support a fulminating aspect for Yahweh's voice as it sets the framework for its use in the remainder of the psalm. This aspect cannot be disregarded when considering further portions of the poem.

Verse 4 also declines to use any verbs with Yahweh's קול. Instead Yahweh's voice is characterized as being powerful (כח) and splendid (הדר). Aside from being theophanic terms, these qualities of Yahweh's voice are not weather-specific. This does not discount a meteorological usage for them, but such a particular usage must remain speculative without further corroboration.

In v. 5 the voice of Yahweh is attributed with breaking (שבר) cedars. Since the origin of thunder is now known, it is common knowledge that thunder cannot physically break anything. On the other hand, lightning can

---

99. Kloos, *Yahweh's Combat*, 51. Kloos's book contains a detailed discussion of Ps 29 from pages 13–129. Less directly relevant, but interesting, is Tournay, *Seeing and Hearing God*, 127–30, 132–35. For the theophanic aspect, see again, Jeremias, *Theophanie*, 30–31.

100. Greenstein, "Yahweh's Lightning," 56, suggests that the occurrence of lightning does not necessitate the context of thunder in this psalm. (He gives Yahweh lightning in the context of v. 7, but he steals Yahweh's thunder.)

and does break trees, often with no evidence of burning.[101] To the psalmist, living long before the connection between lightning and thunder was known, thunder may very well have been assumed the superior force. It can be heard when lightning is not yet seen, and in the wake of a storm, a damage path remains with clues too sophisticated for a pre-scientific observer to unravel. While it is not possible to prove that thunder was thought to break trees, in conjunction with other evidence from the psalm, this should be a possibility not easily discounted. An alternative interpretation is that this verse is making only figurative reference to the breaking of trees.

Verse 6 does not address the voice of Yahweh. The antecedent to the verbs is Yahweh who appears in the second bicolon of v. 5. Thunder and lightning are juxtaposed in v. 7. Given the preponderance of meteorological language in relation to theophanic displays, there is no reason to doubt that the psalmist is referencing a thunderstorm.[102] This verse, along with Ps 42:8 [7], come as close to the idea of "thunderbolt" (addressed above) as any in the Psalms.

Verse 7 has been much discussed. Greenstein provides a very good summary and critique of the major views.[103] His own solution is erudite, but it relies on an emended text, and it brings thunder and lightning together in a way that reflects a stronger sense of their association than I find elsewhere in the Psalms. The suggestion advocated by Ewald, Buttenwieser, and Kissane—that the lightning is the object hewed, or cleaved, by Yahweh's voice—bears consideration.[104] Greenstein admits that this interpretation is possible, but deems it improbable on the grounds of its unique, creative imagery.[105]

In this connection it is worth noting that thunder often appears in the Psalms as a fearful and intimidating weapon. In this psalm thunder even apparently breaks trees. Lightning was conceived in very different terms in antiquity than it is today.[106] Often it is forked in appearance, resembling the fracture lines of a shattered pot. It seems quite likely that the psalmist understood thunder to have been responsible for the great feat of cleaving

---

101. Uman, *All About Lightning*, 35–46.

102. This matches Greenstein's conclusions, which offer a viable way to reconcile the verb with the concept of lightning ("Yahweh's Lightning," 56).

103. Greenstein, "Yahweh's Lightning," 49–57.

104. Ewald, *Commentary on the Psalms*, 1:96; Buttenwieser, *The Psalms, Chronologically Treated*, 154; Kissane, *The Book of Psalms*, 1:127. These sources are all cited by Greenstein.

105. Greenstein, "Yahweh's Lightning," 51.

106. See especially Wilk, "The Meaning of the Thunderbolt," 72–79.

lightning. After all, lightning may be a divine weapon, but thunder is Yahweh's very voice.

If this interpretation is correct, then the flames of fire are indeed lightning and their function here is to display the divine majesty in being split by the thunder. The function of the thunder is to glorify Yahweh by its awesome power.

This mythical "thunderbolt" is pictured as "cleaving" (חצב), which is not really what thunder does, but if conceived in terms of a physical object, it was likely understood in the same terms as the sun, which was corporeal in ancient thought. The comprehension of both thunder and lightning was extremely tenuous and it was certainly not empirically analyzed. With this caveat in mind, we may allow the psalmist poetic license to express thunder in terms that do not actually describe thunder or lightning according to our modern perceptions.

The same kind of relationship prevails in v. 8. Here the juxtaposition is between the voice of Yahweh and an earthquake. Aware of the origin of earthquakes, our modern understanding disallows a causal connection between thunder and earthquakes. We must, however, not hold the psalmist to that level of comprehension. Thunder and earthquakes are elsewhere associated within and outside of the Psalms: Ps 77:18–19 [17–18] (and possibly 18:9 [8]) juxtapose thunder and earthquake in a theophanic context; Isa 29:6 describes a theophanic visit in these terms:

> From Yahweh of hosts you will be visited,
> with thunder and with earthquake and a loud voice,
> storm winds and storms, and consuming flame of fire.

Thunder (רעם) and earthquake (רעש) are paired and associated with the loud voice (קול גדול) of Yahweh. These theophanic verses indicate that thunder and earthquakes were considered related phenomena in the minds of the Israelites. This direct juxtaposition further supports the idea that the voice of Yahweh in this psalm is intended to represent thunder.

The seventh and final reference to Yahweh's voice occurs in v. 9, where the action attributed to the divine voice is the difficult יְחוֹלֵל אַיָּלוֹת. The MT pointing indicates that Yahweh's voice "makes deer writhe"; however, with only pointing changes the phrase could be rendered "causes the oaks to whirl" (NRSV).[107] The latter option probably fits better with the stripping bare of the forests in the second bicolon, and the context benefits from it.

---

107. A. A. Anderson, *Book of Psalms*, 1:237–38; Briggs and Briggs, *Book of Psalms*, 1:254, 256; Cohn, "Hinds in Psalm 29," 258–59.

However, it must be kept in mind that however well this logical development fits the modern, Western perspective, it does not demand this sense for the ancient Hebrew text. The comparison with Job 39:1 is cogent in this context.[108]

In an effort not to force consistent imagery where it is not intended, I have followed the MT text (*BHS* lists no manuscript evidence to support an emendation), where the writhing of the deer is caused by thunder. Causing deer to writhe (in birth pangs) and stripping forests bare are not particularly associated with thunder (or lightning)[109] in the modern meteorological paradigms, but once again, the storm which leaves branches from trees scattered in its wake may have easily been attributed to the destructive connotation of thunder. It is actually wind that causes this kind of damage. Making deer to calve could be an example of "frighting"[110] an animal into giving birth, presumably out of fear of the thunder. If "causes the oaks to whirl" were the translation, this likewise would fall into the category of wind damage attributed to thunder.

The weight of the contextual evidence adds gravity to the suggestion that "voice of Yahweh" throughout this psalm refers to thunder. Its function may be summarized fairly simply, however. The thunder serves to show the glory of Yahweh through its destructive potential and its kinetic energy. This is emphasized by the final tricolon of v. 9 "and in his temple all say 'Glory!'"

SUMMARY OF THUNDER FUNCTIONS

Thunder is utilized in a fairly uniform way in the Psalms. Primarily it is an agent to glorify God. More specifically, it may be representative of the divine battle cry as Yahweh prepares to engage in war (Ps 18:14 [13]; 77:18–19 [17–18]; 104:7), or it may be the thunder of a theophany (Ps 29:3–9, possibly 42:8 [7]), or it may simply be thunder accompanying a storm which shows Yahweh's awesome power (Ps 68:34 [33]; 81:8 [7]). In many ways it appears that thunder was the most feared aspect of the storm in the minds of the psalmists.

Weather terms related to storms in the Psalms are never neutral. Storms represent Yahweh's raw power against which humanity, nature, and even the sea monster, are helpless. Storms do not occur naturalistically or randomly in the Psalms; they are never praised for their own sake. Storms reflect the glory of Yahweh and magnify human appreciation of that glory.

108. Craigie, *Psalms 1–50*, 243; Dahood, *Psalms I*, 178–79.
109. Greenstein, "Yahweh's Lightning," 54.
110. Von Rad, *Genesis*, 301–2.

CHAPTER THREE

The Wind

Rather like Enlil in Mesopotamian thought, Yahweh was the Lord of the Wind in the Hebrew Bible. The purpose of this chapter is to explore aeolian terminology in the Psalms in order to determine how the wind was perceived by the psalmists. An initial exploration indicates that the wind is guided by divine intention. As will become clear as the topic is explored, there are actually seven different categories that reflect how Yahweh utilizes the wind in the Psalms. Never is the wind understood as a "neutral" natural phenomenon—it is always a divine instrument, usually for purposes of destruction.

In this chapter all aeolian references in the Psalms are examined with the goal of suggesting "meteorologically correct" translations of the words that are used to describe the wind. In the process it will become clear that what is often treated as a lackluster element of the weather—with the application of current meteorological terminology—becomes an essential component of Yahweh's array of divine weaponry.

The following words are used to indicate meteorologic air movement in the Psalms: רוּחַ, קָדִים, תֵּימָן, and perhaps סוּפָה and גַּלְגַּל. Each will be examined in turn below. Unlike the previous chapter, the words here lack the specific denotations of varieties of wind—breeze, zephyr, and such connotations are simply not evident in the Psalms.

רוּחַ

רוּחַ, "wind," occurs frequently with a meteorological connotation in the Psalms. Of words indicating air movement, it is by far the most common. In arguably meteorological contexts it occurs in each of the following references: 1:4; 11:6; 18:11 [10], 16 [15], 43 [42]; 35:5; 48:8 [7]; 55:9 [8]; 78:39; 83:14 [13]; 103:16; 104:3, 4, 30; 107:25; 135:7; 146:4; 147:18; 148:8.

The meaning of this word is so well-attested that no comparative material is required to establish its meteorological connotations.[1] Frequently this noun is further qualified in the Psalms. Each individual reference will be examined and classified in order to clarify how the wind was perceived. The categories used to classify these terms are those suggested by the texts themselves.

Psalm 1:4

> Not so the wicked!
> For rather like chaff (are they),
> which the wind drives away.

This verse compares the wicked to wind-blown chaff. This comparison highlights the destructive quality of the wind, in a metaphorical sense, to the wicked. Driving away (נדף) has forceful connotation: the result of this verb in the Hebrew Bible is usually the complete removal of its object.[2] The divine punishment of the wicked classifies this verse as indicating the (metaphorical) destructive potential of the wind.

Psalm 11:6

> He will rain coals (of) fire and sulphur upon the wicked,

---

1. Two early, yet still useful discussions are: Briggs, "The use of רוח in the Old Testament," 132–45, and Shoemaker, "The Use of רוּחַ in the Old Testament," 13–35. For a more recent study see Fabry, " רוח rwḥ," 382–425.

I am working on the basis that the root רוח in general denotes the movement of air, whether connoting wind or breath (discussed in detail by Shoemaker). Semantically these concepts are related, and in some cases either meaning can be argued. On this point see Moscati, "The Wind in Biblical and Phoenician Cosmogony," 305–10.

2. Lev 26:36 and Job 13:25 (a blown leaf); Isa 19:7 (the blowing away of dry soil); 41:2 (the same metaphor as in the current verse); Ps 68:3 (enemies blown away like smoke); Job 32:13 (the driving away of Job, perceived as evil by Elihu); and Prov 21:6 (driven breath).

and a raging wind will be the portion of their cup.

Here the wind is qualified with the word זלעפות ("raging heat" BDB: 273a; "whirlwind" KBS: 272b; "raging" *DCH* 3: 115a): this verse is the only meteorological reference utilizing this thrice-attested word. The wind allusion here is once again the destruction of the wicked: this "raging" or "scorching wind"[3] is paralleled to the raining of fire and sulphur on the wicked—a further meteorological reference (to lightning).[4] The question should be raised concerning the nuance of a "raging" or "scorching" wind. The root זלעף is quadriliteral and does not appear to be related to other Hebrew roots. The suggestion of heat, which the translation "scorching" represents, derives from the heat of the parallel "fire and sulphur" and the heat implied from the other two uses of this noun (Ps 119:53: "indignation," and Lam 5:10: "famine"//"fever," BDB: 273a). The root does not implicitly suggest heat (*DCH*, 3: 115a; KBS: 272b).

This verse also emphasizes the destructive nature of the wind, wielded by Yahweh, with a similar connotation to the previous verse. A phenomenon that actually combines these elements of wind, heat, and destruction is the sirocco. This southeast wind of the transitional seasons is fully detailed by K. Nash, and is often described by early European and American explorers of the region.[5] For the possible meteorological implications of "coals (of) fire" see chapter two above.

Psalm 18:11 [10]

And he rode[6] upon a cherub and flew,
swiftly flew upon the wings of the wind.

This verse makes use of the construct כנפי־ ("wings of") to describe the flying of Yahweh on the wind. Comparison with 2 Sam 22:11 would suggest that Yahweh "appeared" (ירא) on the wings of the wind as opposed to the "flew" (ידא) of the present verse. "Swiftly flew" provides an appropriate parallel to "flew" in the first half of the bicolon, and will form the basis of

3. RSV, NAB, Tanakh, NRSV. This is also the translation used by Dahood, *Psalms I*, 70.
4. The phenomenon of storms in the Psalms is considered in chapter two above.
5. Nash, *Palestinian Agricultural Year*, 21–27; Robinson, *Biblical Researches in Palestine*, 1:195–96, 207; Thomson, *The Land and the Book*, 1:141–43. The latter two sources were pointed out in Nash.
6. The exact connotation of this verb is still debated, but it does not directly affect the discussion at hand.

the discussion here. Several manuscripts of the Cairo Geniza support an emendation to ירא; however, other strong manuscript evidence is lacking. The convergence of flying and wings suggests an apt metaphor for divine travel. Emendation should be supported only as a final resort, and this verse is comprehensible as it stands.

The metaphor is avian, and the image almost certainly has Ugaritic antecedents.[7] The parallelism of the winged wind with a cherub is instructive. In addition to the role of throne-guardian, here we find a cherub utilized in a transportational function (perhaps a similar image to that of Ezekiel's "chariot" in chapters 1 and 10). The function of the winged wind is to transport Yahweh in the event of a theophany and is thus not necessarily the standard form of divine locomotion.

Possible emendations to the MT notwithstanding, the theological statement being made by this verse is of a different category than the previous two. This passage presents Yahweh's appearance to rescue the psalmist in theophanic language rather than focussing on the destructive force of the wind. A similar metaphor, to anticipate, occurs in Ps 104:3, and together they may be classified as verses that portray the wind specifically as a divine vehicle.

Psalm 18:16 [15]

And the beds of the waters appeared,
and the foundations of the world were uncovered,
at your rebuke, Yahweh,
at the breath of the wind of your anger.

Continuing the meteorological metaphors of Ps 18, this verse associates the theophanic imagery with language reminiscent of the exodus. Once again comparison with 2 Sam 22 is instructive. 2 Sam 22:16 has the beds of the sea (ים) appearing rather than the beds of the waters (מים). This comparison does not necessitate emending our text, but it provides further background that points to the exodus: the image is one of Yahweh's breath blowing back the waters to reveal the sea floor.[8] The universality of the uncovering of the

---

7. The Ugaritic material is discussed at length in Dahood, *Psalms*, 1:107–8. Dahood's repointing of the MT would negate the meteorological reference in this particular verse, but as it stands, "flew upon the wings of the wind" is an adequate parallel to riding a cherub.

8. Luyster, "Wind and Water," 3.

earth's foundations is particularly cogent if a cosmological interpretation of the sea is accepted.⁹

The role of the wind here is two-fold: it is the breath of Yahweh and it is the agent of Yahweh's anger. To reduce רוח simply to "breath" is redundant in the light of מנשמת. The use of אפך reinforces the physical aspect of the metaphor, but the translation "anger" also provides an appropriate parallel to "rebuke" in the previous line.

The second role of the wind as the agent of Yahweh's anger demonstrates that, as a meteorological entity, the wind is not simply a natural force but is invested with a divine task. Here, the task is to divide the waters as an expression of the deity's rage.

Psalm 18:43 [42]

And I will pulverize them like dust before the wind,
like mud I will empty them outside.

Comparison with 2 Sam 22:43 again reveals some variation in word choice. The reference to the wind is lacking in the 2 Samuel version: "And I will pulverize them like the dust of the earth." The question of which version is more ancient does not abrogate the fact that the Psalm reference does use the wind as a metaphor for the destruction of the wicked.

The theme of this verse reprises the image of Ps 1:4: the wicked will be driven like dust or chaff before the wind. The wind, at the initiative of Yahweh, blows away the dust, thus providing a fitting paradigm for the psalmist to apply to the wicked.

Psalm 35:5

Let them become like chaff before the wind,
and let the messenger of Yahweh drive them out.

The call for the enemies of the psalmist to be driven like chaff before the wind is a simile in the same vein as 1:4 and 18:43 [42] above. It is of interest that the image of chaff being blown away is paralleled by the enemies being driven out by מלאך יהוה, "the messenger of Yahweh." This is frequently translated as "angel" (NRSV, Tanakh, RSV, NAB, NASB, NEB, REB), but in the light of Ps 104:4 (see below) it should perhaps be translated as its

---

9. Batto, "The Reed Sea," 27–35, and Batto, "Red Sea or Reed Sea?" 57–63.

most basic meaning of "messenger." This would then indicate that the wind (or "breath") was considered one of God's lackeys and it provides a notable parallel to wind in the previous line. The wind, in other words, becomes one of the divine servants. The issue will be considered further under Ps 104.

Regardless of the exact connotation of the parallel of "wind" with "messenger," here is found another reference to the wind as a basically destructive force; the wicked are actively driven away by God's servant, the wind.

Psalm 48:8 [7]

As the east wind shatters the ships of Tarshish,

The destructive force of the wind is primary once again in this passage. The reference is nearly theophanic as it is used to demonstrate the awe of Yahweh instilled at the appearance of Zion. The verse is one in a series of similes[10] used to describe the reaction of foreign kings to the recognition of God's defense of the city.

In this verse רוח is qualified by קדים ("east"). The east wind is a fairly common reference point in the Hebrew Bible, and it often has the connotation of being violent or scorching.[11] In this verse the violent aspect is emphasized since it is regarded as having shattered ships at sea. This east wind is often referred to as "sirocco" by analogy with its Arabic counterpart.[12]

The word "sirocco" denotes a particular atmospheric phenomenon which is sometimes called by its Egyptian name *khamsin*.[13] Frick notes the meteorological differences between a true sirocco, or *khamsin* (strong thermal inversions with east winds), and a *sharav* (east winds originating from a high pressure system centered to the east), and classifies this verse as referring to the latter.[14] Baly, on the other hand, observes that a strong sirocco may clash with the Mediterranean coastal waters at upwards of 60 miles per hour, causing substantial waves which might shatter ships.[15] This verse

---

10. See Dahood, *Psalms*, 1:291, for an explanation of the double-duty simile at work in this series.

11. BDB 870a; Moscati, "Wind," 307; Ben-Yoseph, "Climate in Eretz Israel," 229–30.

12. BDB 870a. For a full description of the sirocco, see Nash, *Palestinian Agricultural Year*, 21–27.

13. Baly, *Geography of the Bible*, 52.

14. Frick, "Palestine, Climate of," 125.

15. Baly, *Geography of the Bible*, 52.

clearly refers to a strong east wind: the description does not provide enough detail to determine whether it describes a *khamsin* or a *sharav*.

Psalm 55:9 [8]

> Let me quickly come to my escape
> from dashing wind and from storm.

Once again the wind is an agent of destruction, but this time it is one that the psalmist seeks to escape: that having been said, the verse still requires clarification. Although the structure of this verse remains open to question the desire to escape a dangerous wind is clear.[16]

The main difficulty in this verse is the hapax legomenon סעה. BDB lists the word as dubious, but suggests "rush, of storm-wind."[17] KBS, with the benefit of Ugaritic, suggests "sweep away, winnow."[18] (KB originally offered "caluminate,"[19] which could have fit the context of the psalm, but was syndetically labored with "wind" and "storm" in the same colon.) Dahood proffered "sweeping wind" based on the Ugaritic *sʿt*.[20] This Ugaritic cognate has a long pedigree and deserves serious attention.[21] The general sense of quick motion may be derived from its context in the Kirta epic (*KTU* 1.14 iii 7); however, the precise meaning of the word continues to be evasive.[22] An Arabic cognate *saʿay*, "go quickly, run, be energetic," is suggested by BDB,[23] and is likely related to Epigraphic South Arabian *sʿy*, "course, area marked out."[24] Although the cognate evidence tends to point in the direction of "quick motion" in some sense, the possibility also remains that the text is corrupt.[25]

I have translated סעה as "dashing" since it provides a sense both of the swiftness and potential violence of the wind that appears to be intended in

---

16. Briggs and Briggs, *Book of Psalms*, 2:19–23: see also the comments on this verse in chapter two above.

17. BDB 703a.

18. KBS 761b–762a.

19. KB 662b.

20. Dahood, *Psalms*, 2:29, 33.

21. Caquot, Sznycer and Herdner, *Textes ougaritiques tome I*, 521, n. l; Gibson, *Canaanite Myths and Legends*, 153; del Olmo Lete, *Mitos y leyendas de Canaan*, 596.

22. Greenfield, "Some Glosses on the Keret Epic," 63, opts for a root meaning of "sweep"; Clines, "Krt 111–114 (I iii 7–10)," 29, prefers "rush."

23. BDB 703b.

24. Biella, *Dictionary of Old South Arabic*, 340.

25. Briggs and Briggs, *Book of Psalms*, 2:27.

this verse. It may thus be classified as an agent of destruction, chiefly by its context in the verse. It may also be classified as indicating the swift passage of the wind, primarily by the cognate evidence.

The second meteorological term in this colon, מסער, "tempest," is discussed fully in chapter two above. The root סער is fairly well-attested in Hebrew, and its stormy denotation is firmly established.[26] Its use in this verse along with סעה affirms a meteorological connotation for the latter.

Psalm 78:39

> But he remembered that they are flesh,
> a departing wind that does not remain.

The reference here could be either to "wind" or "breath." Shoemaker considers this reference to be an exilic example of the ephemeral nature of the wind.[27] Whether "wind" or "breath" is intended here, either meaning obviously suggests the point being made: the swift passing of life. This is a different meteorological use of רוח in the Psalms than those encountered to this point. Without intimating violence, it reiterates the celerity of the wind; however, not in a neutral sense. The swiftness of the wind demonstrates the passing of life which moves Yahweh to be lenient. Its classification would represent a metaphor of swiftness, and perhaps simply the wind as "breath."

Psalm 83:14 [13]

> My God, make them like a whirlwind/tumbleweed,
> like stubble before the wind.

Possibly both of the lines of this bicolon contain aeolian elements. The first, גַּלְגַּל, "whirlwind" is somewhat less certain than the second, רוח.

גלגל is generally translated two ways: either as "whirling dust" (NASB, NRSV, Briggs and Briggs;[28] NAB "whirlwind") or as "tumbleweed" (DCH;[29] REB and Tanakh "thistledown").[30] Both interpretations recognize the cir-

---

26. Lugt, "Wirbelstürme im Alten Testament," 195–204, suggests that the term has cyclonic overtones.

27. Shoemaker, "The Use of רוּחַ," 23.

28. Briggs and Briggs, Book of Psalms, 2:218, 222.

29. DCH, 2:347b.

30. Brettler, "Images of Yahweh the Warrior in Psalms," 147–50, translates "thistledown," yet notes that "[v]erse 14 is comprised of two relatively stereotypical images, of

cularity denotation of the root.[31] Which phenomenon would have been so well-known in ancient Israel that the psalmist could have effectively used it as a metaphor?

Tumbleweeds are not a specific plant; they consist of different species in which a portion drops off a parent plant, or an entire bush breaks off from its root, to be blown around by the wind.[32] In Israel the plant most often associated with tumbleweeds is *Gundelia tournefortii*, still called *galgal* in modern Hebrew.[33] The circular motion of this dead bush when loosed and blown by the wind suggests that "tumbleweed" (or the like)[34] would be an appropriate translation here.[35] This natural phenomenon is still widely known in Israel; it was perhaps so common that it did not require substantial comment by an inhabitant of Palestine in antiquity.[36]

The other option for the meaning of "whirlwind" also raises the question of the audience's recognition of the subject. Whirlwinds are mentioned in various places in the Hebrew Bible—the cases of Elijah and Job come immediately to mind. Supercell tornadoes in the sense of mesocyclonic phenomena are rare in Israel,[37] but lesser vortices such as dust-devils or gust-front tornadoes ("gustnadoes") would conceivably have been observed.

The parallel usage of this word in Isa 17:13 (ורדף כמץ הרים לפני־רוח וכגלגל לפני סופה "and pursued like chaff (to the) mountains before the wind, and like a whirlwind/tumbleweed before a tempest") may support the translation "whirlwind" for גלגל since the position of a gust-front tornado is generally on the leading edge of a thunderstorm.[38] Here too, however, the reference could be to a tumbleweed.[39] The only other parallel usage comes from Ps 77:19 [18], to which attention momentarily must be turned.

---

a floating *whirl* of dust or chaff (cf. Isa 17:13), and of straw blown by the wind" (ibid., 150, emphasis mine).

31. Indeed, a relationship suggests itself with the similar word כרכר, "whirl, pirouette" (see Gruber, "Ten Dance-Derived Expressions," 338–40) as well as the English "circle."

32. Rolling is a central element of tumbleweeds as note in the *Oxford English Dictionary* definition of "tumble-weed."

33. Danin, "Plants as Biblical Metaphors," 20; KBS: 190b.

34. KBS offers "wheel-plant," 190b.

35. Danin suggests that it is the intended metaphor both in this psalm and in Isa 17:13 ("Plants," 20).

36. On the subject of ancient Palestinian plants and the difficulty in coordinating more recent botanical species, see Jacob and Jacob, "Flora," 803–17; Orni and Efrat, *Geography of Israel*, 164–90.

37. Nir, "Whirlwinds in Israel," 109–17.

38. Geer, *Glossary of Weather and Climate*, 105; Grazulis, *Significant Tornadoes*, 53.

39. Danin, "Plants," 20.

Psalm 77:19 [18] contains substantial meteorological terminology:

The voice of your thunder was in the גלגל,
lightnings lit the world,
the earth quaked and shook.

Here גלגל cannot be taken as "tumbleweed," since the context demands a parallel for "lightnings," as well as a place in which thunder could be heard. The whirlwind corresponds to this description and the circular denotation of the root meaning provides further substantiation. This verse will be explored in more detail below.

Comparative philology reveals a uniformity concerning the circularity denotation of the root (usually cited as *gll*),[40] but a specific parallel to the meanings suggested for this verse has not been found.

Prosodically the issue in Ps 83:14 [13] is: with which element of the second line is גלגל parallel? If it parallels "stubble" then "tumbleweed" suggests itself. If it parallels "wind" then "whirlwind" seems likely. Of the other biblical usages of the word, "whirlwind" is fairly certain in Ps 77:19 [18]. There is no definitive method to establish its meaning with certainty here, but comparison with Ps 77:19 [18] and Isa 17:13 may favor "whirlwind." In this verse, if "whirlwind" is the correct interpretation, the metaphor would refer to the "emptiness" of the whirlwind, much as Hos 8:7 refers to the emptiness of severe weather.

If the translation "tumbleweed" is correct, the emptiness aspect is also emphasized. The actual destruction of the wicked is addressed in the second half of the bicolon.

This destruction wish revisits a theme already found in several psalms. The image here is of the wind as a destructive force against the wicked. This idea is paralleled in the first half of the bicolon, regardless of the translation of גלגל: the psalmist wishes for the driving away of the enemy. The wind yet again does not appear as a neutral subject, but one that reflects the divine judgment on evil.

---

40. For Ugaritic *gl*, see Aistleitner, *Wörterbuch der ugaritischen Sprache*, 65; for Ugaritic *glgl*, see del Olmo Lete and Sanmartín, *Diccionario de la lengua ugarítica*, 1:146; del Olmo Lete, *Mitos y leyendas de Canaan*, 532. For Sabaean *gwl*, *gyl*, and its Arabic cognate, see Biella, *Dictionary of Old South Arabic*, 68, 71. For Phoenician *glgl*, see Tomback, *A Comparative Semitic Lexicon*, 65.

Psalm 103:16

> When the wind passes over it, it is not,
> and its place will be regarded no more.

The subject of this verse requires a glance back to v. 15. It is part of an extended simile concerning the frailty of human life. A person is being compared to a flower which is beyond its prime. The wind blows over it and it disappears. In this regard the wind is viewed as a destructive force. The psalmist laments the ephemeral nature of human life as illustrated by the seasonal flower blown away as its time ends. As the metaphorical use clearly indicates, the wind is not viewed as an independent natural force here—it represents Yahweh shortening human life. Thus the wind retains its destructive nature, although on a somewhat smaller scale than that of the tempestuous winds described elsewhere in the Psalms. It might also be classified here as representing the swift passage of the wind as a metaphor for human life.

Psalm 104:3

> The one placing the beams of his roof chambers in the waters,
> the one making cumuli[41] his chariot,
> the one walking upon the wings of the wind.

Before delving into this particular verse, it should be noted that Ps 104 contains an abundance of weather-related terms.[42] In addition to the five verses discussed here, vv. 6–9 appear to describe the coming of a rain storm, and v. 13 also uses a description of rain. Such a preponderance of meteorological imagery should not be unexpected in a poem which reflects on the awesome acts of Yahweh.

This verse contains part of a longer series of awe-inspiring aspects of creation. The initial order roughly follows that of Gen 1: lights, heavens, waters, wind. The aspect of the wind emphasized here we have already seen in Ps 18:11 [10] in the phrase "the wings of the wind." The wind is described in ornithological terms, but that is not the main emphasis of the verse. The focus is on the extraordinary ability of Yahweh, in that even meteorological phenomena have been divinely established and manipulated.

---

41. See below, chapter four, for an explanation of this translation.
42. Dion, "Yahweh as Storm-god," 43–71.

Psalm 18:11 [10] pictures Yahweh as flying (דאה) on the wings of the wind whereas the present verse portrays Yahweh walking (הלך) on the wings of the wind. In other words, the wind here is not so much a vehicle for divine travel as it is a substrate for divine locomotion. Ps 104:3 parallels Yahweh's walking on the wings of the wind to cloud charioteering. This parallel also serves to tie this verse to 18:11 [10]. In both references Yahweh's use of the inaccessible wind for travel serves to increase the wonder associated with the divine power. The wind is not described for its own sake, but for its utilization by Yahweh.

This second use of "the wings of the wind" raises the question whether or not a specific meteorological phenomenon is designated by the phrase. Since the wind itself is invisible, some other atmospheric condition might have been thought to resemble wings. The most obvious suggestion is that some type of cloud may have been perceived as "winged." Many types of clouds, at all atmospheric levels, may easily suggest the presence of wings. The cumulonimbus of a thunderstorm (sometimes associated with a theophany) with a classic incus (anvil top) and relatively flat base would seem particularly appropriate as "winged" wind, but such an identification is certainly not exclusive.

Psalm 104:4

Making winds your messengers,
fire (and) flame your servants.

This verse continues the series of awesome acts of Yahweh reflected in creation. The winds are metaphorically personified into messengers and thus deprived of a meteorologically neutral interpretation.

The role of the wind as "messenger" deserves some consideration. מלאך may be translated as either "messenger" or "angel" as was noted concerning Ps 35:5. Since the most basic denotation of the word is "messenger"[43] and "angel" is a more theologically freighted concept, the use of "messenger" is the more objective term in an ambiguous context. This would not discount the possibility that a mythological allusion is being made in this verse;[44] however, the text does not require it. The metaphor is of the wind as a kind of divine retainer along with fire and flame.[45] Although two fires may

---

43. See, conveniently, BDB 521a-b for comparative usage of the word.
44. Dahood, *Psalms*, 3:35.
45. Dahood (*Psalms*, 3:35) makes the cogent point that "ministers" requires a dual or plural antecedent. This issue was also addressed by Briggs and Briggs, *Book of*

appear in the role of divine messengers in *KTU* 1.2 i 32, no obvious anthropomorphism is yet known in the Ugaritic texts for the wind. In this verse "fire" and "flame" perhaps refer to lightning as parallel to winds (see the previous chapter). These meteorological phenomena have in common the aspect of being sent out: the thundercloud appears to throw out lightning and wind. Together vv. 3 and 4 picture a gathering storm.

"Winds" in this setting may have destructive undertones, as storm winds have destructive potential. In any case, the winds are not presented as an independent natural occurrence; rather, they constitute a divine embassy under Yahweh's orders.

Psalm 104:30

> You send your wind and they are created,
> and you renew the face of the ground.

In this verse the question raised is whether רוח refers to "wind" or "breath." The question cannot be satisfactorily answered without a full consideration of the role of רוח in Gen 1. Such a discussion, although relevant for the larger picture of perceptions of the wind in the entire Hebrew Bible, would unnecessarily lengthen this chapter.[46] At this point it may be said that "wind" stands for one option to translate רוח here. If the wind is referenced here it is specifically designated as belonging to Yahweh and as possessing creative potential.

Psalm 107:25

> And he commanded
> and raised a stormy wind,
> and lifted up its waves.

This verse is discussed under storms in chapter two, but a word about the aeolian aspect will be offered here. Wind is a normal component of storms, and indeed, it is one of their defining characteristics.[47] Naturally enough the storm wind raises waves. The reference to the wind in this verse emphasizes

---

Psalms, 2:332.

46. Luyster, "Wind and Water," 1–10. For a recent discussion with further notes, see Bauks, *Die Welt am Anfang*.

47. Geer, *Glossary of Weather and Climate*, 216.

its danger to those in ships along the lines of Ps 48:8 [7], with the difference that the latter explicitly cites the east wind as being destructive. The source of the destructive winds is the same in both psalms: Yahweh calls out the menacing wind. It remains clear that the natural phenomenon is bent to the divine will rather than presenting its own peril.

Psalm 135:7

> He elevates rising clouds from the end of the earth,
> he makes lightnings with the rain,
> the source of the wind from its storehouses.

This rather literal rendering of the Hebrew lists meteorological elements that demonstrate Yahweh's power over nature. The verse is a fairly accurate description of the development of a thunderstorm: cumulus clouds build into cumulonimbus with a swiftly rising updraft in an unstable atmosphere. Thunderstorms are naturally accompanied by lightning, rain, and gusty winds.

The storehouses (אוצרות) of the wind deserve some comment. The root meaning of אצר, which can also mean "treasury," concerns storage of large quantities of a substance. In the case of a treasury the "substance" is obviously valuables, and this concept was apparently borrowed for meteorological/oceanographic phenomena. Deut 28:12 refers to rain as Yahweh opening the "storehouses of the good."[48] Job 38:22 cites the storehouses of snow and hail. Ps 33:7 mentions the storehouses of the deeps. The image is one of Yahweh saving copious quantities of heavenly provisions for times of divine usefulness. Although not addressing the storage of the wind directly, J. P. Brown suggests that such storehouses, specifically for snow (but applicable to other stored weather), served as a kind of divine arsenal.[49] The contents were used by Yahweh in times of necessity, thus giving a martial quality to their stock-piling. This usage would correspond to what has been noted of the wind in the Psalms to this point: it is a tool of Yahweh, often used metaphorically to destroy the wicked.

Jeremiah 10:13 and 51:16 are either quotes from the current verse, or the psalmist is quoting Jeremiah, or they had a common source.[50] With these two references the citations of natural phenomena storehouses come to a close.

---

48. Dahood, *Psalms*, 1:25; O. Loretz, "Ugaritsch *ṯbn*," 247–58.
49. "Yahweh, Zeus, Jupiter," 186.
50. Holladay, *The Psalms through Three Thousand Years*, 60.

The use of "rising clouds" to translate נשׂאים is perhaps unusual, but it is entirely within the semantic sphere of "rising mist, vapour" cited by BDB.[51] KBS cites an Arabic cognate for "billowing clouds,"[52] a translation that also emphasizes the growth of clouds. Reymond actually classifies this word as *cumuli castellati* (a type of "rising cloud").[53] The phenomenon of clouds will be discussed in detail in the next chapter; however, identifying נשׂאים as "rising clouds" has the benefit of actually providing the background for what follows in the verse (a description of a thunderstorm).

The wind is here presented as a commodity stored by Yahweh against a time of its necessary use. It is also a powerful element, evoking awe in the psalmist.

Psalm 146:4

> His wind goes out,
> he returns to his ground,
> on that day his thoughts vanish.

As in Pss 78:39 and 104:30 this reference may simply be to "breath." Even breath, however, as a movement of the air, may be represented by the wind. Here it is the terminal expiration of the mortal under discussion. Such an event, if understood to involve the wind, is fraught with significance. It is not as a classical meteorological reference, but as a related citation that it is mentioned here. It may be classified as wind representing divinely-given breath.

Psalm 147:18

> He sends out his word and causes them to melt,
> he causes his wind to blow,
> the waters flow.

That which is melting and the receptor of the blowing wind are the ice-phenomena mentioned in verse 17, on which see chapter five below. The context is once again a psalm of praise for Yahweh's great acts, among which are meteorological phenomena. The wind in this verse is once again a divine

---

51. BDB 672b.
52. KBS 728a.
53. Reymond, *L'eau*, 13, 266.

agent, sent to blow across ice and frost and melt them. The verb form used with רוח is a causative (hiphil of נשׁב), demonstrating that even the blowing of the wind is not an independent natural force, but one which is directed by divine command. The category of this verse would be the wind serving to cause awe at Yahweh's activity.

Psalm 148:8

> Fire and hail, snow and dark cloud,
> stormy wind doing his command.

The final meteorological reference to רוח in the Psalms occurs in this verse. The stormy aspect of this verse is discussed in chapter two. As for the aeolian aspect, once again the wind occurs within a context of praise to Yahweh for awe-inspiring phenomena. The list of meteorological elements appears in the middle of a longer "laundry list" of created orders. Lightning ("fire"), hail, snow, and stormy wind (רוח סערה) all have destructive potential, yet are envisioned not only as restrained by Yahweh, but actually performing Yahweh's wishes (דברו). The wind may be classified as a divine agent in this verse.

The last point, while perhaps obvious, reflects the perception of רוח throughout the Psalms: it is a divine agent, acting on Yahweh's initiative. Other weather terms also conform to this paradigm. Four further wind "types" have yet to be examined to complete the picture of aeolian aspects of the weather in the Psalms.

סוּפָה

סוּפָה, "storm-wind," appears in the Psalms only in Ps 83:16 [15] (where it occurs in the form סוּפָתֶךָ, "your storm-wind"[54]).

> Thus you pursue them with your storm,
> and with your storm-wind terrify them.

The root meaning of סופה apparently concerns the violent nature of this type of storm, causing BDB to suggest as a possible connection to סוף

---

54. Also see above, chapter two, where this verse has been previously discussed.

"storm-wind (that *makes an end?*)."⁵⁵ KBS offers simply "storm, gale."⁵⁶ Lugt classifies the word with others meaning "whirlwind" but suggests "storm" (or a synonym) for this particular verse.⁵⁷ The basic meaning may also be determined by the parallel word סער "storm" in the first half of the bicolon. As mentioned above, the meaning of this latter word is well-established, and it likely points to a stormy connotation for סוף. The aeolian denotation of סוף cannot be considered as certain, but it is plausible. The wind is but one terrifying element accompanying a storm.

One term frequently used in modern translations, "hurricane,"⁵⁸ while a powerful image, is technically untenable and meteorologically inaccurate. A hurricane is an ocean-based storm, and Palestine does not receive any true hurricanes.⁵⁹ A more "dramatic" word, which is accurate for Palestine, is "cyclone."⁶⁰ This word refers to a counterclockwise wind circulation (in the northern hemisphere), frequently associated with a low pressure system that often brings rain. Such a weather phenomenon, at least the aspect observable to an ancient Israelite, could conceivably have been utilized by the psalmist.

Psalm 83:16 [15], perhaps an allusion to Judg 4–5,⁶¹ continues the wish for the wicked expressed in v. 14 [13], considered above. Thus perhaps twice in this lament a type of wind is requested as a medium of destruction for the wicked. If this word denotes a wind-type, the divine control and destructive nature of such a storm-wind would confirm the previous connotations of רוח.

---

55. BDB 693a.

56. KBS 747b. See also Grosse, "Le Psaume 83," 10, and Brettler, "Images of Yahweh," 150.

57. Lugt, "Wirbelstürme im Alten Testament," 199–202.

58. See, for example, NRSV; Dahood, *Psalms*, 2:273; Weiser, *The Psalms*, 561.

59. Simpson and Riehl, *The Hurricane and Its Impact*, 10–12; Cotton, *Storms*, 121.

60. "A weather system characterized by relatively low surface air pressure at a given level and a closed cyclonic wind circulation; essentially the same as a low" (Geer, *Glossary of Weather and Climate*, 60). Since "cyclone" is also used to denote tropical hurricanes in the Indian and South Pacific oceans (Geer, *Glossary of Weather and Climate*, 60), and also colloquially to indicate tornadoes, care must be taken not to create the wrong impression with even this word. The rain pattern in Israel is largely determined by cyclonic systems: Baly, *Geography of the Bible*, 47–48; Orni and Efrat, *Geography of Israel*, 140–41; Frick, "Palestine," 122–23.

61. Dahood, *Psalms*, 2:277; Weiser, *The Psalms*, 564.

תֵּימָן and קָדִים

Psalm 78:26

> He led out the eastwind in the heavens,
> and he guided the southwind in his might.

קָדִים, "eastwind," and תֵּימָן, "southwind," appear together in this verse, indicating differences in directional winds. The root meanings of the two words used meteorologically here are "front, east" and "right, south" respectively. Both are utilized synecdochically to refer to the wind coming from the direction cited.[62] Neither word has direct meteorological connotations apart from the context of its use.

Unlike Ps 48:8 [7], קדים (used in this verse without explicit mention of רוח, as noted above) here connotes beneficence. The literary context of the east and south winds is the wilderness wanderings. Ps 78 contains a rehearsal of Israel's tumultuous relationship with Yahweh. Verses 8–53 describe the wilderness wanderings and the complaints of the fledgling community. Verses 26–27 are concerned with the incident of the quails detailed in Num 11:31–35. When the east- and south-winds blow it is for the purpose of bringing quails into the Israelite camp. Given the uncertainties of the setting of the story, an analysis of the local weather is unfruitful.

The main point to note, however, is that the wind is perceived as being controlled by Yahweh, more specifically it is a sign of blessing. As divine tools, the winds bring the birds to the camp from the east and the south. This may be classified as an awe-inspiring use of the wind or in a category by itself of the wind as beneficence.

גַּלְגַּל

גַּלְגַּל, "whirlwind," is the final wind-type possibly referenced in the Psalms. The root meaning of the word indicates circularity, but the specifics of its definition remain to be confirmed. A meteorological interpretation is justified, but cannot be considered as an absolute certainty.

Although Ps 77:19 [18] was used to inform the discussion of Ps 83:14 [13] above, this verse requires further examination in its own right.

> The voice of your thunder was in the whirlwind,
> lightnings lit the world,

---

62. Greenstein, "Mixing Memory and Design," 216, n. 89.

the earth quaked and shook.

The reference to גלגל in the verse is certainly meteorological, whereas in Ps 83:14 [13] it may be taken to refer to a tumbleweed. Most of the mainstream translations understand גלגל as "whirlwind," with the exception of Tanakh, which translates: "Your thunder rumbled like wheels." As this translation demonstrates, there is some reluctance to accept "whirlwind" as a legitimate translation for גלגל here. In all three verses where it is translated as "whirlwind" other viable alternatives are offered. In Ps 83:14 [13] and Isa 17:13 "tumbleweed" remains a possibility. In the current verse, although a meteorological context is evident, how the word acts syntactically may determine the correct translation. The difficulty, however, is determining the syntax of a poetic passage where a word of uncertain meaning occurs.

This psalm also reiterates the mighty deeds of Yahweh. Verses 17–21 [16–20], if "selah" is taken as a poetic break, revisit the crossing of the Red Sea[63] (Moses and Aaron are thus mentioned in v. 21 [20]). If "wheels" is the correct denotation, the psalm recalls the thunder of Pharaoh's chariots rushing into the seabed. Although the possibility exists that the chariot could be that of Yahweh charging against the Pharaoh, a divine chariot is not mentioned in the account presented in Exodus. If the Egyptian chariots are intended, it seems unlikely that Yahweh would have been heard thundering in *their* wheels.

The preposition prefixed to גלגל presents a problem for this interpretation. ב is used rather than the comparative כ. Allowance must be made for poetic license, yet the sense appears to be that the thunder was heard *in* the גלגל.

"Whirlwind" suggests itself as a potential translation. Such an event would have inspired awe, although a whirlwind is not mentioned in the narrative of the Red Sea crossing. The connection with the pillar of cloud may also appear likely here, yet it cannot be considered normative for weather. Support for "whirlwind" may be garnered from the other meteorological references in the verse, yet this is also not definitive evidence.

SUMMARY OF WIND FUNCTIONS

The wind is an aspect of weather often overlooked. In the Psalms, however, it is widely used as an indication of what is happening in the divine realm. Although there are arguably five words used with aeolian connotation, the most common word used to describe wind phenomena is רוח. What are the

---

63. Intentionally named in this form, see Batto, "The Reed Sea."

perceptions of wind in the Psalms? There are seven basic functions the wind performs.

The wind is often described in the Psalms as a medium of destruction, frequently as a harbinger of God's wrath against the wicked or the enemies of the psalmist. This is reflected in Pss 1:4; 11:6; 18:43 [42]; 35:5; 48:8 [7]; 83:14 [13], 16 [15]; 103:16. Once the raging wind is described as threatening the psalmist (Ps 55:9 [8]), thus bringing the destructive aspect again to prominence. The destructive potential of the wind was recognized and applied to divine volition.[64] The psalmists therefore pray for a favorable divine direction of that destruction. It may even be suggested that it appears as the favored medium of destruction requested by the psalmist.

Another facet of the wind is that it is considered a vehicle for divine movement (demonstrated by Pss 18:11 [10] and 104:3). This movement generally occurs as part of a theophany, thus investing the wind with a further supernatural significance. The description of the wind as a divine vehicle has ancient roots: at Ugarit Baal was known to ride the clouds.

The wind, when not a divine vehicle, may accompany a theophany. This is evident in Pss 18:16 [15] and 77:19 [18].

The wind appears as an agent of Yahweh, an embassy doing the divine bidding. Pss 78:26; 104:4, 30; 107:25 and 148:8 indicate that this agent may be personified, but is not necessarily so.

Frequently the wind is listed as one of the elements that inspires awe concerning Yahweh's control over nature. Pss 77:19 [18]; 107:25; 135:7 and 147:18 are cases where it is not theophany, but rather Yahweh's control over the wind which elicits wonder.

At least once (Ps 78:32), and perhaps thrice (Pss 55:9 [8] and 103:16) the wind is a metaphor for swift motion. Its celerity is highlighted in each of these passages, but they may also have further aspects which the wind illustrates.

Finally, the wind may simply be a breath, as perhaps in Pss 78:39 and 146:4. The ancient perceptions range from the terrifying to the necessary, mundane wind of life.

Psalm 78:26 may indicate a further category with one member—the wind as a means of providing blessing.

The wind in the Psalms, no matter in which of the seven classifications it appears, always acts as an instrument of Yahweh.

---

64. Luyster, "Wind and Water," 4–5.

CHAPTER FOUR

Rain and Clouds

Both rain and clouds are necessary components of thunderstorms. Both of these meteorological phenomena, however, often occur independently of thunderstorms as well. Rain may be violent or gentle. Clouds may or may not produce rain. Since these hydrological weather phenomena have a meteorological context of their own, and since they are related yet distinct aspects of weather—rain cannot occur without clouds—they warrant their own separate chapter.

Rain and clouds may be perceived in many different ways. In ancient Israel's agricultural life, rain was necessary for fructifying the land, but its timing was all-important.[1] The evidence of the Hebrew Bible appears to indicate that the causality between rain and clouds was evident: rain does not fall from a clear sky. Hebrew employs different words to refer to different types of rain and clouds, and some of these distinctions are lost to modern readers. One of the issues addressed in this chapter will be the distinctions between these various words. As in the previous chapters the function of these weather terms will be considered as well. Does rain appear as a "natural phenomenon" in its own regard? Are clouds considered apart from any theological implication? These are related issues that will also emerge as the material is examined.

---

1. See especially Futato, *Meteorological Analysis*.

RAIN

Rain language occurs in both nominal and verbal forms in the Psalms. The words מטר, רביב, מים, גשם, and, perhaps זרזיף, תניף, מורה, and טוב refer to rain in nominal forms. מטר, נוה, נטף, משק, and perhaps שקה/שוק, are the verbal roots used with rain. The pluvial functions vary widely, and several of the terms occur in ambiguous contexts. In a land and time dependent on rainfall in the right season, the nuances of different types of rain would have been noted. As Zohary notes "the foremost factor in the climatic conditions is Israel is the precipitation of rain."[2] These three, perhaps as many as seven, words for rain may be supposed to refer to different types of rain, depending on their contexts.[3]

It might be supposed that any term dealing with rain would be necessarily meteorological. The first example below will demonstrate that this is not necessarily the case. Citations of rain terminology used figuratively will be explored in this section as well. Some terms for rain are uncertain, and some are disputed. The word "good" (טוב), for example, is often supposed to refer to rain (see below). In this chapter words that directly denote rain, literally or figuratively, will be considered. Rain is mentioned in Pss 11:6; 65:10–11 [9–10]; 68:8–10 [7–9]; 72:6; 77:18 [17]; 78:24, 27; 84:7 [6]; 104:13; 105:32; 135:7; and 147:8.

מָטַר/מָטָר

The most common word for rain in the Hebrew Bible,[4] and the only word used as both a noun and a verb in the Psalms, מטר will be the first term examined.

Psalm 11:6

> He will rain coals (of) fire and sulphur upon the wicked,
> and a raging wind will be the portion of their cup.

This verse does not describe rain in the usual sense of water falling from clouds to earth. Instead, it uses this action of falling from above (ימתר) to

---

2. Zohary, *Plants of the Bible*, 26. See also Stadelmann, *Hebrew Conception of the World*, 114.

3. Reymond (*L'eau*, 22) catalogues the different nuances of the various Hebrew words used for rain.

4. Reymond, *L'eau*, 22; Scott, "Meteorological Phenomena," 23.

portray the anticipated punishment of the wicked by Yahweh. In doing so, it utilizes three possible meteorological allusions: lightning (coals of fire, see chapter two), the raging wind (see chapter three), and the raining of the coals onto the wicked.

It is difficult to assess the function of the rain here, since it does not indicate actual rain. It does, however, make a straightforward use of the metaphor. Since the punishment is expected from Yahweh, it must come down onto humans. Rain serves as the vehicle for that punishment, and this places no value, positive or negative, upon the phenomenon of rain itself. This verse does indicate, however, that Yahweh makes alternate use of the action of dropping elements from the sky. A further intimation is that rain is a component of the divine arsenal, along with other elements that Yahweh may choose to drop from the sky.

Psalm 72:6

> May he descend like rain upon the mown,
> like drizzle dampening the ground.

This is a royal psalm celebrating the reign of the monarch. The king is compared to three aspects of the celestial world that affect humanity—the sun, the moon, and rain—in a separate stanza marked by the inclusion of "moon" (vv. 5–7). Rain is referred to by two different nouns (מטר and רביבים) and (possibly) two different verbs (ירד and זרף). For a discussion of this latter word, see below.

This particular verse is beset by uncertainty concerning two crucial words in this context: גז and זרזיף. These words cloud the meaning of the entire verse. The sense of this bicolon is often further obscured by translations which follow the Greek in v. 5. The MT reads:

> May they fear you with (the) sun,
> and before (the) moon for all generations.

The usual interpretation is that this is a wish for the longevity of the king, and that the elements of vv. 5–7 point to the goodness that follows from such a lengthy reign.[5] The more likely intension, shown by the sudden shift of person in v. 5, is that the "they" here refers not to God, as commenta-

---

5. A. A. Anderson, *Book of Psalms*, 1:521–22; Briggs and Briggs, *Book of Psalms*, 2:133–34; Dahood, *Psalms*, 2:180–81; Kraus, *Psalms 60–150*, 79; Paul, "Psalm 72:5," 351–55; Tate, *Psalms 51–100*, 224.

tors insist, but the oppressors mentioned in v. 4 and anticipates the foes to be mentioned in v. 8. The phrase "with (the) sun" need not be changed to "as long as" (again, standard practice in the commentaries and translations), since it makes sense as it stands.[6] The enemies of the king are to fear him as soon as the sun rises, and as long as the moon remains in the sky.

With this background, v. 6 should not be forced into a positive meaning, like beneficent rain upon the newly mown grass (גז). As some commentators have noted, in fact, this scenario would be undesirable.[7] This is, I contend, what the psalmist intends to convey. Like the destructive effect of rain on newly harvested fields, so is the effect of the king on his enemies. The simile of the dread of the king continues into this verse from v. 4. This theme of the defeat of the enemies continues through v. 14. It is only with v. 15 that the longevity of the king is raised as a theme for the psalm. If the natural development of the idea is followed from vv. 4–14, the wish is that the king defend those in need from their oppressors. This may be evidenced already in the verb ירד, "come down," which is commonly used to indicate attack.[8]

The semantic sphere of גז is fairly well established as having a connection with cutting,[9] therefore the enemies of the king in v. 6 are like those who have just harvested only to have their work spoiled by the rain.[10]

The second problematic word in v. 6 is the hapax legomenon זַרְזִיף. The major lexica have little comparative philological evidence to establish a meaning and suggest that it may be a verbal form rather than the noun it is understood to be grammatically.[11] The commentaries are equally flummoxed, following the spirit of the Briggses' observation that "by an easy change of a corrupt text"[12] adequate meaning may be found here. Where strong philological evidence is lacking, I suggest that the context is the most reliable guide to the meaning of the word.

---

6. For appeals to Ugaritic see Dahood, *Psalms*, 2:180–81 and Dietrich and Loretz, "Von hebräisch '*m/lpny* (Ps 72:5)," 109–16.

7. A. A. Anderson, *Book of Psalms*, 1:521; Goulder, *The Prayers of David*, 241; Tate, *Psalms 51–100*, 220.

8. As in Judg 1:34; 5:11, 14; 7:10, 24; 1 Sam 14:36; 17:8; 26:10; 29:4; 30:24; 2 Sam 23:21 (so BDB, 432b).

9. BDB, 159; KBS186; DCH 2, 339; Goulder, *The Prayers of David*, 241.

10. Reymond suggests the sense of "averse violente" for מטר here (*L'eau*, 22).

11. BDB (284a) suggests, on the basis of scant comparative philology, a possible hiphil verb form. KBS (281a) suggests a pilpel form of the root זרף. DCH 2 (137b) offers either hiphil or pilpel. Reymond (*L'eau*, 260) gives the meanings "Mouiller, arroser" for the root זרף.

12. Briggs and Briggs, *Book of Psalms*, 2:134.

The immediate context of this verse relates this word to a rain falling upon mown grass, which spoils the cut grain. The larger context of vv. 4–14 relates the simile of rain to the king's dominance over the oppressor. I suggest that the king descends, disastrously, like the rain on his enemies. What could the parallel line add to this aspect of monarchic domination?

The answer, I believe, lies in the proper interpretation of רביבים. The basic connotation of the root רבב is abundance, "muchness." Contextually, Reymond has demonstrated effectively that this word occurs in parallel with מטר "rain" and טל "dew" and should fall somewhere between the two. His suggestion is "drizzle" (*bruine*).[13] Drizzle may be defined as "a type of liquid precipitation composed of very small, numerous, and uniformly dispersed water drops. . . . Unlike fog droplets, drizzle falls to the ground."[14] Reymond's argument from context is cogent and makes perfect sense in this verse. Like drizzle, which dampens the earth, the king covers the enemies. Metaphors of water covering a vast space are used in this way elsewhere in the Hebrew Bible. Micah 5:6 [7] portrays the drizzle (רביבים) and dew covering the land for hostile purposes.[15] As Hillers points out, 2 Sam 17:12 also uses dew to indicate hostile intent.[16]

With this understanding of the function of the rain and drizzle in this verse, it is evident that rain is not always portrayed as beneficial. When its timing is wrong or when it creates widespread dampness, it can be a metaphor for hostility. This is a rare function for pluvial words, but a common one for other meteorological terms (see especially chapter two above).

Psalm 78:24

> And he rained upon them manna to eat,
> and the grain of heaven he gave to them.

This verse does not properly concern meteorology, but a meteorological action, "rain" (מטר, as a verb), is cited in it. It is quite likely that the poet conceived of a literal raining of manna from the sky for the Israelites, notwithstanding more recent attempts to classify what people might have eaten in the desert.

---

13. *L'eau*, 22. Scott ("Meteorological Phenomena," 23) suggests "spring rains or showers" on the basis of various biblical contexts. I find Reymond's analysis more convincing for this verse.

14. Geer, *Glossary of Weather and Climate*, 72.

15. Hillers, *Micah*, 70–71.

16. Ibid., 71.

As noted in chapter two, this psalm is a lengthy didactic hymn concerning Israel's deliverance. The incident is part of a rehearsal of Israel's exodus memories, which constitute a good portion of this psalm.[17]

The purpose of this use of weather language is clearly the beneficence of Yahweh. When Israel was hungry, Yahweh rained down sustenance from above. Yahweh's arsenal is countered with provisions for survival which also fall from the sky.

Psalm 78:27

And he rained flesh upon them like dust,
and like the sand of the sea birds of wing.

The textual and historical[18] contexts are the same as in the previous verse. Once again, there is no inherent reason to suppose that the psalmist was not describing in literal terms imagery involving the raining down of birds. With avian subjects this verse could have been imagined in a more literal sense than the previous one. The purpose is again a display of divine beneficence, demonstrating once again a positive storehouse from which Yahweh dispenses blessings.

This verse contains the final verbal use of מטר in the Psalms.

Psalm 135:7

He elevates rising clouds from the end of the earth,
he makes lightnings with the rain,
the source of the wind from its storehouses.

This psalm, which praises Yahweh for the divine wonders in earth and sky, was also considered in chapters two and three. The four wonders listed in this verse are meteorological in character. Rain (מטר) is placed in a direct relationship with lightning making it likely that the rain here is visualized as part of a thunderstorm. Yahweh's power over such phenomena are cause to offer praise. This verse is immediately followed by the historical wonders of the plagues in Egypt, and then the psalm moves on to other topics. What is

---

17. Greenstein, "Mixing Memory and Design," 197–218.

18. In the sense in which Haglund (*Historical Motifs in the Psalms*, 8) uses "history" divorced from a positivistic point of view.

of interest in this arrangement is that the only "natural" elements for which Yahweh is lauded in this psalm are meteorological ones.

The function of rain is therefore somewhat different than previous usages: here it is not a sign of divine beneficence, but of divine wonder. The rain is one of the aspects of the created order for which Yahweh should be extolled.

Psalm 147:8

> The one covering the heavens with clouds,
> the one preparing rain for the earth,
> the one causing grass to sprout on the mountains.

Psalm 147 is a hymn of praise glorifying Yahweh for wondrous deeds. Other "natural" wonders contribute to the context of praise in this psalm, but the reason for rain's importance is given in the following verse (v. 9), where it is noted that Yahweh provides food for the animals, including non-domesticated ones. The obvious method employed for providing food is the sending of rain, which fructifies the earth, even in the mountains. For the nephological aspect of this verse, see the next section in this chapter.

The function of the rain in this verse, therefore, is to bring glory to Yahweh by fructifying the earth. Once again, rain is a sign of divine beneficence. This is the final occurrence of the noun מטר in the Psalms.

רָוָה, and שׁקה/שׁוק, מַיִם, רְבִיבִים

Many pluvial terms tend to occur in clusters that utilize more than one word for rain. These pericopes often describe rainstorms over more than a single verse, providing some detail concerning how the phenomenon was perceived. The rain description in Ps 65 utilizes the four pluvial words listed here.[19]

Psalm 65:10–11 [9–10]

> You visit the earth and water[20] it,

---

19. Futato (*Meteorological Analysis*) finds the rain in these verses as only a small part of a whole psalm dedicated to rain.

20. This word (תְּשֹׁקְקֶהָ) has gained notoriety in the commentaries. Although the general sense of this section of the psalm is clear, it is also full of translation problems.

you greatly enrich it,
the channel of God is full of water,
you prepare their grain,
for so you established it.
11 [10] Drench[21] its furrows,
break down its ridges,[22]
you soften it with drizzle,
you bless its growth.

In this song of thanksgiving, apparently for an abundant harvest, the psalmist is praising Yahweh for the gift of rain.[23] Given the agricultural cycle of Palestine, the rain after the planting here should be understood as the autumnal rains.[24] Goulder is emphatic about this rain, perhaps more so than the original psalmist:

> Now, suddenly, the land has been soaked: not just showers, inches of rain. God has visited the earth and given it *abundance*—the po'lel of *šuq*, to be abundant. He has *greatly* enriched it. As the farmer irrigates his land with channel or conduit (*peleg*), so has God an enormous canal of water in heaven, which he has sent cascading down. He is making ready his people's ("their") corn, for with this teeming rain ("so") he is making the earth ("her") ready. He *drenches* the furrows (*rawwēh*, inf. abs., to saturate); he *beats down* (*naḥēṯ*, inf. abs. piel, to press down) the ridges

---

The verb שוק is attested otherwise only in hiphil, and then only in Joel 2:24 and 4:13 (see Nash, *Palestinian Agricultural Year*, 173). Because of the reduplicated ק some commentators are unwilling to find a form of the verb שקה in the MT and propose various ways to render the meaning "water." Kraus (*Psalms 60–150*, 27) suggests that this meaning "can be developed from the *hiphil* of the verb (Joel 2:24; 4:13) and from the context." The Briggses (*Book of Psalms*, 2:83) explain the second ק by dittography and translate "and water it." They also note (ibid., 85) that the ancient versions which read "water" could have based this form on the root שקה. Futato notes that whether the root is שוק or שקה, "[b]oth options point to the same event in different ways" (*Meteorological Analysis*, 175). Reymond (*L'eau*, 19) accepts the root שקה. I believe the context strongly commends the translation offered, although the etymological difficulties must, for the time being, remain unresolved.

21. I take this and the following verb, with Dahood (*Psalms*, 2:115), as imperatives.

22. In this verse alone does גדוד have this meaning. The lexica give no comparative examples, and this means that context must supply the meaning. Being in proper congruence (Watson, *Classical Hebrew Poetry*, 118) with "furrows" and being based on a root meaning "to cut" (BDB, 151a; KBS 177a; DCH 2, 316a), "ridges" seems to fit the context. When land is plowed for planting, there are ridges left. These seem to be what is being broken down (נחת) by the rain.

23. Goulder, *The Prayers of David*, 177.

24. Futato, *Meteorological Analysis*, 142, 171, 246.

or clods; he *melts* the earth with the rain (*mug*, po'lel); he gives life to ("blesses") the young shoots. This was not a light drizzle which refreshed the tops: it was a massive downpour.[25]

This description overburdens the semantic range of the words for rain in this pericope. The Briggses likewise picture this as an almost theophanic, sacramental encounter, portraying "God as coming Himself in the storm, and as really present."[26]

From a meteorological perspective, several words associated with rain occur in these two verses. Some of them are conjectural, since the forms used are so rare. Comparative philology is of little assistance since the words with the meanings given in the lexica are unique to the verse in which they occur. The first word encountered with a pluvial connotation is תשקקה, "you water it." The meaning of this word is disputed, but the context gives a clear sense in the following several cola that what God is doing involves irrigation. A verb connoting "to water" does not necessarily denote rain, since there are several ways to irrigate a field. When, however, God is the subject and when words already associated with rain (רביבים) complement it, it is a reasonable supposition that this verb indicates rain in this context. A second pluvial word in this pericope is מים, "water," as a noun. Rain is, of course, composed of water, and water need not refer to rain unless the context necessitates it. In this passage the context makes clear that this is water that comes from God's channel, and therefore is rain. To understand this metaphor, a brief consideration of the cosmology behind such a psalm must be explored. The idea of a channel (or river or brook) appears to express the idea that God has a reservoir of water, likely the defeated and subdued waters of chaos, in the sky.[27] This idea may be compared with the storehouses for the wind discussed in the previous chapter. These waters need to breech the firmament, or dome of the sky, to reach the earth. In this psalm their conduit is a channel that God has opened.[28] Connections with Job 38:25—where, as part of the divine quiz, Yahweh asks Job, "Who cleaved a channel[29] for the flash-flood,/ and a way for the sound of thunderbolts?"[30]—are

25. Goulder, *The Prayers of David*, 177.
26. Briggs and Briggs, *Book of Psalms*, 2:83.
27. Tate, *Psalms 51–100*, 142.
28. A. A. Anderson, *Book of Psalms*, 1:470–71; Goulder, *The Prayers of David*, 177; Tate, *Psalms 51–100*, 142.
29. Pope, *Job*, 298.
30. See chapter two above for a discussion of the meteorologically inaccurate term "thunderbolt." Interestingly, meteorologists now speak of a lightning channel from which the rapidly expanding sound waves cause thunder (see Geer, *Glossary of Weather and Climate*, 136).

cogent.³¹ Although the terminology for rain is different in this Joban verse (שֶׁטֶף, which refers to floods), it is clear that it descends to the earth via a channel (תְעָלָה) cut out (פִּלַּג, which has the same root as "channel" in Ps 65:10 [9]) for it. It is clear in such a setting that the generic word "water" (מַיִם) here refers specifically to rain.

An alternate explanation for this metaphor must be mentioned at this point. Kraus objects to this natural rainfall explanation, preferring to maintain that God's source of water is located in the temple in Jerusalem, and this description is cultic, not natural.³² While possible, this does not seem probable without a more explicit reference to the temple.

The effect of the rain is described firstly by the verb רוה, "drench." This is the most effusive word used for what the rain does in this passage. The ground is thoroughly watered by God's downpour. There is some suggestion that the verb נחת, "descend," here actually acquires a pluvial connotation in this set of verses.³³ This would make it the second verb to describe the effects of the rain. Dahood's reasoning ("The piel imperative *naḥēt* literally means 'Make descend!' Since the lowering of the ridges between the furrows is to be achieved by rainfall, 'soak down' fairly represents its meaning")³⁴ is sound, but lexicographically I feel bound to a more literal translation of the verb. Such meaning is best explained in the notes to a translation.

The third verb describing the effects of the rain is מוג, "soften." This is the obvious effect of rain on dry, hard ground. It may inform us whether the spring or autumn rains are being considered.³⁵ If the ground has just been plowed and planted, the fructifying autumnal rains are the blessing received. The final verb ברך, "bless," is too general to assert a pluvial aspect, but in this context rain is the form that this blessing takes.

The second and final use of the rain-word רביבים, "drizzle," in the Psalms occurs here. The other occurrence is in Ps 72:6 (see above). Goulder's ebullient description of the rain suggests that drizzle is inappropriate to a context where "not just showers, inches of rain"³⁶ are falling. Given the semantic range of רביבים, which falls somewhere between dew and rain, I concur with Reymond that "drizzle" is indeed the word appropriate to use.³⁷ Drizzle is adequate to fructify crops after the initial rains since it falls to the

---

31. A. A. Anderson, *Book of Psalms*, 1:470–71; Tate, *Psalms 51–100*, 143.
32. Kraus, *Psalms 60–150*, 31.
33. Dahood, *Psalms*, 2:115; Tate, *Psalms 51–100*, 138.
34. Dahood, *Psalms*, 2:115.
35. Reymond, *L'eau*, 19.
36. Goulder, *The Prayers of David*, 177.
37. Reymond, *L'eau*, 22.

ground,[38] and it is to be preferred to heavy rains, which may damage crops once growth has begun.

All forms of rain perform the same function in these two verses. They bring glory to God for their fertilizing work. They prepare the ground for planting and moisten it when it is necessary, after the planting. The function of rain here is uniform with previous occurrences.

מַיִם

Psalm 77:18 [17]

> Waters poured forth from cumulus,
> clouds gave out voice,
> indeed your arrows scudded.

Not every occurrence of the word "water" (מים) in the Psalms has a pluvial context. Clearly rain is intended in this verse by virtue of the water pouring forth (זרם) from the clouds. Since this verse will be discussed in more detail below, under clouds, at this point it is necessary to consider only the function of the rain in this context. The psalm utilizes *Chaoskampf* language to bolster the confidence of the psalmist. The primordial waters tremble at God's presence (v. 17 [16]) as revealed in a rainstorm:

> The waters saw you, o God,
> the waters saw you (and) writhed,
> even the deeps were agitated.

The function of the rain in this verse appears purely to demonstrate the response of nature to the presence of God. The chaotic waters that encompass the world[39] see God, and nature's response is to pour out water as the divine voice cries out thunder and flashes lightning. This form of release could be considered a martial challenge to God or a fearful response to the presence of the God who controls the waters. The ultimate result, as revealed in v. 20 [19] is that God's way was through the sea—the waters were divided by divine striding. The ultimate victory and power are thus ascribed to the God in whom the psalmist has put her or his trust. Here the fructifying aspect of rain is not foremost, but the ability of the rain to reflect God's victory over the waters, even the unruly waters of chaos.

38. Geer, *Glossary of Weather and Climate*, 72.
39. Stadelmann, *Hebrew Conception of the World*, 122.

נֹטֵף, גֶּשֶׁם, and נוּף

These three pluvial terms occur in a cluster in another single psalm describing a rainstorm.

Psalm 68:8-10 [7-9]

God, when you went out before your people,
when you marched in the wilderness, (selah)
9 [8] the earth quaked,
indeed the heavens poured (נטף),[40]
from before God, the one of Sinai,
from before God, the God of Israel.
10 [9] Winter rain (גשם),[41] God, you freely sieved (נוף),[42]
your inheritance[43] also was weary,

---

40. Although the lexica indicate that this word properly means "drip" (BDB 642b-643a; KBS 694b), the context of a theophany here demands more forceful language. It is obvious that the root נטף has something to do with releasing liquid, apparently usually, slowly. The use of the conjunction אף to start this colon also indicates something more forceful than the previous reference (BDB 64b), in this case something more intense than an earthquake. "Drip" therefore seems unlikely in such a context. Lipiński suggests that an early misunderstanding of Judg 5:4-5 led to this psalm's use of "distillent" ("Juges 5,4," 200-206). Less satisfying is Vogt's suggestion that because of the similarity of ב and י, that the root should really be נטי —"ja die Himmel wankten" ("'Die Himmel troffen' (Ps 68,9)?" 208-9). For support of my translation "poured," see Caquot, "Le psaume LXVIII," 155; Johnson, *Sacral Kingship*, 71; Kraus, *Psalms 60-150*, 44; and Tate, *Psalms 51-100*, 160, 163, 176-77, and, although basing the form on a different root, also Gray, "A Cantata of the Autumn Festival," 22.

41. גשם is specifically the winter rain, see Reymond, *L'eau*, 19-24; Lipiński, "Juges 5,4-5," 200; Baly, *Geography of the Bible*, 47-50; and Orni and Efrat, *Geography of Israel*, 142, 146. Although he does not use the word גשם, Frick confirms this general winter rain pattern ("Rain," 612). Scott ("Meteorological Phenomena," 23) prefers a more general term.

42. This word is so anomalous that the lexica struggle to explain it. BDB (632a) notes that in this context this "vb. [is] not wholly suitable;" while KBS (682b) posits a second root נוף to account for this verse (and Prov 7:17). I have taken up Lipiński's (ultimately abandoned) suggestion "On pourrait alors traduire le Ps 68,10a 'Tu tamises une pluie généreuse'" ("Juges 5,4-5," 203). This is in keeping with the literal meaning of נוף and it yields an evocative image of how God provides rain. For the cosmological concept of a heavenly sieve, see Feigin "The Heavenly Sieve," 41-42, and Cross and Freedman, "A Royal Song of Thanksgiving," 25, n. 33.

43. Goodwin's suggestion that this should be read "wadi, stream" by dividing the suffix into a separate verb is attractive since a wadi would indeed be established by the winter rains ("A Rare Spelling," 490-91). The proposed rare root of *tkk* is harder to accept. It should not be overlooked, however, that נחל apparently does occur in

you reestablished[44] it.

As noted in chapter two, this psalm is notoriously difficult. Nearly every word offers the translator some dilemma. The various interpretations have been endlessly discussed, but instead of rehashing them here, the reader is referred to the summaries in Miller and LePeau.[45] In keeping with the general aim of this study, I will not be attempting to assign a genre or interpretation to the whole, but rather will attempt to determine the role the weather plays in it.

In its final form this psalm is a hymn. It involves a theophany in which meteorological language is present, although in an unusual way.[46] Rain, as may be noted in the previous passages explored, does not always find mention in theophanic descriptions.

In addition to its use of rare vocabulary, Ps 68 is made difficult by its uncertain context for these verses. The previous verse (8 [7]) is often considered part of this pericope.[47] It sets the stage as God's march in the unspecified wilderness. The psalm also employs at least three words that have been associated with rain in some way: גשם, נטפו, and תניף. Of these, only the first is well-attested and understood, and, in fact, many of the difficulties in these verses revolve around the supposed meteorological terms.[48] In offering a tentative translation, I have relied heavily on context, as several words offer unresolved lexical difficulties. It should not be overlooked that vv. 8–9 [7–8] closely resemble Judg 5:4–5 in the Song of Deborah.[49] In Judg 5, these two verses form a separate unit, which is not necessarily related to the remainder of the Song, other than by their being placed in that precise

---

feminine form in Ps 124:4, and perhaps in Ezek 47:19 and 48:28, although the latter two references may be instances of ה *locale*. If one adjusts the pointing this verse could refer to the restoration of a wadi that has been desiccated by the heat of summer and reestablished by the winter rains.

44. This reiterative force of the po'lel is required by the context, especially if the reading "wadi-torrent" is accepted in the previous line.

45. Miller, *Divine Warrior*, 102–13; LePeau, *Psalm 68*, 6–58.

46. This is close to what Jeremias (*Theophanie*, 7–16) determines is the original form of theophanic description, as found in Judg 5:4–5.

47. Caquot ("Le psaume LXVIII," 149, 155) considers the sense unit (which consists of a protasis and apodosis) to be vv. 8–9 [7–8].

48. Lipiński, "Juges 5,4–5," 185–206; Vogt, "'Die Himmel troffen,'" and "'Regen in Fülle,'" 359–61, illustrate well the difficulties of these verses. In the final analysis, emendation of the text is usually recommended, or a new form based on a questionable root is postulated.

49. This connection may continue beyond these verses in the psalm as well, according to Tournay, "Le Psaume LXVIII," 358–68.

location. These verses are not identical with this passage, but they are close enough to provide helpful comparison.

Adding to the confusion concerning this pericope is the frequent assertion that it refers to the exodus and wilderness wandering traditions.[50] This is largely based on the connection of this verse with Judg 5:4-5.[51] This connection is even pressed to provide a manna interpretation of the abundant rain of v. 10 [9].[52] This connection with the wilderness and exodus traditions should not, however, receive undue emphasis. The wilderness mentioned in v. 8[7], יְשִׁימוֹן, may have undertones of the wanderings, but it may be a generic term as well.[53] This is an important point because the interpretation of the weather terminology depends, in part, on whether or not this is a historical motif. Another option is to see this as a theophanic account of Yahweh's approach from the south,[54] without necessarily referring to Sinai. As long as this uncertainty remains, it is prudent not to build up a wilderness wandering scenario further than this pericope will support one.

What is the function of the rain in this passage? There appear to be at least two main applications of pluvial terminology here: initially, in v. 9 [8], the rain falls at the appearance of God, making it function as an indicator of theophany in a way similar to the lightning and thunder explored in chapter two as well as in Ps 77:18 [17]. It is almost as if at the sight of God, the sky cannot hold back its water, but drops it from fright.

The falling rain is made a bridge to the next idea, in v. 10 [9], that the rain is a sign of divine beneficence. The rain is specified as the winter rain, the rain necessary to begin crop growth. God is portrayed as sieving the rain. Such sieving spreads the rain over a large area, increasing the fertile area of ground.

In keeping with his concept of a sequential development of this theme in the Psalms, Goulder understands this rain as the description of the rain first mentioned in Ps 65.[55] Thematically the ideas are closely connected; they

50. A. A. Anderson, *Book of Psalms*, 1:486-87; Briggs and Briggs, *Book of Psalms*, 2:98; Kraus, *Psalms 60-150*, 52.

51. As noted in Weiser, *The Psalms*, 485. There is undoubtedly some relationship between the two passages.

52. Podechard, "Psaume LXVIII," 507.

53. BDB, 445; KBS 447a.

54. Caquot, "Le psaume LXVIII," 155.

55. "The giving of Psalm 65 to the celebration of the rainstorm, and its understanding there as a sign of forgiveness for 'our transgressions,' gives a satisfactory explanation for the mention of the rainstorm in 68.7-10; once the psalms are understood as a sequence, the two storms are the same, and initiate the royal victory. Without this connection exegetes are thrown back on the hypothesis that the psalm is a reflection of Israel's *Heilsgeschichte*; and all the commentators whom I am following take this general

both indicate the early rains. Seeing an organic connection between such a brief mention in these two psalms requires a concentration which appears to evaporate when the other themes of the psalms are interposed. Rain was, ideally, an annual event. I share Goulder's concern to free the psalm from *Heilsgeschichte*, but not at the price of recognizing one memorable rain only in Israel's life on the land.

גֶּשֶׁם

Psalm 105:32

> He gave (for) their winter rains (גשם) hail,
> fire of flames in their land.

In the literary context of a retelling the tradition of captivity in Egypt, this verse summarizes the plague of hail and fire with which Yahweh punished Egypt (Exod 9:13–35). Instead of the fructifying winter rains (גשם, with reference to the seasonal pattern of Palestine, and not necessarily Egypt, which relied upon the flooding of the Nile for water), destructive hail will be sent. Thus the rains here are not literal, but figurative. Hail may be said to rain from the sky, however, it is a separate meteorological phenomenon, to be considered in chapter five below. For further discussion of the background to this verse (in the context of lightning), see chapter two above.

The function of the rain in this context is clearly divine punishment. This is noteworthy in that rain is generally considered a blessing, but also the rain here described is abnormal—hail was sent instead of rain. It is a further instance of Yahweh's use of various meteors for punishment of the divine enemies, intimating that Yahweh has a heavenly arsenal.

מַשְׁקֶה

Psalm 104:13

> Who waters the mountains from his roof chambers,
> from the fruit of your works you satisfy the ground.

This hymn praising Yahweh's works in nature begins with a hiphil participle of the verb שׁקה, "to give a drink, to water." The participial form fits somewhat awkwardly into the flow from verse 12, but there is no reason to alter

---

position." Goulder, *The Prayers of David*, 196.

the text. The previous verses (10–12) are united by water imagery, some of which may imply rain, but which do not directly mention it. Verses 10–12 focus on streams that Yahweh causes to flow from the mountains to give water to the animals. Such streams ultimately have their source in rain, but the causality should not be assumed to have been understood.[56]

The sense of what is happening in this verse is clear enough—from the divine chambers in the sky Yahweh sends rain onto the mountains. Although שׁקה does not always denote rain, in this context it clearly does. The water comes from the sky (Yahweh's roof chambers, עליות), and falls on the mountains (which is meteorologically correct since mountains force clouds to rise higher, thus inducing rain), and fructifies the ground.

In this verse the function of the rain is to bring glory to Yahweh by watering the earth and making it fruitful.

מוֹרֶה

Psalm 84:7 [6]

> Those traversing the valley of the *baka*,[57]
> will drink[58] (from) springs,
> early rains will cover it with blessings indeed.

This passage, in the context of a pilgrimage psalm, is extremely difficult, forcing some commentators to the conclusion that the text is corrupt.[59] The sense of the verse, however, is fairly clear: pilgrims traversing a certain dry area find it unexpectedly well-watered. For the purposes of this study, the

---

56. Alpert and Neumann, "An Ancient 'Correlation,'" 313–14, note that this correlation between rain and rivers at a distant location is first documented in the third century C.E. Rain in the mountains and streams from the mountains may have been associated in the minds of those who saw both, but this information should not be forced into this psalm.

57. This likely refers to a type of plant. Jacob and Jacob ("Flora," 803–17) do not identify this as a plant type, and the usual rendition of "basalm" has been challenged by A. A. Anderson (*Book of Psalms*, 2:604). Many commentators take Baka to be a place name (ibid., 2:604; Kraus, *Psalms 60–150*, 169; Tate, *Psalms 51–100*, 353–54), which makes for a difficulty with the definite article (הבכא). I take it as a plant, albeit an unidentified one.

58. I can make no sense from the MT as it stands. My translation of this word follows the suggestion of the *BHS* apparatus that יְשִׁיתוּהוּ should be read יִשְׁתּוּ, which I take from the root שׁתה, "to drink," rather than from שׁית, "to set, place."

59. A. A. Anderson, *Book of Psalms*, 2:604; Briggs and Briggs, *Book of Psalms*, 2:227–28; Kraus, *Psalms 60–150*, 166. *BHS* indicates a number of variants in the apparatus.

word for rains, מורה, is also somewhat problematic. The entire final colon is marked as corrupt by *BHS*, and מורה specifically is provided with an alternate reading. The pluvial denotation of מורה is clearly demonstrated in Joel 2:23 where it occurs (twice) in parallel with גשם and מלקוש, words whose meanings are not in doubt.[60]

The word מורה appears to be a simple variant of יורה, the more usual word for early rains. The troubling interchange of the *m* and the *y* should perhaps be compared to the Ugaritic example of the word "beloved," which occurs in two forms: *ydd* and *mdd*. Although obviously not homophones, they clearly have the same meaning and are perhaps used interchangeably.[61] The same perhaps holds true for מורה and יורה. Interestingly, Reymond discusses only the latter form in his section on meteorology, perhaps understanding מורה as corrupt.[62] Since the form מורה in Joel 2:23 is used to contrast the late rains (מלקוש),[63] and since יורה is used elsewhere to denote the early rains, understanding מורה and יורה as synonyms appears to be the most logical interpretation.

The usual problem of finding unseasonable rains in this verse stems from the insistence that it commemorates a certain festival, the timing of which seldom included rain (generally supposed to be Succoth).[64] If the identity of the festival that lies behind the pilgrimage, which is highly speculative, is not presumed, then some of the difficulties in identifying the phenomenon mentioned in this verse evaporate.

Leaving open the possibility of a corrupt text (otherwise it is difficult to make any sense of this verse), the question of the function of the rain in this verse remains unanswered. Primarily the rain appears as relief to travel-weary pilgrims, and it is responsible for leaving them "blessings." With one vowel change and no alteration of the MT, the attractive alternative of "pools" is offered (for example in the NRSV) for "blessings." While this correlates well with the idea of rainfall, it is not a certainty, since rainfall is elsewhere also viewed as a blessing. The early rains here are not viewed as fructifying since agricultural imagery is lacking. They are viewed, however, as refreshing to those on a journey, and thus may be seen as a further example of divine beneficence.

60. See Nash, *Palestinian Agricultural Year*, 104–6.

61. For a discussion of this Ugaritic example see Wiggins, *A Reassessment of "Asherah,"* 52–53.

62. Reymond, *L'Eau*, 9–53. It is not included in his otherwise comprehensive "index des termes hébraïques utilisés à propos de l'eau," 256–71.

63. Scott, "Meteorological Phenomena," 23; Nash, *Palestinian Agricultural Year*, 124–25.

64. For a thorough discussion see Tate, *Psalms 51–100*, 358–60.

POSSIBLE RAIN ALLUSION

טוב

It has been contended that in the relatively dry climate of Palestine, where rainfall at the opportune time is necessary for agricultural success, rain may be referenced by the general word "good" (טוב).[65] טוב is an extremely common word, and its exact referent is not always easily determined. The philological evidence for this specific meaning of "good" as "rain" is not especially strong, and generally the context is the main clue.[66] In none of the generally cited examples is טוב paired in parallelism with a word translated "rain."[67] Not all instances of the word טוב in the Psalms will be examined here, but only one representative reference. Among the four references generally cited, Ps 85:13 [12] is the most convincing.[68] Since this monograph is limited to relatively certain references to meteorological phenomena, a full examination of one possible allusion (to the exclusion of other possible allusions) is out of place. However, the claim that "[t]he 'good' par excellence in Palestine is the rain, so that in a number of texts *ṭôb* without further modification concretely signifies 'rain'"[69] requires at least a cursory investigation here.

Psalm 85:13 [12]

> Indeed Yahweh will give the good,
> and our land will give its produce.

This verse occurs in the context of a list of blessings provided by Yahweh to a grateful people. The psalm as a whole is a prayer for divine mercy, asking for these good things to be restored. By placing a reference to the produce of the land in parallelism with "the good," the psalmist possibly alludes to rain as "the good." In other words, if Yahweh gives rain, the soil gives produce. This is one possible interpretation of this verse which specifically links "the good" and agriculture. The question, however, remains whether this is the

---

65. Dahood, "Hebrew-Ugaritic Lexicography," 411; "A Note on *ṭôb* 'Rain,'" 404; *Psalms I*, xxxii; Gordon, "On BH *ṭôb* 'Rain,'" 111; Loretz, "Ugaritisch *ṭôb*," 247–58.

66. Gordon, "On BH *ṭôb* 'Rain,'" 111.

67. Dahood cites four examples of טוב as rain: Pss 4:7 [6]; 65:12 [11]; 68:11 [10] and 85:13 [12] ("Hebrew-Ugaritic Lexicography," 411).

68. Loretz, "Ugaritisch *ṭôb*," 249–50) adequately dismisses the supposed referents in Pss 4:7 [6] and 68:11 [10].

69. Dahood, *Psalms*, 1:25.

only possible interpretation of "the good" in this verse. Crops require fertile soil and sunshine in addition to rain. It could be argued that Israel had fertile soil and sunshine was never in short supply, but rain was a true variable. In itself this is fair assessment, and the possibility exists that "the good" here is a reference to rain. This would fit well with other psalm references to rain as a blessing.[70]

A dogmatic approach to this interpretation, however, should be avoided. Equating "the good" with rain seems quite probable, but the equation remains open to doubt in that modern interpreters are not privy to the full range of meaning in ancient agricultural terminology. "The good" could be a generic reference to all that Yahweh provides that which is necessary to produce crops, including, but not limited to, rain. Until more specific philological evidence comes to light, it is best to treat this possible allusion as a distinct possibility, but not a certainty.

SUMMARY OF RAIN TERM FUNCTIONS

The first aspect to notice about rain terms in the Psalms is that they are not as numerous as might be supposed, given their necessity for life in Palestine. A second aspect is the clustering of rain terminology in concentrated verses, as in Pss 65:10–11 [9–10] and 68:9–10 [8–9]. A third aspect to consider is the lexical difficulties of several of the words in their larger contexts. Despite these parameters, rain does merit frequent mention in the Psalms, and when it occurs it fulfills a variety of functions, not necessarily divided along the lines of the different words used to indicate rain in the Psalms.

Rain functions in various ways in these verses. Its primary function appears to be to ensure the fertility of the land (Ps 65:10–11 [9–10]; 68:10 [9]; 104:3; 147:8). This aspect is referred to by the term "bless" in Ps 65:11 [10].

Rain is sometimes an attendant phenomenon of a theophany (68:8–9 [7–8]; 77:18 [17]). As such it inspires awe bordering on dread. It may affect people as well as the chaotic, cosmological waters. Ps 135:7 indicates that Yahweh's ability to send rain is a source of wonder, and such awe is not necessarily dreaded.

Once it is the purely beneficial, although not fecundifying, effect of rain which is celebrated; Ps 84:7 [6] may consider rain a blessing to travelers through an apparently dry land.

70. Even though he rejects some of Dahood's suggestions that טוב may mean rain, Loretz accepts such an interpretation of this verse: "In v. 11–14 kann nach alledem nur vom Regen die Rede sein" ("Ugaritisch *ṭôb*," 254).

Sometimes rain is not beneficial. Ps 72:6 presents poorly timed rain as an image of the dread that the king instills among national enemies, Ps 105:32 portrays Yahweh substituting hail for the winter rains.

The concept of rain is also expanded to include various objects dropping from the skies (technically "meteors"). These may be detrimental, as the coals of fire and sulphur understood to "rain" from above in Ps 11:6, or beneficial, as the manna that rained down in Ps 78:24 or the birds in Ps 78:27. Although technically meteorological, such preternatural phenomena are not weather-related. They also provide a glimpse into a cosmology in which Yahweh holds reserves of both weapons and provisions for the chosen people.

CLOUDS

Many words are used in the Psalms to denote clouds. Since clouds occur in many varieties and since the ancients were keen observers of nature, it must be asked whether these several nephological words designate different types of clouds.[71] Naturally, we could not expect scientific distinctions such as cumulus or cirrus (which are based on altitude),[72] but the appearance of cloud types differ from each other making some kind of typology possible, at least theoretically. The contexts of the cloud terminology may well give some indication of what type of cloud was intended by the use of a specific word for it. In such an instance word roots will be important to decipher, as well as the contexts in which the words occur.

There appear to be six main words for cloud types in the Psalms: נשא עב, ענן, שחק, ערפל, and perhaps קיטור. These terms occur in Pss 18:10 [9], 12 [11], 13 [12]; 36:6 [5]; 57:11 [10]; 68:35 [34]; 77:18 [17]; 78:14, 23; 89:7 [6], 38 [37]; 97:2; 99:7; 104:3; 105:39; 108:5 [4]; 135:7; 147:8 and 148:8. The special case of ערבות in Ps 68:5 [4] will also be considered.

---

71. The authority on cloud types is the World Meteorological Organization's *International Cloud Atlas*, 2 vols. (hereafter *ICA*). A well-illustrated source for cloud-types is Scorer and Verkaik, *Spacious Skies*. See also Ludlum, *Field Guide to North American Weather*. Although this source deals with weather in North America, cloud types are a world-wide phenomenon. For a more technical treatment consult Mason, *Clouds, Rain and Rainmaking*.

72. See Geer, *Glossary of Weather and Climate*, 45–46.

עָב

The root of עב (probably עוב) has obscurity as its basic connotation.[73] The root עוב, the basis for the cloud name, appears to be related to the root עבה, "thickness." The thickness aspect of this cloud-type, along with its various contexts explored below, confirms the general opinion that עב denotes cumulus clouds.[74]

Psalm 18:13 [12]

> From brightness before him,
> through his cumulonimbus traversed
> hail and coals of fire.

This verse is in the heart of the theophany of Ps 18 where Yahweh appears to rescue the psalmist. The word order causes some difficulty here since either "cumulonimbus" or "hail and coals of fire" could be the subject of ערב ("traversed"). As noted in chapter two, however, the imagery is clearly that of a thunderstorm with its attendant clouds.

The clouds that produce thunderstorms are cumulonimbus. Cumulonimbus clouds are also, in fact, the generators of both hail and lightning ("coals of fire"), which travel through them. The psalmist would not have known the scientific origins of these phenomena, but to the eye both lightning and hail appear to descend from the clouds. Hearkening back to the root meaning of עב, obscurity, what is obscured in this psalm is the divine presence. The clouds that most effectively obscure the sky are cumulonimbi, which often appear gray or very dark.[75] Although in basic terms עב is intended to denote cumulus clouds generally, the context here strongly suggests that thunderstorm clouds, cumulonimbi, are intended.

The function of the cloud in this verse is at least two-fold. The towering cumulonimbus obscures the divine personage, so that Yahweh cannot be seen, but it also is the vehicle of a theophanic event. As theophanic instruments, clouds produce lightning and hail, the dangerous aspects of the divine presence. Here they are used in the context of Yahweh as a divine

---

73. The comparative material in both BDB (727b) and KBS (773a) indicates that cloudiness or darkness, both of which obscure, are the concepts that define this root.

74. Scott, "Meteorological Phenomena," 25; Stadelmann, *Hebrew Conception of the World*, 97–98. This was a conclusion at which I arrived independently of Scott and Stadelmann, but their work confirmed my choice of nephological terms.

75. Geer, *Glossary of Weather and Climate*, 58–59.

warrior who intimidates the enemies of the psalmist. Theophanic events both reveal and obscure Yahweh and cloud-language is functional in both aspects.[76]

Psalm 104:3

> The one placing the beams of his roof chambers in the waters,
> the one making cumuli his chariot,
> the one walking upon the wings of the wind.

Psalm 104 is a hymn praising the creative acts of Yahweh. Verses 2–4 address atmospheric aspects of Yahweh's glory. Here Yahweh is pictured as establishing a dwelling amid the waters beyond the dome separating the chaotic waters outside the created order from those within. Two methods of divine locomotion are presented: Yahweh walking on the wings of the wind[77] and riding on the clouds as a chariot.

As suggested by Stadelmann, I have translated עבים in this verse as "cumuli."[78] This particular cloud-type is distinguished by its thickness and its propensity to produce rain. In this verse such clouds constitute a divine chariot. The imagery is distinctly martial and its connection with the Ugaritic notion of Baal as charioteer of the clouds has not gone unnoticed.[79] Yahweh theophanically rides the rain-cloud,[80] not so much in this case to discomfit an enemy as to display the divine oversight of the skies. The pluvial aspect of this cloud-chariot will reappear in v. 13.

The function of the cumulus clouds in this passage appears primarily to be a demonstration of divine power. Yahweh is able to build among the unstable waters. Further, Yahweh is also able to ride the chariot of cloud in order to designate when and where its rain might fall. The veiling and revealing effect of thick clouds is also an essential element in the choice of עבים here.

---

76. Also concluded by Stadelmann, *Hebrew Conception of the World*, 97.

77. On this aspect, see above, chapter three.

78. Stadelmann, *Hebrew Conception of the World*, 97–98.

79. Allen, *Psalms 101–150*, 33; A. A. Anderson, *Book of Psalms*, 2:719; Stadelmann, *Hebrew Conception of the World*, 101.

80. Jeremias, *Theophanie*, 70; Allen, *Psalms 101–150*, 26; Weiser, *The Psalms*, 29, 667.

Psalm 147:8

> The one covering the heavens with clouds,
> the one preparing rain for the earth,
> the one causing grass to sprout on the mountains.

The pluvial aspect of this verse is described above. This hymn offers Yahweh's feeding of creatures (v. 9) as a cause for praising God. In order to feed creatures, rain must fall. For rain to fall, the correct clouds must fill the skies. This verse indicates clearly that the causality between clouds and rain were under the direct control of Yahweh.

This verse also serve as a warning against simple equations of only one cloud-type with a Hebrew root. As mentioned above, Stadelmann made the astute observation that "'ʿb designates the 'cumulus.'"[81] The difficulty here is that not only cumulus clouds produce rain, and often the torrential, frequently brief, nature of cumulus rains is inadequate for agriculture. The low-lying, sky-blanketing nimbostratus cloud usually produces a prolonged, steady rain.[82] The terse reference to clouds in this verse make it difficult to determine which variety of cloud is more likely. Cumulus clouds may be localized, but still large enough apparently to cover the entire sky. In such a context "clouds" is a safer translation than a more specific term.

The function of the clouds here is similar to that of the rain. The clouds are sent to provide the rain, which, in the next verse, fructifies the earth. Fecundity is therefore the function of the clouds in this verse.

Further references to עב in the Psalms also employ the root שחק to denote clouds as well.

שְׁחָקִים and עָבוֹת/עָבֵי שְׁחָקִים

The root meaning of שחק seems to relate to dust or fine powder.[83] By extension this has been applied to fine, wispy clouds, or cirrus.[84] Perhaps by coincidence, or by the commonality in the Psalm verses where the word occurs, it appears to apply to cirrus only when it is not used in conjunction with עב. Even in several of the less obvious occurrences of the word (it is generally masked in English translations by the word "sky"/"skies") it is difficult

---

81. Stadelmann, *Hebrew Conception of the World*, 98.
82. ICA, I, 30; Ludlum, *Field Guide to North American Weather*, 86.
83. BDB 1006b–1007a; KBS 1464; Scott, "Meteorological Phenomena," 25.
84. Reymond, *L'Eau*, 15; Scott, "Meteorological Phenomena," 25; Stadelmann, *Hebrew Conception of the World*, 98.

to define it specifically as cirrus, although it is generally not ruled out. שׁחק is used to denote clouds in Pss 18:12 [11]; 36:6 [5]; 57:11 [10]; 68:35 [34]; 77:18 [17]; 78:23; 89:7 [6], 38 [37]; and 108:5 [4].

Psalm 18:12 [11]

> He made darkness his covering around himself,
> his booth (the) hiding-place of waters, thick, towering clouds.[85]

This verse offers an intriguing challenge to a precise meteorological description. In the context of a theophany in which Yahweh comes to the aid of the psalmist, the divine form is veiled by darkness and clouds. The challenge centers on the two cloud terms appearing together in the phrase עבי שׁחקים. If this is a construct relationship (as the MT is pointed) the nomen regum, עבי, would be the usual word for thick clouds (cumulus), while the nomen rectum, שׁחקים, would be the usual word for thin clouds (cirrus). Another possibility is that the pointing is slightly incorrect. With only minor vowel changes עבי could be a noun based on the root עבה: "thickness."[86] The essential characteristic of cirrus clouds is their height: in addition to actually being higher in the atmosphere, they obviously appear to be higher than stratus and cumulus clouds. Instead of understanding שׁחק as "cirrus" here, it might be taken to mean tall clouds, thus "the thickness of high clouds" might be a possible connotation. Although the translation presented above is less literal, it allows for either grammatical construction by distilling the adjectival force from each noun and striving for the fundamental sense of the combination. Towering castellanus clouds (cloud turrets) would be adequate to veil a figure of considerable size and would penetrate to high altitudes. As noted above, strict precision correlating cloud types with various Hebrew nephological words is frustrated by the evidence.

Some of the usual sources of help are lacking here: the wording of this phrase is precisely the same in 2 Sam 22:12, and the observation of purely natural phenomena is precluded by the theophanic aspect—we cannot see what the psalmist saw. The most straightforward way to translate the meteorological aspect in this verse, therefore, is one which leaves some ambiguity.[87]

---

85. The wording is difficult here. The combination of עב (generally cumulus) and שׁחק (often cirrus) will be discussed in the text.

86. Although I consider textual emendation as a final resort, the shift here would be from *qameṣ* to *ḥaṭep-pataḥ* in the first position and from *ṣere* to *ḥireq* in the second position, a shift which does not even violate any vowel classes. This pointing is reflected in Reymond, *L'eau*, 13. For the root see BDB 716a.

87. Mention should be made here of Sarna's evocative translation "Dark

The function of the clouds here, however, is fairly clear. The clouds are intended to obscure the divine form and to reveal the divine presence in a theophany.

Psalm 77:18 [17]

> Waters poured forth from cumulus,
> clouds gave out voice,
> indeed your arrows scudded.

Like Ps 18, the psalmist of Ps 77 is in trouble. The thought of God's great power as revealed in both *Chaoskampf* language (v. 17 [16]) and in meteorological terminology in the present verse, provide a source of comfort. God terrifies the chaotic waters in the previous verse with the result that a theophanic storm ensues.

Justification for the use of "cumulus" for עבות[88] arises from the quantity of rain denoted by its pouring forth (זרם). Although a steady rain may fall from low-level nimbostratus clouds, this rain, although persistent, is not like the heavy shower produced by a cumulus cloud.[89] עבות is paralleled by שחקים. Once again translation of שחקים by the standard "cirrus" is controverted by the context: cirrus clouds are not associated with thunder, which is the likely meaning behind "gave out voice" in this clause.[90] When עב and שחקים are used together they tend to indicate cumulus clouds, if not a cumulonimbus. Such towering thunderheads are entirely appropriate in the context of a divine manifestation.

Two main possibilities present themselves regarding the function of the clouds here. One is that they, as participants in the great mass of chaotic waters, are terrified at God's approach and show their discomfiture by pouring down rain and raging thunder and lightning. More likely is the second alternative that the clouds act as the vehicle of God's epiphany. As the divine approaches, this is made known, not by a direct sighting, but by the profuse rain, the divine voice of thunder, and the divine arrows of lightning.

---

thunderclouds, dense clouds of sky" (*Exploring Exodus*, 112).

88. The noun עב occurs in both feminine and masculine plural forms.
89. *ICA*, 1:38; Ludlum, *Field Guide to North American Weather*, 86.
90. Reymond, *L'eau*, 12. See chapter two above.

שְׁחָקִים/שַׁחַק

When the word שׁחק occurs in the Psalms without עב, it generally takes the meaning "cirrus," the high, wispy clouds that are not associated with imminent rain.

Psalm 36:6 [5]

> Yahweh, your lovingkindness is in the heavens,
> your fidelity [stretches] up to the cirrus.

Despite the grammatical conundrum of בהשמים, the sense of this verse is forthright. The previous four verses of this lament describe the immorality of the wicked, which this verse contrasts with the virtues of Yahweh. This verse is an example of two adverbial prepositional phrases in verbless clauses. Generally some form of the verb "to be" is supplied in such circumstances,[91] although many modern translations supply a verb of extension in this case.[92] Such a verb choice is justified by the use of עד in the second clause, which implies duration in space or time.[93] Although Dahood's use of "from" for ב here is attractive,[94] I have followed the more cautious approach of the Briggses.[95] The choice of verb in the second clause must be informed by the context, and so there is some latitude for the translator.

In this verse we possess a fine example of how שחקים indicates the highest variety of cloud, the cirrus. The cirrus clouds are interestingly paralleled with the very heavens; Yahweh's fidelity extends to the highest clouds, that is, to the brink of the firmament itself. This expansive statement indicates that clouds may function as delineators of great distance, a function hitherto unseen in the Psalms.

Psalm 57:11 [10]

> For great is your lovingkindness up to [the] heavens,
> and up to [the] cirrus your fidelity.

---

91. Waltke and O'Connor, *Introduction to Biblical Hebrew Syntax*, 72–73.
92. For example, NRSV, REB, NAB, NJB, and the Tanakh.
93. GKC §103o.
94. Dahood, *Psalms*, 1:220.
95. Briggs and Briggs, *Book of Psalms*, 1:317–18. Interestingly, they name the clouds as one of "the four great objects in nature" (317), a sentiment that indirectly demonstrates the thesis of this book.

The closeness of this verse to Ps 36:6 [5] (immediately above) has long been noted. They share all of the same nouns, including שחקים, "cirrus." Again the verse consists of two verbless clauses. In this case no verb of extension is necessary since "is" may capture the sense adequately.

The function of this verse in another lament is also parallel to 36:6 [5]: to declare that God's merits are as high as the highest clouds.

Psalm 68:35 [34]

> Ascribe strength to God,
> his majesty is over Israel,
> and his strength is in the clouds.

Textually this verse presents few problems, unlike many of the other verses considered for this particular psalm. It represents the first verse of a two-verse closing doxology to the psalm, and, as such, it need not be divided as proposed by Albright.[96]

It is difficult to assert that שחקים denote any specific type of clouds in this verse since the context is deliberately vague. The strength (עז) of God is supposed to be in the clouds, a term often translated "heavens" in this verse because of its obvious generality. If cirrus clouds are denoted here, the height aspect would be the emphasis, and this would be an appropriate way of exalting the power of one's God: not only does the deity display might in the clouds, but control over even the highest clouds. While this cannot be established with any certainty, it should remain a possibility in this verse.

The function of the clouds in this verse is to serve as a display of the might of Israel's God. Control over the clouds demonstrates the divine ability for Israel to see.

Psalm 78:23–24

> 23 And he commanded the clouds from above,
> and the doors of heaven he opened.
> 24 And he rained upon them manna to eat,
> and the grain of heaven he gave to them.

---

96. Albright, "A Catalogue of Early Hebrew," 35, 39.

As a demonstration of divine care in the wilderness tradition, God provided manna for the Israelites. This psalm, as already noted, is a long rehearsal of that tradition. Exod 16:13–14 narrates the arrival of the manna with the dew, which was considered a kind of precipitation in the Hebrew Bible (see below, chapter five). Perhaps assuming dew to be precipitation, the psalmist associates the appearance of the manna with the opening of the doors of heaven, the storehouses of weather elements.[97] Specifically stated in this verse, is that the clouds were commanded. Often concealed in the translation "skies," שחקים here is likely intended to denote clouds, although not specifically cirrus in this verse. Clouds were considered the source of the dew, as they were the source of any hydrometeor.[98] The connection is made explicit in this psalm by v. 24, where manna is said to have rained down upon the Israelites.

The function of the clouds in this verse is the specific aspect of providing manna. The precise mechanism is, naturally, not spelled out, but the general conception is certainly clear.

Psalm 89:7 [6]

> For who among the cloud(s) compares with Yahweh,
> or is like Yahweh among children of gods?

In the context of a hymnic celebration of Yahweh's power, this verse asks who may be compared to the God of the king. For the purposes of this study, the verse is fairly straightforward; among those dwelling in the skies, among the clouds, none is comparable to Yahweh. שחק occurs as a singular here, which is unusual in the usage of this word in the Psalms. The use of the singular, however, conveys no apparent difference in meaning from the use of the plural.

The related issue of monotheism is relevant to this verse since the other deities, "children of gods" (בני אלים), are in parallel with those among the clouds. Clearly this is not a monotheistic context, but the other deities, judged inferior by the psalmist, live in the clouds. Since gods were generally considered to have lived on mountains, this may indicate that שחק in this

---

97. Specifically cited as the storehouse of snow in Job 38:22. For attempts to draw a more specific picture of the clouds as sources of water, including dew, see Torczyner, "The Firmament and the Clouds," 188–96; Sutcliffe, "The Clouds as Water-Carriers in Hebrew Thought," 99–103.

98. See Stadelmann, *Hebrew Conception of the World*, 117–18. On dew, see Uval, "The Dew of Heaven," 117–18.

verse is a lower-level cloud which obscures the tops of the mountains. If such is the case, then it is likely not a cirrus cloud.

The function of the cloud in this verse is to hide the gods, Yahweh presumably among their number. Those "among the clouds" is used as a trope for "gods," as it appears in parallel with "children of gods." The function is somewhat specialized, but unambiguous.

Psalm 89:37–38 [36–37]

His seed will remain forever,
and his throne, like the sun, before me.
As [the] moon[99] it[100] is established forever,
and a witness in the cloud(s) is faithful, (selah).

The verse under immediate consideration (v. 38 [37]), continues an idea begun in v. 37 [36]. With this reference a new section of Ps 89 has been entered with respect to the last verse considered in this psalm (v. 7 [6], above). Rather than hymnic, this section is rather more a lament for some difficulty which the king is experiencing. Among the woes a reminder of the perpetual promise to David is offered in this verse.

An extended debate concerning this verse has recently transpired centering on the identity of the witness.[101] Within the context of this verse, cloud (שחק, singular), has an expansive meaning. The only two singular references to this word meaning "cloud" occur in this psalm.[102] Etymologically there is no basis for the usual English rendition of "skies," since the basic connotation of שחק ("powdery") is applied specifically to dust or to clouds.[103] Semantically, by extension, the meaning of "skies" may be derived from "clouds," but this circumlocution is not necessary. As Veijola has demonstrated, in Hittite treaties, the clouds are summoned as witnesses

---

99. The reference to moon (ירח) without the definite article suggests the possibility that the deity Yariḫ ("Moon") is intended here. For a summary of this deity's role see Schmidt, "Moon," 1098–1113. For a summary of this deity's role in a neighboring culture see Wiggins, "What's in a Name?" 761–79. As noted in the comments on the previous verse, Ps 89 is clearly not monotheistic in outlook.

100. The "it" referenced here is clearly the line of David, the subject of the previous verse.

101. Mullen, "The Divine Witness," 207–18; Mosca, "Once Again the Heavenly Witness," 27–37; Veijola, "The Witness in the Clouds," 413–17.

102. Mullen, "The Divine Witness," 215, n. 34.

103. See also Veijola, "The Witness in the Clouds," 414, n. 12.

themselves.[104] Since this verse notes that the witness is "in the clouds," and not the clouds themselves, Veijola makes a strong case for Yahweh as the witness cited.[105]

In this context, שחק may indicate "cirrus" clouds as the "highest sphere of heaven," to borrow Mosca's phrase.[106] However, the function of the cloud in this verse is apparently that of veiling the witness. This is particularly appropriate given Veijola's cogent arguments that the witness is Yahweh, who is frequently veiled by clouds. As noted earlier, a precise correlation of cloud-types with the Hebrew lexica is problematic, although there are some general trends to be observed. In verses such as this one, the obscuring nature of the clouds would seem to gainsay a translation of "cirrus" since cirrus are generally thin clouds. On the other hand, they are the highest clouds, and as such, may demonstrate the distance of Yahweh from the courtroom scene presented in the psalm, namely, in the highest heavens.

Psalm 108:5 [4]

> For great is your lovingkindness in comparison to [the] heavens,
> and up to [the] the cirrus your fidelity.

This third parallel to Pss 36:6 [5] and 57:11 [10] (see above) differs by only one word from the latter. The similarity between these verses has long been obvious. Once again the term "cirrus" is used to indicate the ultimate height of God's integrity. This psalm, unlike the previous two discussed, is more hymn than lament, but the meteorological function remains identical.

Perhaps a reflex of these three verses being variants of each other, the only references to שחקים in the Psalms apart from עב appear to indicate cirrus clouds. When שחקים appears in conjunction with עב, however, it takes on a different cast, denoting the height of clouds which are thicker than the wispy ice clouds of the troposphere.

עָנָן

Although עָנָן is the common term for "cloud" in general,[107] it also has a specialized use in the Psalms in that it is used to denote the "pillar of cloud"

---

104. Veijola, "The Witness in the Clouds," 415.
105. Ibid., 415–17.
106. Mosca, "Once Again the Heavenly Witness," 35.
107. Scott, "Meteorological Phenomena," 24.

from the wilderness accounts. The only passage in which it occurs without referring to this specialized sense is in Ps 97:2, where it occurs with the term ערפל. In other words, ענן used alone in the Psalms does not refer to natural weather terminology, but it will be considered for its symbolic use of a primarily meteorological phenomenon.

Psalm 78:14

> And he led them daily with a cloud,
> and all the night with a light of fire.

In the context of a psalm rehearsing Yahweh's powerful deeds in Israel's memory, the cloud here clearly refers to the pillar of cloud introduced in Exod 13:21. This verse does not refer to it specifically as a "pillar," but uses instead simply the word "cloud" (ענן). The origins of the cloud imagery used to indicate the divine presence are disputed, but it is unlikely truly meteorological.[108] Sarna describes the pillar as a symbol of God's presence which encompasses "the mysterious, intangible, incorporeal elements of fire and cloud—[it is] actually a diaphanous, luminescent mist visible both by day and by night."[109] The literary usage may, however, rely on a basic understanding of ענן as a weather term. In Stadelmann's words concerning the rainbow: "meteorological elements combine to reproduce something ethereal and ineffable."[110]

The function of this non-meteorological utilization of a meteorological term is divine guidance and protection in the wilderness. This specific function occurs in the Psalms weather citations only when the exodus tradition is referenced.

Psalm 99:7

> From a pillar of cloud he spoke to them,
> they kept his testaments,
> and the statutes [which] he gave to them.

---

108. For a discussion of the origins of the cloud imagery, see Sarna, *Exploring Exodus*, 110–13. Plastaras (*The God of Exodus*, 186) suggests that the origin could have been meteorological, "possibly a whirlwind or a storm cloud."

109. Sarna, *Exodus*, 70.

110. Stadelmann, *Hebrew Conception of the World*, 110.

Rain and Clouds

This hymn celebrating Yahweh's kingship contains a second reference to עָנָן as the pillar of cloud (here it is stated explicitly: עַמּוּד עָנָן). The "them" to which the psalmist refers is Moses and Aaron mentioned in the previous verse (along with an anachronistic Samuel). No specific incident is apparently cited, but rather a general tendency of Yahweh to speak to Moses and Aaron (and Samuel) and for their tendency to obey.

The function of the cloud-pillar is slightly different in this verse than in Ps 78:14. The cloud pillar here acts as a medium for divine instruction. Yahweh speaks to Moses and Aaron via the cloud.

Psalm 105:39

> He spread out a cloud for a covering,
> and a fire to illuminate [the] night.

Once again the context of a mnemonic hymn recounting the deeds of Yahweh in Israel's wilderness wanderings, this verse mentions the cloud and fire elements. The spreading out of the cloud does not recall an event narrated in Exodus,[111] but it does symbolize the divine protection. Following, as it does, the expulsion from Egypt, the verse could refer to the moving of the cloud to a position between the Israelites and Egyptians, narrated in Exod 14:19. This, however, does not describe the cloud as a covering.

Clearly the function of this non-meteorological cloud is that of protection, leading back into the realm of Ps 78:14. The parallel between "cloud" (עָנָן) and "fire" makes the identification of the object certain.

עָנָן and עֲרָפֶל

As a type of meteorological phenomenon, עְרָפֶל is typically defined as "heavy cloud" (BDB, 791b) or "thick darkness" (KBS, 888a). A directly cognate form in Ugaritic (ġrpl)[112] helped to define the word more clearly. Cohen has recently demonstrated that the meteorological aspect is best captured by a connotation of "dense fog."[113]

---

111. Briggs and Briggs, *Book of Psalms*, 2:347.
112. See del Olmo Lete and Sanmartín, *Diccionario de la lengua ugarítica*, 1:160.
113. Cohen, "The Basic Meaning," 7–12.

Psalm 97:2

> Cloud and dense fog envelop him,
> righteousness and justice are the foundation of his throne.

Psalm 97 celebrates Yahweh's enthronement, and verse 2 begins the description of the awe-inspiring vision of the deity. The first aspect addressed is the divine invisibility. Here the general word for cloud (עָנָן) is paired with עֲרָפֶל, a word denoting darkness or obscurity. In meteorological contexts the darkness of עֲרָפֶל seems to connote dense fog particularly,[114] a meaning which fits the present context well. Fog is "a cloud in contact with the earth's surface,"[115] and, as such, has obscuration as one of its essential characteristics. The word primarily appears in contexts where it serves to hide the divine presence. Verses 2–5 describe the theophanic appearance using nephological, fulgurous, and volcanic images.

The function of both types of cloud in this verse is clearly to obscure the divine personage. This obscurity brings further mystery and majesty to Yahweh, who is known to rule and control meteorological phenomena, but who cannot be seen.

עֲרָפֶל

Psalm 18:10 [9]

> He even pitched the heavens and descended,
> and dense fog was under his feet.

The marshal, meteorological, theophanic language of Ps 18 is prominent in this verse. Yahweh is portrayed as pitching the heavens as a tent,[116] then descending into the fray with an obscuring blanket of fog beneath the divine feet. The divine warrior thus comes to the aid of the psalmist with a theophanic display. The fog, as the base of a low cloud, serves to hide Yahweh's form from the heavens down to the battlefield itself.

The nephological language in this verse once again utilizes the recondite nature of clouds to keep Yahweh from view during a theophany. This

---

114. Cohen, "The Basic Meaning," 8–9.

115. Geer, *Glossary of Weather and Climate*, 89. This corresponds to Scott's ("Meteorological Phenomena," 25) and Stadelmann's (*Hebrew Conception of the World*, 100) "lowering clouds."

116. This is one of the basic meanings of נטה. See BDB, 640a. The idea of God stretching out the heavens like a tent is prominent in Deutero-Isaiah; see KBS, 693a.

function corresponds to the primary usage of this imagery in descriptions of God's manifestations in the Psalms.

נְשִׂאִים

The meaning of the common root נשׂא is to lift or carry. Its use in a meteorological context is relatively rare,[117] but its root connotation remains intact. The combination of clouds and rising has led Reymond and Stadelmann to propose cumuli castellati as the operative description.[118] Since water vapor cannot be seen, it is best to avoid using "vapor" as descriptive word for a cloud,[119] although water vapor is a primary element in the formation of clouds.

Psalm 135:7

> He elevates rising clouds from the end of the earth,
> he makes lightnings with the rain,
> the source of the wind from its storehouses.

Cumuli castellati are towering clouds,[120] and this definition is descriptive and precise. As this verse describes clouds growing into rain clouds, it may be too precise a term. Taking castellati form is one way in which cumulus clouds may grow into rain clouds, but it is not the only way that this may happen.[121] It is clear from the remainder of this verse that rain, as well as lightning and wind, are the outcome of these rising clouds. These phenomena often accompany the larger varieties of storm-cloud, particularly the cumulonimbus, rather than the castellatus variety.

The verb used to describe the lifting of these clouds, מעלה (a hiphil participle), indicates the causality of Yahweh behind the coming storm in this hymn. It is also presented as one of the reasons for which Yahweh is being praised. Since weather systems in Israel tend to move from west to east, the phenomenon of rain clouds forming over the Mediterranean Sea was likely a familiar one. To all appearances the end of the earth, the

---

117. It occurs only in Jer 10:13; 51:16; Prov 25:14, and the present verse.
118. Reymond, *L'eau*, 13; Stadelmann, *Hebrew Conception of the World*, 99.
119. As suggested in BDB, 672b.
120. Scott, "Meteorological Phenomena," 25.
121. *ICA*, 1:41; Scorer and Verkaik, *Spacious Skies*, 31.

Mediterranean, gives rise to the fructifying clouds for which Yahweh is lauded. Indeed, Yahweh is given the credit for causing these clouds to build.

Clouds function in this verse as the bearers of rain and stormy conditions availing further cause to praise Yahweh.

קיטור

Related to the usual term for "smoke," קיטור remains disputed. Suggestions range from thick fog,[122] dense cloud,[123] mist,[124] vapor,[125] smoke,[126] to frost.[127] The point of comparison with smoke would seem to be opacity or perhaps the rising, billowing nature of smoke. Contextual data must be considered in the assessment of this term, since neither the other occurrences in the Hebrew Bible nor comparative philology give weight to any of the particular suggestions.

Psalm 148:8

> Fire and hail, snow and dark cloud,
> stormy wind doing his command.

This verse is remarkable in its concentration of meteorological phenomena. This is noteworthy in that it is the only reference to weather-related subjects in the entire psalm. If fire is understood to reference lightning,[128] then all the other phenomena mentioned in this verse are meteorological. It would be incongruous to have a non-meteorological term in the middle of a list of weather-related occurrences for which Yahweh is being praised. In other words, the context supports a meteorological phenomenon interpretation.

Given the root, the starting place for determining the meaning of קיטור must be the comparison with smoke. If the argument for a meteorological referent is cogent, then this word must denote a weather-related occurrence that resembles smoke in some way. Smoke, from a meteorological

---

122. Reymond, *L'eau*, 15; Kraus, *Psalms 60–150*, 560.
123. Scott, "Meteorological Phenomena," 25; Stadelmann, *Hebrew Conception of the World*, 100; Weiser, *The Psalms*, 836.
124. Allen, *Psalms 101–150*, 312; A. A. Anderson, *Book of Psalms*, 2:950.
125. Briggs and Briggs, *Book of Psalms*, 2:538.
126. Dahood, *Psalms*, 3:354.
127. NRSV at Ps 148:8.
128. See above, chapter two.

perspective, is "[s]uspended particular matter in the air resulting from combustion."[129] As such, smoke is classified as a lithometeor, or particulate matter in the air that reduces visibility to less than nine kilometers.[130] Simply put, smoke interferes with vision. Furthermore, smoke necessarily rises, often resembling a billowing cloud. If these basic criteria are considered, vapor and frost are ruled out as possibilities.[131] If all of the phenomena listed, lightning, hail, snow, and storm winds, are considered to be part of one meteorological event, then קיטור would also participate in it. What is noticeably missing from the picture of a weather event is the mention of any clouds. "Thick cloud," "dense cloud," and "mist" are three further suggestions that actually describe types of clouds. Since fire and hail tend to form a conceptual pair (although not technically a word-pair), it might be asked if snow and קיטור likewise form a conceptual pair. If so, קיטור would be a snow-bearing cloud, but this is not a specific cloud type. Any cloud capable of producing precipitation may produce snow if the air is cool enough.

It cannot be considered a foregone conclusion that all the elements do belong to the same event, but if they do, they would tend to indicate a nephological component for קיטור. Otherwise the meaning likely remains in the nephological realm because of the root of the word. Given these considerations, I have translated קיטור as "dark cloud" since the darkness may reflect either a smoke-like appearance or a cloud laden with snow or other precipitation. Any cloud heavy with snow would also function to obscure the view of the divine. The function of the potential cloud here is, like the other elements mentioned, to bring praise to Yahweh.

עֲרָבוֹת

This difficult word has led to considerable speculation about a corrupt text. Often it is suggested that an emendation would solve the difficulties. The two usual candidates, which *BHS* also proposes, are עָבוֹת or עֲרָבוֹת, both taken to mean "clouds" in a general sense.

Psalm 68:5 [4]

Sing to God,

---

129. Geer, *Glossary of Weather and Climate*, 203.

130. Ibid., 137.

131. "Frost" is generally considered as belonging to a root separate from קטר I, "smoke;" see Allen, *Psalms 101–150*, 312.

sing praise [to] his name,
lift up the charioteer of the clouds!¹³²
Yah is his name,
therefore exalt before him!

As noted above, Ps 68 is notoriously difficult in places. The main difficulty with this verse involves the word under discussion, ערבות. As a term for "cloud" it would be a hapax legomenon, and thus it has often been emended. This is, however, one of the instances where the discovery of the Ugaritic texts has offered a straightforward solution to a difficulty in Hebrew.¹³³ These texts provided a parallel epithet applied to the god Baal, *rkb ʿrpt*,¹³⁴ which is clearly related to the title for Yahweh in this psalm: רכב ערבות (*rkb ʿrbwt*). Dahood has pointed out the instances in which the bilabials *b* and *p* have interchanged within Semitic languages,¹³⁵ and the ו is readily explained as a *mater lectionis*. There should be no reluctance to seeing this isolated occurrence as the one Hebrew attestation of the word ערבות as "cloud."¹³⁶ Both the ancient West Asian context and the context of this hymnic psalm itself provide support for this interpretation. Furthermore, the same concept of Yahweh riding the clouds occurs in Ps 104:3 and Isa 19:1: Deut 33:26 notes that El (God) rides the heavens, a concept likewise cited further on in this psalm (68:34 [33]). The weight of the evidence appears to support the image of Yahweh riding on the clouds.

A related issue is how to translate רכב. The root of the word denotes mounting and riding,¹³⁷ and the nominal forms often denote "chariot." Some years ago Mowinckel demonstrated that, although horses were ridden in the biblical period, for purposes of warfare, they were used to draw chariotry.¹³⁸ The meteorological imagery in the Psalms quite often draws upon martial terminology when Yahweh manipulates the phenomenon. The same is likely true here—God's manifestation brings hopes of deliverance to the psalmist. The tone with which the psalm opens is distinctly martial. Considering all of this, רכב should probably be translated as "charioteer" rather than "rider"

---

132. For this title see Mowinckel, "Drive and/or Ride," 278–99; Wyatt, "The Titles of the Ugaritic Storm-God," 420–22.

133. Cooper, "Divine Names and Epithets," 458–60; Dahood, *Psalms*, 2:136; Miller, *Divine Warrior*, 105.

134. Attested fifteen times: *KTU* 1.2 iv 8; 1.2 iv 29; 1.3 ii 40; 1.3 iii 38; 1.3 iv 4; 1.3 iv 6; 1.4 iii 11; 1.4 iii 18; 1.4 v 60; 1.5 ii 7; 1.10 I 7; 1.10 iii 36; 1.19 i 44; 1.92 37; 1.92 40.

135. Dahood, *Psalms*, 2:136. See also Caquot, "Le psaume LXVIII," 152.

136. See LePeau, *Psalm 68*, 79–81.

137. BDB, 938b; KBS, 1230–31.

138. Mowinckel, "Drive and/or Ride," 278–99.

here. This verse describes Yahweh driving the divine chariot, that is, the clouds, in a theophanic context.[139]

Clouds in this verse function as the chariot of Yahweh in the context of a theophany. The type of cloud cannot be determined with certainty, but other references to the divine chariot favor the cumulus, particularly the cumulonimbus, as the nephological form that best hides and reveals Yahweh.

SUMMARY OF CLOUD TERM FUNCTIONS

Clouds of various types frequently attend theophanic events in the Bible. This is true particularly in the Psalms. In the theophanic contexts, clouds hide Yahweh's actual form, which allows for the divine presence, yet the divine form cannot be seen. Clouds also reveal the divine, since this is an essential function of theophany. Examples of this occur in Pss 18:10 [9], 12 [11], 13 [12]; 68:5 [4]; 77:18 [17]; 97:2; and 104:3. An example of the clouds hiding, without revealing, the divine, occurs in Ps 89:7 [6], 38 [37]. Also in a theophanic context, clouds serve as the vehicles of lightning and hail production (Ps 18:13 [12]). These are considered the weaponry of the divine warrior.

Psalms 68:5 [4] and 104:3 also describe clouds functioning as Yahweh's chariot. This imagery combines divine locomotion and the ability, in the context of Ps 104, to decide where rain should fall. In 68:5 [4] the chariot is part of a theophanic display. This may also be the imagery behind Ps 77:18 [17].

The more pragmatic aspect of clouds providing rain is another function attested in the Psalms (135:7; 147:8). As such, the clouds and their attendant rain provide a reason for which to praise Yahweh.

Psalms 36:6 [5]; 57:11 [10]; 108:5 [4], and perhaps 89:38 [37], indicate that cirrus clouds may be used to illustrate great distances. Inherent in this function is the awareness that the atmosphere stretches far into the sky, to the limits of the comprehensible world. As such, these high clouds were likely used to assert the control God possesses over even the most distant of meteorological phenomena, as demonstrated in Ps 68:35 [34].

In three psalms, 78:14; 99:7; and 105:39, a specialized theological use of the pillar of cloud is made. This meteorological image is utilized to indicate divine protection and guidance in 78:14 and protection alone in 105:39. In 99:7 the cloud serves as a vehicle for divine instruction to Moses and Aaron. In each of these cases it does not refer to an actual weather phenomenon. Also associated with the wilderness tradition, the clouds are once cited as the source of the manna in Ps 78:23–24.

139. LePeau, *Psalm 68*, 83.

CHAPTER FIVE

Hail, Snow, Frost, Rime, and Dew

The phenomena considered in this chapter are linked in three ways: most obviously, they all are formed from water. The second connection concerns the first four subjects; hail, snow, frost, and rime are elements that consist of ice. The third association ties the final three subjects together; frost, rime and dew are all forms of "ground weather." These forms of ground weather do not occur together, but they appear only on plants near the ground, and they do not fall from the sky. This grouping, as noted in the introduction, is somewhat arbitrary; however, each category of weather relates to the others discussed in this chapter.

HAIL

Although generally produced by a thunderstorm, hail is a weather phenomenon that consists of ice. The frozen water droplets high in a cumulus cloud begin to fall, but in a severe storm an updraft lifts the falling ice back up within the cloud. Coated with water from liquid precipitation and its own melting, the ice droplet adds a new layer which then freezes. When it becomes heavy enough to resist the updraft, or moves out of it, the hailstone begins to fall again. This process may repeat itself several times resulting in large chunks of ice capable of damaging crops, livestock, structures, or people.

בָּרָד

One term is generally used for hail in the Psalms: ברד. The fact that the Hebrew Bible knows of hail indicates that severe weather was a part of the life of the people, and one with which they had to reckon.[1] Hail is mentioned in Pss 18:13–14 [12–13]; 78:47–48; 105:32–33; and 148:8.

Psalm 18:13–14 [12–13]

13 [12] From brightness before him,
through his cumulonimbus traversed
hail and coals of fire,
14 [13] Yahweh even caused thunder in the heavens,
and Elyon gave his voice,
hail and coals of fire.

The theophanic nature of this pericope has been observed above in chapters two and four. The psalmist is in trouble, and in response to a cry to Yahweh, the deity appears in a thunderstorm. The theophanic storm language continues through v. 16 [15]. In the course of describing the divine rescuer, hail is mentioned two times, once in each of the verses translated here. Although hail benefits the moisture level of the soil, like lightning, it is primarily cited for its destructive effects in the Hebrew Bible.[2] Yahweh's descent here is described with the concomitants of a severe thunderstorm, which comforts the psalmist, but which the enemy is unable to resist.

In both verses hail is paired with "coals of fire," a poetic description of lightning.[3] These two elements of the thunderstorm are potentially the most dangerous, and therefore demonstrate most clearly why Yahweh should be feared by the enemy. Elsewhere, notably Josh 10:11, Yahweh uses hail as a weapon, pointing the reader of this psalm toward the discernment of the divine warrior motif in conjunction with the appearance of hail.[4] The hail is not actually directed at the enemy here, but rather it appears that the display of the weapon is sufficient to dishearten the foe.

---

1. Mané, "A Severe Rainstorm," 115–19 describes a heavy rainfall. The wind speed (maximum gusts of 55 km/h) and the lack of hail would generally not qualify as a severe storm by current meteorological standards. Severe storms, however, have been attested in Palestine/Israel. See Nir, "Whirlwinds in Israel," 109–17.

2. For the benefits of storm phenomena, including lightning and hail, see Kessler and White, "Thunderstorms in a Social Context," 5–6.

3. Brown, "Yahweh, Zeus, Jupiter," 186. See also chapter two above.

4. Miller, *Divine Warrior*, 121–22; Lind, *Yahweh is a Warrior*, 83.

Psalm 78:47–48

> 47 And he killed their vine[s] with hail,
> and their sycamores[5] with lightning (חנמל).[6]
> 48 And he delivered up their livestock to the hail,
> and their cattle to the flames.

Psalm 78 recounts the story of Israel's past through a series of vignettes. One of these vignettes, vv. 44–53, recounts some of the traditions regarding the plagues in Egypt and Israel's deliverance. In vv. 47–48 the plague of hail is recollected (traditionally the seventh plague, Exod 9:18–26). The second half of v. 47 utilizes a hapax legomenon, חנמל, to parallel "hail" (ברד). Based on the LXX, many early translations used "frost" to explain חנמל, although no known etymological evidence supports this meaning. Few commentaries address the issue, and many are content to use "hailstone" to parallel "hail." Goulder argues for "great hailstones," noting, no doubt correctly, "it takes a lot to kill a sycamore."[7] BDB tentatively offers "frost,"[8] KBS "devastating flood,"[9] and *DCH* "frost (?), flood (?)."[10]

This poetic rendering of the plagues does not find a precise correspondence in the Exodus narrative, which leads Haglund to suggest that Ps 78 is the earlier of the two accounts.[11] I would suggest, without venturing into the thorny question of date, that the two accounts be mutually considered for the resolution of the meteorological conundrum of these verses.

Exodus 9:23–24 reads "And Moses stretched out his staff to the heavens and Yahweh gave voices and hail, and fire went earthward and Yahweh rained hail upon the land of Egypt. (24) And there was hail and fire taking ahold of itself throughout; the like of the very heavy hail in all the land of Egypt has not been from the time that Egypt became a nation."[12] If, as I sug-

---

5. Zohary, *Plants of the Bible*, 68–69.
6. For justification of the translation for this term, see the text below.
7. Goulder, *Psalms of Asaph*, 122; see also Kraus, *Psalms 60–150*, 120.
8. BDB 335b.
9. KBS 334b.
10. *DCH*, 3:272b.
11. Haglund, *Historical Motifs in the Psalms*, 94–95. Campbell ("Psalm 78," 51–79) suggests that the plagues in Ps 78 were composed "before the pentateuchal selection and sequence had become traditional" (69–70). Clifford ("In Zion and David," 121–41) refers to it as "the ancient pattern found also in Exod 15:1–18" (133). Coats (*Rebellion in the Wilderness*, 202–3) offers a good summary of the situation. Greenstein, "Mixing Memory and Design," 197–218, questions this method of the dating the psalm.
12. See also above, chapter two.

gest in chapter two, the fire referenced in these verses denotes lightning, this would support such a meaning for חנמל in Ps 78. Furthermore, every other reference to hail in the Psalms is accompanied by lightning. This reflects a basic correlation in nature, but also a conceptual pair in the mindset of the Israelites—hail and lightning form a poetic pair. Specifically with regard to v. 47, lightning is capable of destroying hardy sycamores, indeed, any kind of tree. "Flames," that is, lightning, parallels hail in v. 48. All of this taken together strongly recommends that the hapax חנמל be translated so as to reflect lightning as the destructive agent. Since comparative philology has suggested no other viable etymology to date, the context almost demands a keraunic meaning.

If this translation is allowed to stand, it also obviates the need for emending the text because of the repetition of "hail" in v. 48.[13] Taken together these two verses form a pleasing parallel account which emphasizes the severity of this meteorological plague. The function of hail in these verses would be a means of divine punishment, perhaps even a weapon of the deity. It is a punishment used against Egypt in a tradition regarding Israel's past.

Psalm 105:32-33

32 He gave (for) their winter rains hail,
fire of flames in their land.
33 And he smote their vine and fig tree,
and he shattered the tree(s) of their territory.

As in Ps 78:47-48, this verse also recounts the tradition of the punishment of Egypt prior to the exodus. Clearly the reference is to the same plague—the scourge of hail and lightning. The hail in this verse is described in insidious terms; rather than the fructifying winter rains (more characteristic of the Levant than of Egypt), hail came down on the immature crops. Corresponding to the Exod 9 account, the hail was accompanied by fire. In meteorological terms fire associated with a storm denotes lightning (see above, chapter two). The result of this disaster is given in v. 33, the fruits of the land, vine and fig tree, were destroyed. This was the immediate result of the hail and lightning.

---

13. So Symmachus. See Briggs and Briggs, *Book of Psalms*, 2:188, 195; Kraus, *Psalms 60-150*, 120, 122; A. A. Anderson, *Book of Psalms* 2:572; Tate, *Psalms 51-100*, 283; Goulder, *Psalms of Asaph*, 122.

The actual shattering of trees may be hyperbole, or it may be the result of lightning. Hail generally does not shatter trees. The function of hail in this context is therefore that of a divine weapon used for the chastening of a recalcitrant Egypt.

Psalm 148:8

> Fire and hail, snow and dark cloud,
> stormy wind doing his command.

Psalm 148, a hymn of praise, adjures all orders of creation to join in the praise of Yahweh, their creator. In this verse five meteorological phenomena are invited to join the celebration, including the coupled lightning (here once again "fire") and hail. Together these elements present a formidable display of divine power. The list begins with the destructive elements of lightning and hail, which are presented as being under divine control: "doing his command" likely applies to all the aforementioned constituents of weather.

Hail functions as one of the elements that praise Yahweh, or demonstrate the divine greatness. As always in the Psalms, it is paired with lightning.

SUMMARY OF HAIL TERM FUNCTIONS

Hail serves as a weapon in the divine arsenal. This is shown most clearly in passages depicting the deity as warrior. Such a portrayal is clear in Ps 18:13–14 [12–13] where hail parallels lightning.

Psalms 78:47–48 and 105:32–33 recite Yahweh's use of hail as an instrument for punishing the recalcitrant Egyptians. In this respect hail may also be classified as a weapon in the divine arsenal, or at least a meteorological phenomenon with no humanly redeeming value in the eyes of the psalmists. In both references lightning accompanies hail, in accordance with the narration of the plague in Exod 9:23–24.

A final function of hail is its role in praising Yahweh. Ps 148:8 presents five aspects of the weather invoked to glorify their creator. Among the impressive quintet is hail.

It is important to note that hail never occurs in the Psalms without its concomitant phenomenon of lightning. These two phenomena form a conceptual poetic parallel, although they do not occur as parallel elements within a verse, they always occur together. Since cumulonimbus clouds, which generally produce hail, are characterized by thunderstorms, this should not be unexpected. In current scientific understanding a more natural pair would be thunder and lightning, but such a coupling betrays a modern bias as much as lightning and hail demonstrates an ancient one.

A further significant aspect of hail is that it is never portrayed as a beneficent form of precipitation.[14]

SNOW

The root denoting snow, שׁלג, occurs both in nominal and verbal form in the Psalms. As a noun there are three references: Pss 51:9 [7]; 147:16; and 148:8. The verbal form occurs only once, in a difficult passage—Ps 68:15 [14].

Although the modern reader from a Western cultural context may find references to snow surprising, it is actually an important component of the water cycle of Palestine and its neighbors. Snow tends to fall on the higher elevations in the rainy season (winter), and its melting supplies wadis with water. The fertility of the land, in turn, depends on this melt-water. Nevertheless, the relative rarity of snow does demonstrate the impact it had upon the religious understanding of the Israelites.

שֶׁלֶג/שָׁלַג

Psalm 51:9 [7]

> Purify me with hyssop[15] and I will be clean,
> wash me and I will be whiter than snow.

The sin-sick psalmist pleads with God for purification in this lament. Aware of personal sins, the psalmist displays several facets of guilt, and includes a suggestion as to how it may be removed. The technique of guilt removal is briefly described, and the result is that the psalmist's absolution may be compared to the whiteness of snow.

Snow functions in a metaphorical, comparative sense in this verse. A specific characteristic of snow, its albescence, or whiteness, is the point of comparison. If God cleanses the psalmist, the suppliant will be spotlessly white, like snow.

---

14. Stadelmann, *Hebrew Conception of the World*, 117.
15. Zohary, *Plants of the Bible*, 96–97.

Psalm 68:15 [14]

> When Shaddai scattered kings in it,
> snow fell in Zalmon.

Nearly legendary in its difficulty, this verse affords little certainty concerning its meaning.[16] It contains the only use of שלג as a verb in the Hebrew Bible. The verb תשלג may be either a second person masculine singular or a third person feminine singular form.[17] Once a person is assigned, the verb has no proper antecedent. The prepositional phrase "in it" also lacks a proper antecedent, and here must refer to what follows. An added difficulty is that this verse fits uneasily in its context—relating it to either the preceding or following verses requires considerable imagination.[18] Emendation is widely practiced on this verse.[19]

The crux for the modest function of this exercise, determining the meteorological significance of snow in this verse, is the identification of Zalmon.[20] Where is Zalmon?[21] What does it mean for snow to fall in Zalmon? Is it surprising or expected? What event provides the antecedent for this particular paean?[22] Exegetes and commentators differ widely on these issues.

There is no known mythical or historical event to which this verse refers,[23] therefore the verse must be interpreted on its own merit. Zalmon is assumed to be a mountain for two reasons: there is a Mount Zalmon, referred to in Judg 9:48, to which this verse is generally considered not to refer,[24] and

---

16. In the words of Cheyne, "Still a heavy stress upon the interpreter" (*The Book of Psalms*, 1:188). The difficulties are well summarized by LePeau, *Psalm 68*, 125–32.

17. Dahood ("Third Masculine Singular," 103) has argued that this could be a third person masculine singular form.

18. This lends support to Albright's suggestion that this psalm is a collection of incipits, linked into a whole ("A Catalogue of Early Hebrew," 7–9).

19. Podechard ("Psaume LXVIII," 503, 508–9) cuts the Gordian knot by treating the snow reference as a gloss and omitting it.

20. As noted by Gray, "A Cantata of the Autumn Festival," 16, "here the emphasis would fall on the statement that it snowed on/from Ṣalmon."

21. Or should Zalmon be translated? See Gray, "A Cantata of the Autumn Festival," 16, LePeau, *Psalm 68*, 129, Caquot, "Le psaume LXVIII," 162, for an affirmative answer to this question.

22. Iwry, "Notes on Psalm 68," 162.

23. LePeau, *Psalm 68*, 132. Some scholars have suggested that it refers to the siege of Shechem by Abimelech, although this is a minority view. See Tournay, "Le psaume LXVIII," 364–67.

24. For example, Albright, "Catalogue of Early Hebrew," 23; followed by Dahood,

the following verses question the mountain of Bashan concerning its envy. If verse 15 [14] is not closely tied to the following verses, then Zalmon does not necessarily refer to a mountain in Bashan. Indeed, if the reference is not to Zalmon near Shechem (Judg 9:48), then Zalmon is not even necessarily a mountain. The added evidence of Claudius Ptolemy's reference to a mountain *range* called Asolmanos[25] has led most commentators to assume this is the evasive Zalmon.[26] This association is extremely problematic, and there is clear evidence of assumptions being made without the evidence having been weighed.

Goulder traces the association of Zalmon with "the Jebel Hauran" to Wetzstein, cited by Delitzsch.[27] Many commentators simply cite Albright's support of that location, usually under the name of "Jebel Druze," as ample evidence.[28] Jebel Druze, located in the region of Hauran,[29] consists of several volcanic peaks. This mountainous region is located about 100 kilometers east from the eastern shore of Lake Kinneret (Galilee), to the southeast of Damascus, within present-day Syria. It is quite remote from biblical Israel. Part of the difficulty in this identification lies in the multiple names used of the same location, as well as the general confusion concerning the geography of this part of Syria in the various sources. The highest peak is Tell al-Jēnnah, according to Orni and Efrat.[30] To add further confusion, the names are different again in Ritter's geography, where he notes that looking east from Safed (the southwest branch of the Hermon system), "beyond that the limits of the Leja (the Hauran) can be discerned, from which rises in marked pre-eminence a single peak, Jebel Kuleib, or Kubeib (Kelb) Hauran, the Hauran dog, which Col. Leake considers to be the Mount *Alsadamus* of Ptol. v. 15" (my emphasis).[31]

Psalms, 2:142. A. A. Anderson, *Psalms* 1:490 states "[m]ost commentators identify Zalmon with 'the modern Ǧebel Ḥaurân'" (citing Johnson, *Sacral Kingship*, 72). This point is, however, disputed by some, notably Tournay, "Le psaume LXVIII," 364–67. Weiser (*The Psalms*, 487) suggests a connection with Sihon and Og and their defeat in Num 21: Goulder (*The Prayers of David*, 191) asserts that it refers to Absalom's defeat at Zalmon.

25. As noticed already by Cheyne, *Book of Psalms*, 188.
26. This correlation may be seen in Abel, *Géographie de la Palestine*, 377–78.
27. Delitzsch, *The Prayers of David*, 202.
28. A. A. Anderson, *Book of Psalms*, 1:490; Dahood, *Psalms*, 2:142; Johnson, *Sacral Kingship*, 72; Tate, *Psalms 51–100*, 108. Albright's reference is found in "Catalogue of Early Hebrew," 23.
29. Orni and Efrat, *Geography of Israel*, 119.
30. Ibid.,119.
31. Ritter, *Comparative Geography of Palestine*, 221.

The reference to Alsadamus is of vital importance here. Ptolemy's *Geography* is one of the works of antiquity (Claudius Ptolemy lived c. 90–168 C.E.) which was lost and was reconstructed by its Arabic recoverers. As such it exists in both Greek and Latin in a variety of manuscripts, mostly fragmentary.[32] The maps that accompany the geography are important for linking the sites listed with their citations in Ptolemy's text. The maps of the *Codex Ebnerianus*, housed in the New York Public Library, were prepared by Donnus Nicolaus Germanus, and represent "the important Roman editions of Ptolemy of the years 1478, 1490, 1507, and 1508, in which the Ptolemaic maps are reproduced more accurately than in most other editions."[33] Comparison of these maps with the text translated by Stevenson indicate that the mountain range in Syria is called Alsadamus "near Arabia Deserta are the Alsadamus mountains, the middle part of which is in 71 33."[34] Following these coordinates on map 4 of Asia, in the Stevenson edition, the name reads "Alsadamus."

Until Stevenson's 1932 translation, no English editions of Ptolemy's *Geography* existed, and to the time of this writing no critical edition had yet been produced. Already in 1888 Cheyne had noted that the suggested "Asalmanos" was one of three variant readings for this range (the other two cited as "Alsalamos, and Alsadamos").[35] Alexander Jones, editor of an authoritative translation of the *Geography*, indicated that "Alsadamos" is the preferred reading.[36] "Asalmanos" is therefore a textual variant, and to base an identification on what is likely a misspelled word in a document lacking a critical edition is problematic indeed.

I have spent some time on this problem since it has not been satisfactorily addressed to date. The simple equation of Zalmon with the mountains of Alsadamos does not hold up to close scrutiny. Biblical scholars must await a critical edition of Ptolemy's work before attempting a correlation. In the text as we now have it, Zalmon either remains unidentified, or the reference is to the mountain mentioned in Judg 9:48.

What is noteworthy in this reference is the snow. This has also led investigators of this psalm to conclude that Zalmon must have referred to a mountain, since snow tends to cover only the highest elevations in the Mediterranean climate of Israel. Snow, however, may occur throughout Israel,

---

32. Stevenson, in his preface to Ptolemy, *The Geography*, xiv.

33. Fischer, in his introduction to Ptolemy, *The Geography*, 3.

34. Ptolemy, *The Geography*, book 5, chapter xiv, page 126 of Stevenson's edition. The numbers represent the longitude and latitude, respectively.

35. Cheyne, *Book of Psalms*, 188.

36. Private communication, 17 July 2000.

as the snowstorm of 28–30 January 2000 demonstrated.[37] What remains, therefore, is that Yahweh once scattered kings in an otherwise unrecorded incident. In some way this event resembled snow falling in the unspecified location called Zalmon (which appears to mean "dark" or "black").[38] Given the lack of geographical certainty, an attractive hypothesis is presented by Gray, who sees the reference not to a geographical location, but to a meteorological phenomenon.[39] Taking ṣlm as cognate with Arabic ẓalm, Gray translates "As snow is scattered from the dark cloud."[40] More lexical support would render this an even more attractive option, since as a geographical reference Zalmon is problematic.

Regardless of which interpretation of צלם is followed, the question remains about the point of comparison between kings scattering and snow. The whiteness of the snow has been compared to the salt scattered after the siege of Shechem by Abimelech,[41] the sun-bleached bones of the defeated kings on Zalmon,[42] or in contrast to the blackness of Mount Zalmon.[43] The reference to snow has been seen as a metaphor of kings scattering like snow,[44] enemies disappearing like the melting of snow,[45] a symbol of Yahweh's theophanic presence during the battle,[46] Yahweh's weaponry,[47] or simply the unforgettable snow itself.[48] Any of these functions could be argued cogently, given the ambiguity of the verse.

With the infrequent mention of snow in the Psalms, it is worth considering that Ps 147:16 (immediately below) refers to the scattering (פזר) of hoarfrost in parallel with the giving of the snow. This psalm has snow falling when Shaddai scattered (פרש) kings. Although different roots are use for the scattering, perhaps this meteorological comparison would tentatively

---

37. This snow may be read about in issues of the *Jerusalem Post* dated from 30 January 2000. Back issues of the *Post* may be consulted online.

38. For example, Albright, "Catalogue of Early Hebrew," 23; Dahood, *Psalms*, 2:142; Goulder, *The Prayers of David*, 201; Kraus, *Psalms 60–150*, 53; LePeau, *Psalm 68*, 129; Tate, *Psalms 51–100*, 166, 180.

39. Gray, "A Cantata of the Autumn Festival," 16.

40. Ibid.

41. Tournay, "Le psaume LXVIII," 365.

42. Caquot, "Le psaume LXVIII," 162; Briggs and Briggs, *Book of Psalms*, 2:100.

43. Mowinckel, *Der achtundsechzigste Psalm*, 37; Tate, *Psalms 51–100*, 180.

44. LePeau, *Psalm 68*, 132.

45. Based on a textual emendation, Iwry, "Notes," 161–65, followed by Albright, "Catalogue of Early Hebrew," 23–24.

46. Weiser, *The Psalms*, 487.

47. Brown, "Yahweh, Zeus, Jupiter," 186.

48. Goulder, *The Prayers of David*, 202; Kraus, *Psalms 60–150*, 53.

support LePeau's suggestion that the point of comparison is that kings scatter like snow.[49]

Psalm 147:16

> The one giving snow like the wool,
> he scatters hoarfrost like the ashes.

Psalm 147 has a collection of meteorological terms spread over verses 16–18. The first two mentioned, snow (שׁלג) and frost (כפור, see the next section below), are cited as signs of Yahweh's power. A seasonal development transpires in vv. 16–18. Yahweh is praised for giving snow, hoar frost, and ground frost during the cold season (vv. 16–17), then for melting the ice-based elements with the divine wind (v. 18). The end result of this meteorological activity is that the water flows (v. 18), that is, the earth is irrigated by melt-water. This aspect of the water cycle is sufficiently wonderful for the psalmist to praise the deity capable of performing the acts of scattering frost and snow and melting them into the necessary water. In the words of Kraus, the verses "portray a living picture of natural processes of the winter and rainy season."[50]

In the light of this ordinary, yet vital, aspect of hydrologic cycle, the psalmist was compelled to offer praise to Yahweh. The snow therefore functions in this verse as an agent of awe at the divine power, and perhaps even foreknowledge of a God who plans in advance to supply water. Snow is an element for which to praise Yahweh.

Psalm 148:8

> Fire and hail, snow and dark cloud,
> stormy wind doing his command.

In the catalogue of elements and beings called upon to praise Yahweh in this psalm, occur the five meteorological phenomena of this verse. It has been discussed in the sections concerning lightning, wind, clouds, and hail, above. According to the arrangement adopted in this book, the final element called upon to praise its creator is snow. The context does not further clarify why any of these particular elements have been chosen, other than

---

49. LePeau, *Psalm 68*, 132.
50. Kraus, *Psalms 60–150*, 558.

Hail, Snow, Frost, Rime, and Dew

that they are essential aspects of the weather of the Levant. There may be a conscious grouping together of related phenomena, such as lightning and hail, snow and dark clouds. If so, snow is paired with its parent cloud. Dark snow clouds are usually cumulus clouds, which produce snow in winter, even in Israel/Palestine. By grouping all five together, however, the psalmist does indicate some awareness of the relationship between meteorological features.

As with the other elements listed, the function of snow in this verse is to praise its creator, Yahweh.

SUMMARY OF SNOW TERM FUNCTIONS

Snow serves four separate functions in its rare appearances in the Psalms. The scarcity of the references compounds the marvelous aspect of the phenomenon itself.

Snow functions as a comparative element to the pardon of human peccability in Ps 51:9 [7]. Snow is pictured not as a purifying agent, but as a symbol of purity because of its pristine color.

Psalm 68:15 [14] offers many possibilities for snow functions. Snow could symbolize the flurry of scattering kings or the whiteness of their bleached bones. It could be an image to contrast the whiteness of the snow against the darkness of "black mountain" (supposed meaning of Zalmon). Although no comparative word occurs here, snow could be a metaphor for the falling kings; however, the kings are said to have been scattered, not felled. Regardless of interpretation, the image is a martial one, with kings being scattered.

Two of snow's functions are corollary aspects of divine approbation. Ps 147:16 utilizes snow as a phenomenon for which Yahweh is extolled; it is an agent evoking the praise of the psalmist. Ps 148:8 indicates that snow functions also to praise Yahweh, along with the other meteorological elements.

FROST/RIME

קֶרַח and כְּפוֹר

Psalm 147:16–18

> 16 The one giving snow like the wool,
> he scatters hoarfrost like the ashes,
> 17 throwing his rime like crumbs,

before his cold who will stand?
18 He sends out his word and causes them to melt,
he causes his wind to blow,
the waters flow.

The references to frost in this passage are unique in the Psalms. The immediate difficulty facing the interpreter of these verses is the uncertainty of the meaning of individual words for frost. The general meaning of "frost" is established by the divine melting which takes place in v. 18. כפור occurs as a word for "hoarfrost" only in two verses beyond the present citation: Exod 16:14, describing manna, and Job 38:29, where Yahweh questions Job about phenomena associated with cold. קרח appears a total of six or seven times (Gen 31:40; Jer 36:30; Job 6:16; 37:10; 38:29; possibly Ezek 1:22; as well as the citation here under consideration). All of the citations of both nouns are metaphorical. The one characteristic of both words which is certain is that they are related to coldness, as the parallel words in many of these references demonstrate. Perhaps the main difficulty is that with metaphors a comparison is being made, and the point of that comparison is often obscure.

כפור is generally translated as "hoarfrost." BDB unaccountably places it under the root כפר IV, perhaps meaning "to dig."[51] A more logical connection might be כפר I, "to cover."[52] Hoarfrost is a "deposit of interlocking ice crystals (hoar crystals) formed by direct deposition on objects, usually those of small diameter freely exposed to the air."[53] It should not be confused with frozen dew, or rime.[54] In particular it seems appropriate for a description of manna, as in Exod 16:14, since hoarfrost appears as a thick and flaky covering to leaves and stems of plants. Hoarfrost may occur when temperatures drop below the freezing point (0° C) often at night, and thus it is a plausible candidate for כפור.[55]

The case of קרח is more difficult. It is fairly certain that the word concerns some kind of ice and that Yahweh is supposed to have "thrown" (שלך) it. Further, קרח is compared with crumbs and paralleled with "cold."

---

51. BDB 499a. KBS (492b) and *DCH* (4:453) give this word a separate root.

52. *DCH* connects כפור with כפר, "to cover" (4:453).

53. Geer, *Glossary of Weather and Climate*, 112. See also *ICA*, 69.

54. Geer, *Glossary of Weather and Climate*, 94; *ICA*, 69. This mistake is made by Stadelmann, *Hebrew Conception of the World*, 120: "'hoarfrost,' which is dew formed on clear nights when the temperature falls below freezing." Such fine points of detail indicate why periodic revisitation of meteorological investigations of the Hebrew Bible is necessary. Scientific understanding of the weather continues to change in the light of further information, and this, in turn, effects correct translation of ideas.

55. Reymond, *L'Eau*, 28.

The main difficulty is that various forms of ice either fall as precipitation or form at the ground level. This is reflected in the various translations and commentaries which often translate קרח as "hail," presumably since Yahweh has "thrown" it. Further help may be obtained by comparing the use of קרח elsewhere in the Hebrew Bible. First, however, the information provided by this pericope will be examined.

This verse itself provides two pertinent clues: the throwing of the קרח, and the comparison with crumbs. Neither piece of evidence offers an unambiguous answer to the conundrum, but both must be considered.

Throwing has the connotation of forceful removal. This being the case, an object thrown from God would, depending on where God was considered to have been, have fallen to the earth. That is the clear implication of this verse, the thrown object has landed on or near the ground. The end result is that the object is scattered, a further connotation of שלך.[56] Yahweh's throwing of קרח, if the forceful aspect were emphasized, could suggest "hail," which falls with force from a storm cloud. If the point of the throwing is the scattering that results from קרח being flung, then hail remains a candidate, but not the only candidate. It should also be noted that whatever form hydrometeors[57] take (dew, hail, rime, or frost), the Bible conceives of their having "come down" from the sky, as a general survey of the many references indicates.

Comparison with crumbs likewise leaves some question as to the precise referent. What is the point of comparison between ice and crumbs? Commentators sometimes suggest that it is the size of the hydrometeor that is being compared to crumbs.[58] The difficulty here is that crumbs may come in many sizes, and it is difficult to discern the dimensions envisioned by the psalmist in this verse. Crumbs are also characterized by their fragility and their tendency to scatter. Either of these aspects could describe frost or hail, as well as other hydrometeors.

Since internal evidence of this verse cannot resolve the ambiguity, further references to קרח must be considered. Gen 31:40 and Jer 36:30 place קרח in the context of night and contrast it with the heat of day. Job 6:16 and 37:10 cite קרח as frozen water. The final certain meteorological reference

---

56. KBS 1528b suggests "to tip out, scatter" for 2 Kgs 2:21; 4:41, and Ezek 43:24.

57. This is a general meteorological term for any form of water that precipitates, and since קרח, represents such an ambiguous term, "hydrometeor" is perhaps its best counterpart in this discussion.

58. Allen, *Psalms 101–150*, 306, suggests "The size of hailstones is exuberantly extolled with some hyperbole." Briggs and Briggs, *Book of Psalms*, 2:536, note "These various forms of cold . . . compared respectively to *wool* for whiteness, to *dust* for quantity, and to *morsels* for a comparatively large size . . . ."

to קרח occurs in Job 38:29 where it is once again ambiguously paralleled with כפר, as in the current pericope. If these sparse attributes are compiled, it may be discerned that קרח occurs characteristically at night and that it consists of frozen water. The former of these attributes has the potential of narrowing the field of choices, since hail characteristically coincides with thunderstorms, which may occur either in day or night, while frost and rime tend to form at night. Frozen precipitation of the night is clearly the meaning of the word in Gen 31:40 and Jer 36:30.

To this discussion may be added that the parallel of קרח with קרה, "cold," may well point the translator away from "hail" in this verse. Although hail itself is cold when handled, it occurs in the context of thunderstorms, which tend to form when warm surface air is destabilized by cold air aloft. The ground-level sensation tends to be warmth and not chilly conditions. Rime becomes apparent on noticeably chilly mornings, after a cool night.

All of these factors taken together tip the balance in favor of some form of frost or rime. Technically the two are different phenomena: frost is a deposit of distinct ice crystals formed in the air while rime is dew or fog frozen after attaching to an object.[59] Either may form after a warm day, and both appear to have been scattered. Rime, as a form of frozen dew, occurs on clear nights as a result of radiational cooling. As such, it contrasts well with the heat of the day mentioned in Gen 31:40 and Jer 36:30. For this reason as well as for purposes of comparison I have translated "rime" above. Since "frost" occurs in the context of "hoarfrost" in v. 16, a warmer weather variety of frozen "ground weather" suggests itself. However, "frost" remains a viable alternative. No matter which term is chosen, hoarfrost and rime/frost function to stress the wonder of a God who sends and then melts them.

SUMMARY OF FROST AND RIME TERM FUNCTIONS

The function of frozen ground hydrometeors, either frost or rime, in this psalm is the same as the snow mentioned in v. 16. Their function is to give cause to praise Yahweh. They give multiple reasons to laud their sender: they demonstrate the divine facility with cold, a type of weapon; they may cover a large area, indicating Yahweh's wide-spread influence; they melt into the water (v. 18), which is so necessary for life.

---

59. Geer, *Glossary of Weather and Climate*, 94, 191; *ICA*, 66–70.

DEW

Dew is water condensed on objects on or near the ground from water vapor present in clear air.[60] It does not precipitate,[61] and therefore appears to form miraculously, from thin air. It is a water source in otherwise dry seasons.[62] The standard word for "dew" is טל, which is the only word used for it in the Psalms. The metaphorical representations of dew as a source of blessing have continued to attract the interest of present-day interpreters of the ancient world.[63]

For all that, dew occurs only twice in the Psalms (110:3; 133:3). Both references to טל are metaphorical.

טַל

Psalm 110:3

> Your people are a freewill offering
> in the day of your strength,
> in the majesty of holiness,
> from the womb, from dawn,[64] go forth!
> Like (the) dew, I have begotten you.[65]

This verse has the dubious honor of being dubbed "le plus obscur de tout le psaume."[66] It is intriguing in every line; slight emendation is required to make any sense of it. Although I have tried to make the translation coherent, any translation of this verse must be tentative. The general thrust of the verse appears to be the willingness of the youth of the kingdom to accompany the

---

60. *ICA*, 69; Geer, *Glossary of Weather and Climate*, 67.
61. Geer, *Glossary of Weather and Climate*, 67. Compare Stadelmann, *Hebrew Conception of the World*, 117.
62. Uval, "Dew of Heaven," 117–18; Reymond, *L'eau*, 25; Stadelmann, *Hebrew Conception of the World*, 117–18; Scott, "Dew," 839b.
63. Brown, "Yahweh, Zeus, Jupiter," 191.
64. Given the obscurity of this reference, not much may be asserted with confidence concerning this reference to dawn. It is perhaps a reference to a deity, which would fit the context, but this must remain uncertain. See Parker, "Shahar שחר," 1424–28, and the discussion below.
65. I have followed the suggestion of Brown ("A Royal Performance," 94–96) here. See the discussion in the text for my justification in doing so.
66. Tournay, "Le psaume CX," 10.

king in a show of strength, and presumably, into battle.[67] Other than the fact that it celebrates the loyalty of the subjects to the king, little may be determined with certainty on the basis of the apparent disparity of ideas present in this verse. For the purposes of this study, I will concentrate on only the final two lines since they are the lines that address the subject of dew.

מֵרֶחֶם מִשְׁחָר is often translated "from the womb of (the) dawn," a phrase that is "poetic with a vengeance,"[68] but which appears to introduce a new idea outside of the day of the king's strength, the subject of the previous lines. The Masoretic pointing suggests a repetition of the preposition מן, "from" on both words. "Womb" is designated with a definite article, "dawn" is not. The suggestion that משחר is a variant of שחר remains a possibility, but the form would be attested only in this difficult context.[69] I prefer to retain the MT wherever possible, and by retaining a repetition of the preposition, sense can be made of this verse with the minor alterations suggested by Brown.[70] Recognizing that the stichometry is itself an interpretative device, I follow Brown in adding לך to the fourth line and repointing it from לְךָ to לָךְ.[71] This has the effect of continuing the "day of your strength" motif—the king is being sent out. Haplography must be the cause of the missing כ in line five. This is the only consonantal change required in this verse.[72]

טַל יַלְדֻתֶיךָ is often translated "the dew of your youth," or the like. The form of יַלְדֻתֶיךָ is problematic no matter how the interpretation is approached; there is no possibility of simply following the MT here.[73] Brown has demonstrated that ילדתיך is an anomalous form and that, considering the textual evidence of the LXX, it cannot be simply based on Ps 2:7.[74] On the force of his arguments, and the widespread recognition that the concept of begetting follows naturally the reference to "womb" in the previous line, I have adopted the reading יְלִדְתִּיךָ, "I have begotten you," which involves only repointing.[75]

---

67. Sterk, "An Attempt at Translating," 440.

68. Ibid.

69. BDB, 1007b.

70. Brown, "A Royal Performance," 93–96.

71. Ibid., 95–96.

72. Certainly Allen (*Psalms 101–150*, 81) and Brown ("A Royal Performance," 95) are correct that the LXX omits לך טל because of difficulty, and not because it was missing in the *Vorlage*.

73. As cogently demonstrated by Brown, "A Royal Performance," 95.

74. Ibid.

75. Kraus, *Psalms 60–150*, 344; A. A. Anderson, *Book of Psalms*, 2:770; Kilian, "Der 'Tau,'" 418.

To discuss this verse adequately the issue of whether "dawn" here is a reference to a pre-Israelite goddess must be addressed. Usually this suggestion is traced to Grelot and McKay.[76] The discussion revolves around the deity Shachar, "dawn," known from the Ugaritic text *KTU* 1.23.[77] Shachar is, however, a male deity.[78] The association with a goddess is often made with the supposition that the morning and evening star aspects of the planet Venus represent the male and female aspects of Athar, respectively.[79] Naturally the issue meets some resistance in this verse since "dawn" is the male aspect, and is therefore not a likely candidate for having a womb. Following the pointing of the MT, however, "the womb of the dawn" is not likely, since שחר does not have the definite article, and since the preposition reinforces the same preposition on "womb." Dawn is therefore compared to a womb, but is not said to possess one.

Given these details, it appears unlikely that Shachar is referenced here. That "dawn" may have been hypostatized as a goddess without a direct pre-Israelite correlation is also possible, however.

The reason that this issue is important for the current discussion is that some connection exists between the dawn and the dew.[80] Dew condenses at night, but offers relief only after the dawn. The exact point of comparison, however, has yet to be determined. If my translation above is correct, the popular connection of dew with many youths, like dew in abundance,[81] is not likely. Another usual interpretation is that the vitality of the king is like dew.[82] What exactly this means is not clear. To specify further how dew is used in this verse, the perception of dew elsewhere in the Bible must briefly be considered.

Elsewhere in the Hebrew Bible the dew has a sire. Job 38:28 asks "Is there a father to the rain, or who begets drops of dew?" Mettinger suggests that Yahweh is the father here,[83] a role that would place Yahweh in alignment

---

76. Grelot, "Isaïe XIV 12–15," 18–48; McKay, "Helel and the Dawn Goddess," 458.

77. This deity is often associated or equated with Athtar: Craigie, "Helel, Athtar and Phaethon," 224. See also the recent works on this god by Smith ("The God Athtar," 627–40) and Heiser ("The Mythological Provenance of Isa. xvi 12–15").

78. As pointed out by Mettinger, *King and Messiah*. 264; Booij, "Psalm CX," 400.

79. Smith, "The God Athtar," 629–30; McKay, "Helel and the Dawn-Goddess," 458.

80. Jefferson, "Is Psalm 110 Canaanite?" 155.

81. Gammie, "A New Setting for Psalm 110," 13; Briggs and Briggs, *Book of Psalms*, 2:377; Weiser, *The Psalms*, 695.

82. A. A. Anderson, *Book of Psalms*, 2:770; Kraus, *Psalms 60–150*, 350; Johnson, *Sacral Kingship*, 121.

83. Mettinger, *King and Messiah*, 264.

with Baal as the father of "dew" in Ugaritic thought.[84] Although this belated paternity suit does not necessarily implicate Yahweh here, there is obviously a sexual connotation to the dew in this verse,[85] both because "like the dew" the king is "begotten," and since the place of the king's setting forth is said to be "from the womb."

What does it mean to have been begotten like the dew? The point of comparison would involve dew being associated with semen in some way—an idea with an ancient pedigree.[86] As semen impregnates, the dew leads to the production of crops. The fructifying aspect of dew must be kept in mind when dealing with ancient concepts.[87] Ultimately royal legitimation is symbolized by the dew: the king has been begotten, presumably by Yahweh, to ride out to victory. The function of dew is one of watering the earth in this context, and being compared with the king who refreshes Israel.

Psalm 133:3

> Like the dew of Hermon
> which descends upon the mountains of Zion.
> For there Yahweh appointed the blessing,
> life for all time.

This verse begins mid-sentence, and adds a simile to the sacred oil which spills over Aaron's collar onto his robe, cited in the previous verse. The similes both compare the amiability of consanguineous harmony with soothing substances. Simply put, the meteorological aspect is purely metaphorical in this citation.

The word טל is in the construct state, being associated with Mount Hermon. Dew does occur on Mount Hermon,[88] but it was also known for

---

84. One of Baal's standard epithets includes his being the father of *ṭly bt rb* "Tallay ['Dewy'] Daughter of Showers" (for example *KTU* 1.3 i 24–25; 1.3 iii 7; 1.3 iv 51; 1.3 v 42). See Wiggins, "The Weather under Baal."

85. As demonstrated for other texts by Brown, "Yahweh, Zeus, Jupiter," 191. See also de Savignac, "Théologie pharaonique et messianisme d'Israël," 86. This is an image that persists into current times, to judge by what I used to hear in secondary school in the early 1980s.

86. Enlil's "water" impregnates Ninlil in the Sumerian myth (see Kramer, *Sumerian Mythology*, 44).

87. Uval, "Dew of Heaven," 117–18.

88. Arav, "Hermon, Mount," 159. This reference is independent of the author's citation of Ps 133 as a source of meteorological information on p. 158.

its snow, which can last into the summer.[89] Melt-water from Hermon supplies the headwaters of the Jordan River,[90] making the association of the mountain with water obvious. Goulder points out, somewhat ironically, "[t]he surprising element in the image is that it is the dew of Hermon which is said to come down upon the hills of Zion; for beyond question the dew of Hermon comes down on Hermon, not on Zion, 150 miles to the south."[91] He goes on to note that "heavy dew" is intended by this verse.[92] Dew is a sign of blessing in the Hebrew Bible, a function that is also reflected in this verse.[93]

The context makes the function of dew in this verse obvious. It is the soothing quality of the dew that is compared to siblings living in peace. The dew of Hermon is a simile for this concord.

SUMMARY OF DEW TERM FUNCTIONS

Dew is used only in a metaphorical sense in the Psalms. It occurs in two verses only. The reference in Ps 110:3 is a complex simile that emphasizes the fructifying aspect of dew, which is perhaps compared with semen. Dew also appears to have a refreshing effect in this verse as well, since the king is being commissioned to ride out from the womb at the dawn, full of strength.

The second use of dew, in Ps 133:3, focuses on the soothing, cooling aspect of dew. It is used as a simile for peace in the family, compared to the cooling oil with which Aaron was anointed.

---

89. Baly, *Geography of the Bible*, 193; Arav, "Hermon," 159.

90. Baly, *Geography of the Bible*, 14.

91. Goulder, *Psalms of the Return*, 105.

92. Ibid.

93. This association continued well into the Rabbinic period. See Kern-Ulmer, "Consistency and Change in Rabbinic Literature," 55–75.

Chapter Six

Temperature

All weather phenomena set in motion a series of effects which eventually encounter all of the physical entities on the surface of the earth. It is difficult, therefore, to determine precisely when a literary meteorological image ceases to be weather and begins to be another feature of the natural world. When does rain cease being rain and begin being groundwater? When does extreme heat cease to be weather and begin to be the cause of wilting plants? Arguably there is not substantial difference in the phenomena involved: water remains water and heat remains heat. This issue nevertheless is acute in exploring biblical perceptions of temperature; the psalmists make no distinction between air temperature and its effects. However, since temperature is a major aspect of weather, and since heat and cold are specifically mentioned in Psalms, some parameters concerning when temperature effects are weather must be established.

Heat is more commonly cited than cold in the Psalms, and the sun is obviously a source of heat. Many Psalms mention the sun, most notably Ps 19:5–7 [4–6]. The sun, although it causes much of what we recognize as weather, is not itself a meteorological phenomenon. The sun directly affects air temperature, and is recognized as a source of heat in the Psalms. The sun is also luminous, and it marks the end of night. Its position in the sky marks seasons. Not all Psalm references to the sun are concerned with its meteorological effects.

The sun is cited as a source of light and times (Pss 74:16; 104:19, 22; 113:3; 136:7–8). Sometimes God is referred to as the source of light (Pss 18:29 [28]; 27:1; 36:10 [9]; 43:3; 94:1; 118:27). God's face is frequently mentioned as shining (Pss 4:7 [6]; 31:17 [16]; 44:4 [3]; 67:2 [1]; 80:4 [3], 8 [7], 20 [19]; 89:16 [15]; 90:8; 119:135) or as being visible in the morning (Pss 17:15; 50:1–3) or some opportune time (Ps 42:3 [2]). These facts have led some to conclude that the appearance of the sun was in some way associated with God's face.[1] The wrath of God is perceived as burning (Pss 21:10 [9]; 50:1–3; 69:25 [24]; 79:5; 85:4 [3]; 89:47 [46]), and virtue is described as light (Ps 37:6). Emotion may cause heat (Pss 39:4 [3]; 119:53), and theophanic heat may melt mountains or the earth (Pss 46:7 [6]; 97:5; 144:5). The sun praises Yahweh (Ps 148:3). The sun is also a metaphor for longevity (Pss 72:5, 17; 89:37 [36]). In all of these cases, however, sunshine, or solar radiation, cannot be classified specifically as weather.[2] The psalmists appear to consider the sun an appropriate metaphor for light, which is more often the metaphrand than heat.[3] Often it appears that the element of heat was taken for granted, while the light aspect of the sun was eagerly anticipated.

The sun shines and heats the earth regardless of atmospheric conditions. Solar radiation becomes weather when it is perceived as heat, that is, when it is directly experienced as the air temperature. How much of this process was understood by the ancients is uncertain, and the psalmists make no attempt to spell it out precisely.

Although many of the references in the psalms do not make this solar-thermal association explicit, there are sufficiently numerous references to merit an exploration of how the psalmists perceived air temperature in a few of the psalms.

SUN

One psalm makes a direct, if metaphorical, equation of Yahweh with the sun.[4]

---

1. See Smith, "'Seeing God' in the Psalms," 171–83. It should be noted, however, that if the sun was thought of as Yahweh's face this would indicate another association of God's control over weather.

2. The reference to the sun in Ps 50:1–3 will be explored below, but on a basis quite different from the wrath and shining of God aspects.

3. The term "metaphrand" is borrowed from Jaynes, *The Origin of Consciousness*, 48–49.

4. For a brief introduction to the relationship of Yahweh to the sun see Lipiński, "Shemesh שמש," 765–66. See also Wiggins, "Yahweh: The God of Sun?" 89–106.

Psalm 84:12 [11]

> For Yahweh is sun and shield,
> God gives grace and honor,
> Yahweh does not withhold good
> from those walking with integrity.

This verse is meteorologically noteworthy in that one of the aspects of solar radiation is heat. In this verse, since the precise aspect of the sun to which Yahweh is likened is not specified, heat may be an implied point of comparison. More likely, however, the referent is the light of the sun, which is the more common solar aspect cited in the Psalms. Nothing else in this passage suggests that heat is specifically produced by Yahweh, but, the verse does mention the "good" (טוב), which Yahweh bestows. "Good" in the Psalms is sometimes probably understood to be rain (see chapter four). Since this verse mentions the sun, however, warmth may be the good for which the writer is thankful. As a set of one, this verse may be offered as the sole exemplar of this possible, tentative, association between Yahweh, the sun, and heat.

HEAT

Concerning the thermal aspect of the atmosphere, the Psalms use two terms to describe heat: חמם and חרבן. Each of these terms occurs in a meteorological context in a single psalm. In addition to these words, a potential thermal image may occur in Ps 50 with the use of the words יפע and אש, but this is unlikely. Some of the direct effects of heat are also noted below for purposes of comparison.

חַמָּה

Psalm 19:7 [6]

> From the end of the heavens is its [the sun's] coming out,
> and its course to their end,
> and nothing is hidden from its heat.

Psalm 19:2–7 [1–6] contains a paean to the sun. This leads some to conclude that the psalm originated as a hymn to the sun. If the psalm has such an origin, it has been adjusted so that God is cited as the source of the solar splendor. The verse under consideration is the only verse in the psalm that specifically attributes heat to the sun.

This verse presents no translation problems, but its interpretation is widely varied.[5] Of particular concern here is the meteorological function of the reference to the sun's heat (חַמָּתוֹ). Clearly the psalmist celebrates the omnipresent aspect of the sun's heat, since nothing is hidden from it. Just when the reader might expect some further explanation, the subject of the psalm shifts to praise of Torah. Is there an aspect of the sun's heat that is specifically being celebrated? If so, what is it? This psalm tacitly abstains from providing more information on why heat is isolated in this verse. Elsewhere in the Psalms, heat is a sign of divine wrath, although such an aspect is not obvious here. Perhaps the most straightforward referent here is the ubiquity of the sun's heat. This, like Yahweh's control of nature, is universal in the eyes of the psalmist.

The use of the word סתר, "hidden," however, suggests that the heat leads to a desire for relief. In this respect, heat is a negative element of the weather. It may have been understood as part of the divine arsenal.

חֲרְבֹנִי

Psalm 32:4

> For by day and night heavy upon me is your hand,
> my cream[6] has turned into the dry heat of summer.

The precise sense of this verse eludes current understanding. Three of the words are disputed in meaning, with two of these being quite rare.[7] The three disputed words are all directly involved in the comment about temperature; the words translated "cream," "turned," and "dry heat" fit uneasily together. Commentators disagree concerning the referent, and emendation is generally proposed. Any potential weather information gathered from this context must therefore be treated with considerable reserve.

Clearly the psalmist laments the heavy-handed aspect of God. The complaint is that the "cream" of the psalmist has become the dry heat of summer. The word "cream" (לשד) occurs only once elsewhere, in Num 11:8,

---

5. For one interpretation, see my "Yahweh: The God of Sun?" 98–99. Note also Sarna, "Psalm xix," 171–75.

6. See the following two notes.

7. The meaning of הפך ("turned") in this context is unclear. לשדי ("my cream") is a rare word, occurring elsewhere only in Num 11:8, and חרבני ("dry heat of summer") is a hapax legomenon.

where it is used to describe the taste of manna. Commentators generally do not give pause to this rare word in Numbers, but in this psalm, it becomes a crux. I have followed the translation suggested by Milgrom, since he alone offers philological support for his translation.[8]

The meteorologically significant word in this verse, חרבני, is a hapax legomenon. The major lexica agree that there is some aspect of heat and/or dryness in the word, relating it to the root חרב I, "be dry."[9] The primary association of חרבן with dryness highlights the difficulty of determining the function of its potential meteorological referent. Dryness is an aspect of humidity, which is a weather element, namely, the relative dearth of moisture in the air. Dryness, in the form of a lack of precipitation, may lead to drought. חרבן is often translated as "drought."[10] If drought is the actual meaning, then this is not a meteorological reference, but an indication of one of the results of meteorological activity, as discussed above.

If "heat" or "dry heat" is the referent, then the image is meteorological. How would this potential meteorological image function in the context of this verse? What does it mean for cream to turn into heat? The associations of cream include a soothing feel, and it appears that the psalmist feels that God is not soothing, but rather hot and/or dry. These conditions, although both heat and dryness are associated with the sirocco, are explicitly stated to be the conditions of summer. Rain is quite rare in the Levantine summer, and it appears that the psalmist has chosen this aspect to compare with the anticipated divine relationship, which should be like cream. If this interpretation is correct, then heat has a decidedly negative association in this verse. Beyond this minimal assessment, precision is currently unattainable.

יָפַע and אֵשׁ?

The final potentially thermal signals in the Psalms occur in Ps 50. The juxtaposition of language involving the physical sun, Yahweh's shining, and fire consuming before Yahweh suggest a possible reference to heat.

Psalm 50:1–3

The God of gods is Yahweh!

---

8. Milgrom, *Numbers*, 84, notes that Akkadian *lishdu* also has the meaning "cream."
9. BDB 351; *DCH* 3: 311b; KBS 350a.
10. See, for example, Cheyne, *Book of Psalms*, 87; Craigie, *Psalms 1–50*, 263; Dahood, *Psalms*, 1:193.

He speaks and calls forth the earth,
from the rising of the sun to its going in,
2 from Zion, the perfection of beauty,
God shines forth.
3 Our God enters and is not silent,
fire consumes before him,
and around him it storms severely.

The meteorological referent in this verse is uncertain. Like many other psalm passages, this pericope makes note of Yahweh's shining (יפע). This would appear to be a solar metaphor, and would therefore not necessarily be meteorological. It is included here because of the reference to fire (אש) consuming before Yahweh in v. 3. The use of fire language in combination with solar language suggests the possibility of a thermal, meteorological image. If so, fire is used as a metaphor for heat. On the other hand, it is possible, and probably preferable, to understand אש in association with the storm mentioned in v. 3, which would make reference to lightning rather than heat. If the reference is a thermal one, it is unique in its use of combining יפע and אש to express the idea of air temperature. The function of the "fire" is to reveal Yahweh's glory in a theophanic appearance. While this pericope must remain a potential heat reference, it is more likely a metaphor for lightning (see chapter two).

FUNCTIONS OF HEAT LANGUAGE

It is difficult to determine with any precision how atmospheric heat was perceived by the psalmists. Clearly, it is considered in a negative way, since heat is something from which to be hidden (Ps 19:7 [6]) and since it is contrasted to a positive substance (cream, Ps 32:4). Ps 84:12 [11] may indicate that the good produced by Yahweh, equated with the sun, was heat. Far more likely, however, is the possibility that Yahweh's association with the sun is based on its light-giving aspect, and that "the good" is used generically.

COLD

קָרָה

Only one verse in the Psalms directly mentions coldness. The reference occurs in Ps 147:17 and utilizes the word קרה. In order to make sense of the verse, it will be presented within the context of v. 16 in the translation here.

Psalm 147:16–17

> 16 The one giving snow like the wool,
> he scatters hoarfrost like the ashes,
> 17 throwing his rime like crumbs,
> before his cold who will stand?

After listing various meteorological phenomena associated with ice, and, particularly in the higher elevations of Palestine, the author of this particular psalm asks who can stand before Yahweh's cold. The straightforward interpretation of this rhetorical question is that cold is an element to be avoided. Although not enough detail is recorded to assign cold as a divine weapon, it functions in a similar way to other weapons, in that it is an element under divine control which causes humans discomfort. In this it is similar to heat, in that both temperature extremes, heat and cold, are given a distinctly negative slant in the Psalms.

SOME EFFECT OF TEMPERATURE

Temperature effects have an all-embracing aspect. Heat and cold cause further phenomena such as drought, abundant harvests, and crop failure. In extreme cases exposure may lead to the death of fauna or of humans. It is not possible to cover all of the further effects of temperature in the Psalms, since the effects ramify and transform into other phenomena, which themselves have multiple associations. Nevertheless, four specific effects of the weather mentioned in the Psalms appear to have temperature as one of their main constituents: season references, the melting of ice, the wilting of plants, and the ability of the sun to smite human beings.

SEASONS

חֹרֶף/קַיִץ

Psalm 74:17

> You established all the boundaries of the earth,
> summer and autumn you fashion them.

Seasonal references are reflexes of the basic fact that the northern and southern hemispheres annually tilt toward and away from the sun. This change in orientation leads to temperature differences at various times of the year. In Israel/Palestine the shift in seasons is accompanied by changes in the precipitation pattern, and the temperature differential is less pronounced than in many temperate climates. The reference in this psalm to summer (קיץ) and autumn (חרף) coincides with heat reflexes only minimally: it cannot be determined with any certainty that heat is the primary referent. Another obvious potential candidate is an agricultural metaphor.

In the context of the psalm, this seasonal citation has primary reference to boundaries. Verse 16 states that God establishes the boundaries of day and night, sun and stars. Verse 17 explicitly mentions the boundaries (גבולות) of the earth before introducing summer and autumn. Although temperature has an integral role in the changing of the seasons, here it is far from view. God is praised as the establisher of boundaries, and heat is incidental to one of the confines that happens to be mentioned.

MELTING

מָסָה

Psalm 147:18

> He sends out his word and causes them to melt,
> he causes his wind to blow,
> the waters flow.

Immediately following the sole reference to cold in the Psalms in 147:17, this verse points to Yahweh's ability to control that cold. The most obvious effects of cold weather include frozen precipitation and frozen ground water. In order for these to melt, heat must be applied, thus the connection of this verse to temperature suggests itself.

All melting requires the application of heat. The ancients surely understood the general principle, as the widespread use of smelting indicates. References to the melting of mountains (see for example Ps 97:5) seem to show an awareness of volcanic activity, and the comparison to wax demonstrates that the application of heat was understood as essential to melting substances.

Temperature effects in this verse are not explicitly stated as being positive, but the sense the reader derives from the context may be one of relief that the cold is ending. The totality of cold and warmth is under the control of Yahweh, which gives the psalmist cause to praise the divine ability to melt what has frozen. The temperature effect here functions as an active cause for which to ascribe wonder to Yahweh.

WILTING

מָלַל and נָבֵל

Psalm 1:3

> And he will be like a tree planted by water channels,
> which gives its fruit in its time,
> and whose leaves do not wither (נבל),
> and all that he does is brought to success.

Psalm 37:2

> For as vegetation quickly wilts (מלל),
> and as greenness of grass withers (נבל),

Psalm 90:6

> In the morning it blossoms and revives,
> at evening it withers (מלל) and dries up.

The interaction of agriculture with weather is both complex and direct.[11] The terms used in the Psalms for the wilting of plants, נבל and מלל, are not precise enough to determine what environmental factor may have been causing stress to the flora. Both high temperature and lack of precipitation may cause plant damage.[12] As with the weather in general, the psalmists did not have the physical causes of plant stress as their focus. It was the ability of Yahweh to control these realities that was of primary concern.

All three references cited here are used to compare human longevity with the ephemerality of plants. Ps 1:3 likens the vitality of the righteous to a well-watered tree. Ps 37:2 notes that the wicked vanish as shortly as the grass. Ps 90:6 compares all human life to the brief period of plants blossoming. It is clear that although heat may play a role in the blighting of plants, it is not the thermal aspect that is central. The primary aspect under view in

---

11. Rosenzweig, "Agriculture and Climate," 20–25.
12. Ibid., 21–22.

these verses is a matter-of-fact observation that plants are short-lived, and thus make a good contrast to human life.

SMITING

נָכָל

Psalm 121:6

> By day the sun will not strike you,
> nor the moon by night

A final example of a potentially thermal reference in the Psalms mentions not heat, but the smiting power of the sun. The sun is cited as having the ability to strike (נכה) people, although the psalmist assures the reader that this will not happen. The possible thermal reference arises in an attempt to understand how the sun might "strike" a person. While being stricken by light is an evocative image, heat-stroke is a reality, and is perhaps the phenomenon to which the psalmist refers. If so, this is not a direct meteorological reference, but rather one of the effects of heat on a human agent. Specifically, it may be an instance of the use of heat as a weapon. This weapon does not seem to be wielded by Yahweh, however, but is a direct effect of the sun.

The parallel with the moon striking a person calls for caution with this interpretation. Nowhere is the moon depicted as generating heat, but the baleful influence of the moon was obviously feared.

FUNCTIONS OF THERMAL REFERENCES

With few direct references to air temperature, thermal phenomena do not constitute a large category of Psalms weather references. When the temperature is a significant factor it is almost always a source of discomfort. In the three definite references to temperature (Pss 19:7 [6]; 32:4 (heat) and 147:17 (cold)), the extremes of hot and cold are noted as worthy of avoidance. Since the sun may strike a person (Ps 121:6), it may have been thought to be a weapon, but it is more likely a reference to the sun's own ability to generate a negative influence. Both heat and coldness may have potential functions as weaponry, especially in the light of other weather phenomena acquiring such a function. This negative perception may be true of other effects of temperature noted in the Psalms: heat may play a role in the wilting of greenery (Pss 1:3; 37:2; 90:6). Positive effects of thermal conditions may have been associated with the change of seasons (Ps 74:17) and the melting of ice (Ps 147:18).

CHAPTER SEVEN

Synthesis and Development

In the Hebrew Bible the weather in general is understood as a kind of "barometer" of Yahweh's interaction with humankind. This sweeping statement also reflects the modern mind-set in popular culture, as reflected in the 1998 film "Twister" in which a meteorologist answers the question of a layperson about the definition of an F5 tornado[1] by stating that it is "the finger of God!" Such thinking is present even in sophisticated reflections on natural phenomena.[2] The idea of the weather as a divine instrument is clearly "biblical" as well, as this study has demonstrated.[3] This biblical perception has been raised to the surface by demonstrating how prevalently the concept of weather in the divine sphere is used in the book of Psalms.

---

1 The F scale, or Fujita scale, is named after the late University of Chicago physicist Ted Fujita, who first classified tornadoes according to their damage paths on a scale of 0 to 5. Since the original writing of this book it has been modified somewhat, but the reference in the movie remains to a classic F5.

2. Increase Mather's, *Remarkable Providences Illustrative of the Earlier Days of American Colonisation*, which, appropriately opens and closes with a quotations from Psalms, is a good seventeenth-century example of this. At least three of his chapters are predominantly about the weather. For a more recent citation of this phenomenon see, Fleming, *Meteorology in America*, 8–9. Even the extremely reputable *Encyclopedia of Climate and Weather* contains an article entitled "Religion and Weather" (by S. Young, 2:639–43).

3. Note especially Reymond, *L'eau*, 35–53; Brown, "Yahweh, Zeus, Jupiter," 175–97. For useful introductions to biblical weather see Scott, "Palestine, Climate of," 621–26 and Frick, "Palestine, Climate of," 119–26. For more detailed information see Orni and Efrat, *Geography of Israel*, 135–63; Baly, *Geography of the Bible*, 43–68.

Weather references, or obvious allusions to the weather, occur in some forty-two psalms.[4] This number of citations constitutes a fairly important theme in the book, as it is some 28 percent of the Psalter. Many of these psalms have multiple or extended references to weather. In no case does the weather appear as a natural occurrence—it is always within the purview of Yahweh.

This monograph has considered only the direct references or transparent allusions to meteorological phenomena in the Psalms. It is quite possible that abstract allusions to the weather exist in the Psalms as well. There are strong indications that some common words, such as "the good" (הטוב)[5] and "blessing" (ברך)[6] became *technicus termini* for rain in some contexts in the Psalms and elsewhere in the Bible. The problem is that their metaphrands are not clear. If these associations were secure, they would provide yet further evidence for the centrality of meteorotheological thought in the Psalms. Yahweh was intimately associated with the weather.

"Meteorotheological" is simply a neologism that indicates that the weather is a divine phenomenon and that it may be approached from a modern meteorological perspective. This provides advice to translators concerned with precision, but also maintains the mythical world where weather, indeed, nature, is not "natural." It is a balancing act between religion and science.

Rather than rehearse the results of the survey of Psalms material above, this final chapter will attempt to demonstrate the relevance of the biblical understanding for the twenty-first century. The evidence has been examined, but what is to be made of it? Is it only a reflection of a quaint, but antiquated viewpoint, fit for an interesting but irrelevant museum display? I would contend that it is not. The biblical themes are deeply imprinted on human thought processes. Whether it is in our blaming God for the weather, or in our looking for the face of Jesus in gaseous nebulae millions of light years from our own earth, we seem to be incapable of removing God from the sky.

---

4. The psalms are: 1, 7, 11, 18, 19, 29, 32, 35, 36, 38, 42, 48, 50, 51, 55, 57, 58, 65, 68, 72, 77, 78, 81, 83, 84, 85, 89, 97, 99, 103, 104, 105, 107, 108, 110, 133, 135, 140, 144, 146, 147, and 148.

5. Dahood, *Psalms*, 1:25.

6. Nash, *Palestinian Agricultural Year*, 114, n. 7.

YAHWEH, GOD OF THE SKY

It has become axiomatic in some circles that Yahweh was understood as a sun-god or the God of the sun in ancient Israel.[7] This kind of construct, which I have elsewhere suggested be called the "divine genitival construct,"[8] is problematic. It is problematic in several respects, but here I focus on two: 1. The divine genitival construct is a faulty construct in general, and 2. Yahweh's role and character in the Hebrew Bible encompass much more than a solar role.

1. The divine genitival construct is a faulty construct. This method of explaining ancient deities projects an enormous amount of Victorian, eurocentric interpretation into ancient perceptions of deities. From the evidence available to current-day researchers it is quite evident that ancient West Asian cultures had more sophisticated and complex roles for their deities than what is implied by relegating a deity to a particular sphere of nature using the phrase "god/goddess of—." In order to understand what an ancient deity was, the evidence for that deity must be studied and analyzed. Over the course of my academic career, I had attempted to apply this method to various deities of the Ugaritic pantheon, and always their role in that pantheon emerges and being much more complex than simply as a "rain god" or "goddess of the sun." These terms have become so heavily freighted with faulty constructs that it is time to abandon them for more accurate terms.

2. Yahweh's role and character in the Hebrew Bible encompass much more than a solar role. In general terms, Yahweh is conceived of as a deity interacting with other supernatural beings, intervening in human affairs, both interpersonal and international relationships, and controlling terrestrial, atmospheric, and celestial phenomena. In what sense could Israel have understood a deity with this broad of a sphere of activity as a solar god? In the light of what has been written above, I would suggest that Yahweh was much larger, much more complex than even a God of the weather *in toto*.

The book of Psalms frequently brings the weather into the realm of Yahweh's immediate and direct control, but this does not make Yahweh into a "weather god." What this study has demonstrated is that the weather fell under the purview of Yahweh in the book of Psalms, but that this relationship had some specific categories into which it fit. I have summarized these paradigms at the end of each section in the text above, and here I examine some of the more striking conclusions that might be drawn from those associations: how does weather conceal and reveal Yahweh, what is the

---

7. For example, Taylor, *Yahweh and the Sun*. See also the section on "Sun" in chapter six above.

8. Wiggins, "What's in a Name?" 761–79.

relationship between weather and warfare, and how does it relate to the divine glory? These associations lead naturally to the question of how science informs the understanding of the Bible. Here the question will be examined in particular reference to the weather, but in terms which also apply to current understanding of other natural phenomena as well.

WEATHER REVEALS AND CONCEALS GOD

The terrifying and awe-inspiring effects of the weather urge the sensible person to flee, or at least keep a distance from, the danger they represent. At the same time, the individual is drawn toward that very source of danger out of sheer fascination.[9] This is amply demonstrated by the conflicting subtones on much modern film footage of severe weather, where the filmer, sotto voce, says to himself or herself that they must seek cover, and yet find themselves unable to remove their gaze from the approaching source of danger.[10]

This same dynamic is evident in the Psalms. The psalmists are continually describing the much-anticipated arrival of Yahweh with the language of the storm. The person of God is never described, but the closest image to be found is meteorological. For the deity associated so closely with the sky, the unexplained atmospheric elements are the obvious accoutrements. Lightning—unsurpassed in brilliance; wind—invisible yet full of destructive power; hail—stones from the sky; thunder—the very voice of God; all of these elements combine in the severe thunderstorm which drives the enemy away. At the same time, these dazzling armaments cause the psalmists to let their gaze linger over a few verses and impress the reader with this sense of being in the presence of the divine warrior.

WEATHER AND WARFARE

Throughout the Psalms Yahweh has access to, and sometimes utilizes, thunder, lightning, winds, storms, and hail as weaponry. These elements were thought to have been stored in an arsenal, a storehouse in the heavens, along

---

9. These competing aspects of the storm might rightly be related to the categories of the holy as devised by Otto (*The Idea of the Holy*), many years ago.

10. As with newspaper stories and television news interviews with individuals after a storm, in which personal interpretations of God's role in the weather figure prominently, the number of film segments demonstrating this phenomenon is immense. One need only watch the tornado footage contained in such collections as The Tornado Project's series "Tornado Video Classics" to hear many examples of this.

with more benevolent elements such as rain and snow. This martial imagery matches one of the ancient aspects of God as presented in the Hebrew Bible, which is that of Yahweh the divine warrior.[11] As a warrior, Yahweh was thought to be an independent operator—the divine weapons could be turned on Yahweh's enemies, on Israel, or even on the psalmists. There was an apparent arbitrariness to this choice of victim which is sometimes reflected in the pleas of the psalmists to turn the divine wrath in a direction in which it is not headed. The divine warrior is ultimately not constrained by human assessments of fairness or justice. Weather weaponry remained a threat.[12] In a way unknown to the psalmists, this perception of the weather concurs with a scientific understanding.

Ironically, the scientific study of weather took a major leap forward with the military application of supercomputers. No Psalmist ever foresaw, even with a warrior God, that the military of a much later millennium would devise the means partially to understand the divine arsenal. A study such as this also owes some of its information to humanity's warlike tendencies.

Weather in all of its aspects involves motion. The motion of wind and precipitation are obvious. Humidity involves the changing amounts of moisture in the air, and this change is caused by the motion of water vapor. Temperature involves the speed of molecular motion—the faster the motion, the higher the temperature. This constant motion, of the world turning on its axis, of the atmosphere heated by the sun, cooled by the surface of the earth, creates the planet's restless, apparently arbitrary weather. Here the divine warrior and the psalmists' perception of the weather coalesce.

Although this could not have been known to the ancients, this restless, constant activity of the atmosphere was revealed in the metaphor of Yahweh the divine warrior.[13]

WEATHER AND GLORY

Throughout the Psalms the weather serves to bring glory to Yahweh. Evident not only in Psalms categorized as "hymns," but in other genres as well, humans were awestruck by the ability of Yahweh to control the weather. From the perspective of humankind, the weather is immense and its effects immediate. Some 2,500 years have not changed this aspect of life. Even in

---

11. Miller, *Divine Warrior*, is the standard study of this motif.

12. This imagery of the thunderstorm as warfare reemerged in late seventeenth-century Britain. See Janković, *Reading the Skies*, 27–28.

13. Janković, (*Reading the Skies*, 55–77) provides a discussion of a rather more recent, European application of meteorology to warfare.

today's rational, scientifically oriented cultures the helplessness of humanity in the face of the weather is frequently expressed.[14] Even today people quickly attribute weather disasters directly to the intervention of God.[15] In its own way, this blaming of the divine is related to the awe expressed by the psalmists. Knowing that the weather is beyond human governance, those adversely affected by it have recourse to the God-of-the-gaps.

This study brings to a conscious level the fact that, as far as the weather is concerned, popular sentiment as to its origin has not noticeably changed since biblical times. Rationally we may know that the atmosphere can be studied and explained by the principles of physics and fluid dynamics, but emotionally we are reluctant to let God escape the process. The glory attributed to the God who controls the weather by the psalmists is now systematically examined by scientists who equally appreciate its wonders. Empirical study has not diminished the scope or the awe of humanity's heavenward gaze, but it has shifted the focus.

Herein lies the crux of the issue: how can biblical study and science coexist? This monograph has applied the science of meteorology to the science of textual study in the hopes of discerning something of the history of religion. Although many of the issues addressed above have been specifically textual, the more penetrating question of the relationship between science and Bible is the catalyst for this study. To understand adequately how a modern reader of the Psalms can apply the weather theme to a twenty-first century viewpoint requires some consideration of the role of science in the study of the Bible.

SCIENCE, CHAOS, AND YAHWEH

Clearly the psalmists had no designs on providing an accurate record of meteorological events, let alone a scientific account of the weather.[16] The relationship between science and the Bible enters this discussion in the application of a scientific understanding of the weather to the imagery used to express weather phenomena in the Bible. This application does not draw

---

14. During the writing of this book two journalistic accounts of weather events climbed the best-sellers' lists: Larson, *Isaac's Storm*, and Junger, *The Perfect Storm*.

15. This is evident in any number of interviews found in newspapers after a violent storm. My own collection of such clippings is too large to begin to cite here.

16. Janković, (*Reading the Skies*, throughout) demonstrates just how recently weather observation became associated with science. Even after that connection was established, weather was still particularly associated with the divine.

lines of battle between science and the Bible, but perhaps surprisingly, reveals an underlying correlation.

Scientific theories to explain natural phenomena consist of continually increasing zones of influence. This study also leads to ever-expanding areas of related interest, interlocking into the global enterprise of the scientific study of natural phenomena and literary and theological developments. Science is the means of such study, the result is a more informed understanding of what the Psalms say about God. Both science and the Psalms interestingly converge on the concept of chaos.

The weather cannot be understood in isolation. As a part of the global environment, the atmosphere is affected by whatever happens on the surface of the earth as well as whatever astronomic events occur near enough to influence it. Over time the collective effects of the weather are classified as climate. It has long been recognized that climate is intimately connected to the oceans.[17] The climate, like the oceans, is constantly in a state of flux, and each passing hour alters the climatic records that are kept for any given region by adding further data to those records. In other words, climate is a continually unfolding set of data. The practical difficulties of studying it are immense. This immensity is embraced by chaos theory.[18]

In Mesopotamian and Syro-Palestinian religions, chaos was a kind of primeval first substance. The earlier forms of this thought actually hypostatize this unformed, unruly matter into a deity associated with the great deeps. This deity may actually be a king or queen and is an adversary with whom to be contended.

Chaos is frequently associated with water in the ancient mind. Water was understood to be a, or *the*, primordial element, but when chaos is personified, or is used as building material, it is clearly not only water.

At some point a challenge is issued to the reign of chaos. In Mesopotamia the challenge is a result of the previous decision on the part of chaos (named Tiamat) and her cohorts to wipe out the younger generation of gods, who are making too much cosmic noise. In response, the younger gods choose a champion to eradicate the chaotic, primeval gods. In Ugarit the basis of the challenge has not been preserved, but Baal is the champion. He must eradicate Yam (chaos) in order to become king of the gods. It appears that this was a self-motivated act on the part of Baal. In Israel Yahweh was the champion. This theme is preserved in the book of Psalms. Like Baal, Yahweh had to do combat with and overcome chaos. In at least the last two

---

17. This is evident in the classic study by naturalist Rachel Carson, *The Sea Around Us*, 156–72; see also Raikes, *Water, Weather and Prehistory*, 15–16.

18. Gleick, *Chaos*, is a good introduction to the tenets of chaos theory.

of these cosmologies, chaos was not eradicated, but defeated. The possibility still remains that chaos will break back in upon creation.

After the defeat of the chaos monster, creation can take place. Often creation is formed out of chaos or the remains of the chaos monster. Normally creation is the work of the deity who actually did the defeating and it signifies their preeminence over the other gods.

In order to construct a paradigm, the Ugaritic version is useful, since it is more closely associated with the biblical image than the Mesopotamian one is. This suggests some level of cultural continuity. Interestingly, the deity who defeats chaos is also the deity who controls the weather. Baal determines where and how much it rains, he uses lightning and thunder as weapons, and he may even be responsible for dew. I maintain that Baal's role is much larger than this, but this larger role is often culture-specific, so it is less useful for constructing a paradigm. In the Psalms Yahweh controls the weather, and it is Yahweh who defeated and controls chaos. This situation conforms to the paradigm.

In scientific studies of chaos theory the weather is often used to illustrate the principle of ultimate unknowability. If a butterfly flaps its wings in China, it rains in Wisconsin. More precisely this principle might be cited as the interrelatedness of the entire atmosphere; every incident which has an impact on the atmosphere affects the whole atmosphere. The atmosphere affects all of geology and, in some sense, all of space. The effects in space, given its size, must be minimal, but even the light generated on the earth travels on to infinity. The effect on the earth is more measurable, in that the atmosphere influences climate and surface erosion. Climate, as stated above, impacts all living things.

Once again chaos emerges as a central aspect of the paradigm. Ironically, it is the sphere of activity of the deity the ancients deemed the victor over chaos—the god who controls the weather (which is the prime example of what chaos is)—to control the weather.[19] In a sense, then, scientific chaos may be recognized as the force that, according to the paradigm of ancient religions, defeated mythological chaos. Perhaps the ancients were right and chaos does rule the cosmos.

If the perceptions of the weather in the Psalms are brought into contact with science, both may point to chaos. In science, chaos theory is characterized by fractals, an underlying pattern of infinite repetition. There is order within chaos. If the present-day reader of the Psalms could view the cosmos through the lenses of a pre-scientific era, the picture would not

---

19. The Greek philosopher Theophrastus, however, argued that the divine had no control over the weather, or better, meteors; meteorological phenomena exhibited no order. See Janković, *Reading the Skies*, 20.

be that different. Yahweh, the deity who controls the weather, is the victor over chaos. Yet chaos is not destroyed, it is formed. Creation, order, occurs within the realm of chaos. Science and the Bible have come to a kind of consensus. Fear of mythology often prevents modern Bible readers from noticing how well science and the Bible fit together.

It is important for the modern reader constantly to keep in mind that the current understanding of causality and connectedness of weather are not always the same as those of the ancients. The Psalms demonstrate this fact repeatedly. Most important is the suspension of value judgments on the perceptions of the ancients; they were products of their era and their *Zeitgeist* as much as we are. I consider it likely that as sciences continue to advance our understanding of our universe, weather will be viewed from unexpected quarters and revolutionized in ways that we cannot imagine. It is my hope that even with such advances, students of natural phenomena in the Bible may find such a work as this a useful starting point for further discussion.

Afterword

It is a sobering task to return to a work that was written over a decade ago. Perspectives change and mature, and I realize that if I were to approach this task anew, much would have been different. There would have been less repetition. The writing would have been crisper, and maybe a little less parsimonious at times. I still stand by the results, however. This was intended to be the beginning of a research agenda that was cut short by career exigencies. I hope that others will understand this and take the work forward.

I tremble to take the risk of mentioning sources that I would have incorporated into this study had they appeared in time. This is by no means an attempt at a comprehensive list, but reflects works I found in a period of optimism that I might be on my way back to my academic calling. Aloysius Fitzgerald, F.S.C., had written a dissertation on this topic. He did not respond to my requests to locate a copy, but after this book was finished, the published version, *The Lord of the East Wind*, finally appeared. The *Festschrift* dedicated to him, *Imagery and Imagination in Biblical Literature*, edited by Lawrence Boadt and Mark S. Smith, came onto my radar about the same time, although it was published a year earlier. Some of the essays therein would have been useful. Alberto R. W. Green, some of whose courses I subsequently took over at Rutgers University, published his *The Storm-God in the Ancient Near East* in 2003. The same year saw Menashe Har-El's *Landscape, Nature and Man in the Bible*. Studies of the Psalms continued apace, and there are many useful sources now available that did not exist when I was working on the book. Noteworthy is the collection edited by Lowell K. Handy, *Psalm 29 through Time and Tradition*, at least one essay of which would have been utilized. I also, in my small way, continued to publish on the topic, with the articles "Pidray, Tallay, and Arsay in the Baal Cycle," and "Wheel, Tumbleweed or Whirlwind? *galgal* in the Hebrew Bible."

I am certain that many more studies have appeared, but as a very hot place will freeze over before the academic job situation thaws, I will have to leave this assumption untested.

In the light of continuing denials of the fact of global warming, the strange coincidence of scientific and biblical perspectives on the weather may shed some wisdom. It is to be hoped that humanity will pay attention.

The bibliography that follows reflects the time at which this book was written. Only minimal updates have been made in the case of books that have forced themselves onto the attention of a lay-person who cares deeply about meteorotheology in the Psalms.

Bibliography

Abel, F.-M. *Géographie de la Palestine*, Tome I, Géographie physique et historique. Paris: J. Gabalda et Cie, 1933.
Aharoni, Yohanan. *The Land of the Bible: A Historical Geography*. Rev. ed. Philadelphia: Westminster, 1979.
Ahlström, G. W. *Psalm 89: Eine Liturgie aus dem Ritual des leidenden Königs*. Lund: Gleerups Förlag, 1959.
Aistleitner, Joseph. *Wörterbuch der ugaritischen Sprache*, Berichte über die Verhandlungen der Sächsischen Akademie der Wissenschaften zu Leipzig, Philologisch-historische Klasse 106/3, 2nd ed. Berlin: Akademie-Verlag, 1965.
Albertz, Rainer, Hans-Peter Müller, Hans Walter Wolff, and Walther Zimmerli, eds. *Werden und Wirken des Alten Testaments: Festschrift für Claus Westermann zum 70. Geburtstag*. Göttingen: Vandenhoeck & Ruprecht, 1980.
Albright, W. F. "A Catalogue of Early Hebrew Lyric Poems (Psalm LXVIII)." *HUCA* 23 (1950-51) 1-39.
Allen, Leslie C. *Psalms 101-150*, WBC 21. Waco, TX: Word, 1983.
Alpert, P. "An Ancient 'Correlation' between Streamflow and Distant Rainfall in the Near East." *JNES* 48 (1989) 313-14.
Altmann, Alexander, ed. *Biblical and Other Studies*, Philip W. Lown Institute of Advanced Judaic Studies Brandeis University, Studies and Texts 1. Cambridge: Harvard University Press, 1963.
Amiran, D. H. K. and M. Gilead. "Early Excessive Rainfall and Soil Erosion in Israel." *IEJ* 4 (1954) 286-95.
Anderson, A. A. *The Book of Psalms: Volume 1, Introduction and Psalms 1-72*. New Century Bible. London: Oliphants, 1972.
―――. *The Book of Psalms: Volume 2, Psalms 73-150*. New Century Bible. London: Oliphants, 1972.
Anderson, Bernhard W., ed. *Creation in the Old Testament*, Issues in Religion and Theology 6. Philadelphia: Fortress, 1984.
Anderson, Robert T. "'A Man Asleep in a Storm at Sea' as a Biblical Motif." *Proceedings of the Eastern Great Lakes and Midwest Biblical Societies* 6 (1986) 32-39.
Arav, Rami. "Hermon, Mount." *ABD* III:158-60.
Aristophanes. *The Clouds*. Translated by Benjamin Bickley Rogers in *Aristophanes I: The Acharnians, The Knights, The Clouds, The Wasps*. The Loeb Classical Library. Cambridge: Harvard University Press, 1967.

Ashbel, D. *Bio-climatic Atlas of Israel and the Near East.* Jerusalem: Meteorological Department of the Hebrew University, 1949.
Assaf, Ali Abou. "Die Ikonographie des altbabylonischen Wettergottes." *Baghdader Mitteilungen* 14 (1983) 43–66.
Atlas of Israel: Cartography, Physical Geography, Human and Economic Geography, History. Jerusalem: Survey of Israel, Ministry of Labour, 1970.
Auffret, Pierre. "Essai sur la structure litteraire du psaume 133." *BN* 27 (1985) 22–34.
Austin, Richard Cartwright. *Hope for the Land: Nature in the Bible.* Environmental Theology Book 3. Atlanta: John Knox, 1988.
Baly, Denis. *Geographical Companion to the Bible.* New York: McGraw-Hill, 1963.
———. *The Geography of the Bible*, rev. ed. New York: Harper & Row, 1974.
Baly, Denis, and A. D. Tushingham. *Atlas of the Biblical World.* New York: World, 1971.
Barr, James. "Man [sic] and Nature—The Ecological Controversy and the Old Testament." *Bulletin of the John Rylands University Library of Manchester* 55 (1972) 9–32.
Barré, Michael. "The Formulaic Pair טוב (ו) חסד in the Psalter" *ZAW* 98 (1986) 100–05.
Batto, Bernard F. "The Reed Sea: *Requiescat in Pace.*" *JBL* 102 (1983) 27–35.
———. "Red Sea or Reed Sea? How the Mistake was Made and What *Yam Sûp* Really Means." *BAR* X/4 (July/August 1984) 57–63.
Bauks, Michaela. *Die Welt am Anfang: Zum Verhältnis von Vorwelt und Weltentstehung in Gen 1 und in der altorientalischen Literatur.* WMANT 74. Neukirchen-Vluyn: Neukirchener Verlag, 1997.
Ben-Yoseph, Jacob. "The Climate in Eretz Israel during Biblical Times." *HS* 26.2 Abraham I. Katsh Festschrift (1985) 225–39.
Beyerlin, Walter. *Origins and History of the Oldest Sinaitic Traditions.* Oxford: Blackwell, 1965.
———. *Werden und Wesen des 107. Psalms.* BZAW 153. Berlin: de Gruyter, 1979.
Biella, J. C. *Dictionary of Old South Arabic: Sabaean Dialect.* HSS 25. Chico, CA: Scholars, 1982.
Bintliff, J. L. "Climatic Change, Archaeology and Quaternary Science in the Eastern Mediterranean Region." In *Climate Change in Later Prehistory*, edited by A. F. Harding, 143–61. Edinburgh: Edinburgh University Press, 1982.
Bintliff, John L., and Willem Van Zeist, eds. *Palaeoclimates, Palaeoenvironments and Human Communities in the Eastern Mediterranean Region in Later Prehistory.* BAR International Series 133 (i). Oxford: B.A.R., 1982.
Birkeland, Harris. "Hebrew *zē* and Arabic *ḏū*" *Studia Theologica* 3 (1948) 201–2.
Blidstein, Gerald J. "Nature in 'Psalms.'" *Judaism* 13 (1964) 29–36.
Block, Joel. "The Ten Plagues of Egypt." *Religious Education* 71 (1976) 519–26.
Boadt, Lawrence, and Mark S. Smith, eds. *Imagery and Imagination in Biblical Literature: Essays in Honor of Aloysius Fitzgerald, F.S.C.* CBQMS 32. Washington, DC: The Catholic Biblical Association of America, 2001.
Booij, Th. "Psalm CX: 'Rule in the Midst of your Foes!'" *VT* 41 (1991) 396–407.
Borger, R. "Weitere ugaritologische Kleinkeiten III. Hebräisch *mḥwz* (Psalm 107, 30)." *UF* 1 (1969) 1–4.
Bowker, J. W. "Psalm CX." *VT* 17 (1967) 31–41.
Branick, Michael. *A Comprehensive Glossary of Weather Terms for Storm Spotters.* 2nd ed. NOAA Technical Memorandum NWS SR-145. Online: http://www.nssl.

noaa.gov/~nws/branick2.html [accessed 2002 (current location: http://server.maxdiamonds.com/images/GLOSSARY_NWS-SR145.pdf, accessed 2/22/2014).

Bratcher, Robert G. "Biblical Words Describing Man [sic]: Breath, Life, Spirit." *The Bible Translator* 34 (1983) 201-9.

Brettler, Marc. "Images of Yhwh the Warrior in Psalms." *Semeia* 61 (1993) 135-65.

Briggs, C. A. "The Use of רוח in the Old Testament." *JBL* 19 (1900) 132-45.

Briggs, C. A., and E. G. Briggs, *A Critical and Exegetical Commentary on the Book of Psalms*, vol. 1. ICC. New York: Scribner's Sons, 1908.

———. *A Critical and Exegetical Commentary on the Book of Psalms*, vol. 2. ICC. New York: Scribner's Sons, 1909.

Brock, S. P. "ΝεΦεληγερέτα = rkb 'rpt." *VT* 18 (1968) 395-97.

Brown, John Pairman. "The Mediterranean Seer and Shamanism." *ZAW* 93 (1981) 374-400.

———. "The Sacrificial Cult and its Critique in Greek and Hebrew (I)." *JSS* 24 (1979) 159-73.

———. "The Sacrificial Cult and its Critique in Greek and Hebrew (II)." *JSS* 25 (1980) 1-21.

———. "Yahweh, Zeus, Jupiter: The High God and the Elements." *ZAW* 106 (1994) 175-97.

Brown, Margaret H. "Psalm 72: The Giftedness of the Anointed King." In *The Psalms and Other Studies on the Old Testament Presented to Joseph I. Hunt*, edited by Jack C. Knight and Lawrence A. Sinclair, 28-33. Cincinnati: Forward Movement, 1990.

Brown, William P. "A Royal Performance: Critical Notes on Psalm 110:3aγ-b." *JBL* 117 (1998) 93-96.

Bryson, Reid A. "The Paradigm of Climatology: An Essay." *BAMS* 78.3 (1997) 449-55.

Bryson, Robert U., and Reid A. Bryson. "Application of a Global Volcanicity Time-Series on High-Resolution Paleoclimatic Modeling of the Eastern Mediterranean." In *Water, Environment and Society in Times of Climate Change: Contributions from an International Workshop within the Framework of International Hydrological Program (IHP) UNESCO, held at Ben-Gurion University Sede Boker, Israel from 7–12 July 1996*, edited by Arie S. Issar and Neville Brown, 1-19. Dordrecht: Kluwer Academic, 1998.

———. "High Resolution Simulations of Regional Holocene Climate: North Africa and Near East." In *Third Millennium BC Climate Change and Old World Collapse*, NATO ASI Series 149, edited by H. Nüzhet Dalfes, George Kukla, and Harvey Weiss, 565-93. Berlin: Springer-Verlag, 1997.

Budd, Philip J. *Numbers*, WBC 5. Waco, TX: Word, 1984.

Burkert, W., and F. Stolz, eds. *Hymnen der Alten Welt im Kulturvergleich*. OBO 131. Göttingen: Vandenhoeck & Ruprecht, 1994.

Buttenwieser, Moses. *The Psalms: Chronologically Treated with a New Translation*. Chicago: University of Chicago Press, 1938.

Butzer, K. W. *Quaternary Stratigraphy and Climate in the Near East*. Bonner Geographische Abhandlungen 24. Bonn: Verlag Ferdinand Dümmler, 1958.

Calmet, Augustin. "Actions de graces pour la pluie que le Seigneur a donée et pour la fertilité qu'il rendue à la terre, après une longue sécheresse: Psaume 65." *Bible et Vie Chrétienne* 64 (1965) 24-32.

Campbell, Antony F. "Psalm 78: A Contribution to the Theology of Tenth-Century Israel." *CBQ* 41 (1979) 51-79.

Canaan, T. "Plant-lore in Palestinian Superstition." *JPOS* 8 (1928) 129–68.
Caquot, André. "Le psaume LXVIII." *RHR* 177 (1970) 147–82.
———. "Remarques sur le psaume CX." *Semitica* 6 (1956) 33–52.
Caquot, André, M. Sznycer, and A. Herdner. *Textes ougaritiques tome I: mythes et légendes. Introduction, traduction, commentaire.* Paris: Cerf, 1974.
Carroll, R. P. "Psalm lxxviii: Vestiges of a Tribal Polemic." *VT* 21 (1971) 133–50.
Carson, Rachel L. *The Sea around Us.* Signet Science Library. Rev. ed. New York: The New American Library, 1961.
Chappell, John E. Jr. "Lake Levels and Astronomical Causes of Climatic Change." In *Desertic Terminal Lakes*: Proceedings from the International Conference on Desertic Terminal Lakes held at Weber State College, Ogden, Utah 84408, May 2–5, 1977, edited by Deon C. Greer, 27–35. Logan, UT: Utah State University, 1977.
Cheyne, T. K. *The Book of Psalms or the Praises of Israel: A New Translation, with Commentary.* New York: Whittaker, 1888.
Childs, Brevard S. *The Book of Exodus: A Critical, Theological Commentary.* Old Testament Library. Philadelphia: Westminster, 1974.
Chinitz, Jacob. "Psalm 147." *JBQ* 27 (1999) 115–18.
Church, C., and D. Burgess, C. Doswell, and R. Davies-Jones, eds. *The Tornado: Its Structure, Dynamics, Prediction, and Hazards.* Geophysical Monograph 79. Washington, DC: American Geophysical Union, 1990.
Clifford, Richard J. "The Hebrew Scriptures and the Theology of Creation." *StTh* 46 (1985) 507–23.
———. "In Zion and David a New Beginning: An Interpretation of Psalm 78." In *Traditions in Transformation: Turning Points in Biblical Faith*, F. M. Cross Festschrift, edited by Baruch Halpern and Jon D. Levenson, 121–41. Winona Lake, IN: Eisenbrauns, 1981.
———. "Psalm 89: A Lament over the Davidic Ruler's Continued Failure." *HTR* 73 (1980) 35–47.
Clines, D. J. A., ed. *Dictionary of Classical Hebrew*, vol. 1. Sheffield, UK: Sheffield Academic Press, 1993.
———, ed. *Dictionary of Classical Hebrew*, vol. 2. Sheffield, UK: Sheffield Academic Press, 1995.
———, ed. *Dictionary of Classical Hebrew*, vol. 3. Sheffield, UK: Sheffield Academic Press, 1996.
———, ed. *Dictionary of Classical Hebrew*, vol. 4. Sheffield, UK: Sheffield Academic Press, 1998.
———. "Krt 111–14 (I iii 7–10): Gatherers of Wood and Drawers of Water." *UF* 8 (1976) 23–26.
Coats, George W. *Rebellion in the Wilderness: The Murmuring Motif in the Wilderness Traditions of the Old Testament.* Nashville: Abingdon, 1968.
Cohen, Chaim. "The Basic Meaning of the Term עֲרָפֶל 'Darkness.'" *HS* 36 (1995) 7–12.
Cohn, Herbert. "Hinds in Psalm 29." *JBQ* 24 (1996) 258–59.
Collon, Dominique. "'The Smiting God' A Study of a Bronze in the Pomerance Collection in New York." *Levant* 4 (1972) 111–34.
Cook, Stephen L. "Apocalypticism and the Psalter." *ZAW* 104 (1992) 82–99.

Cooper, Alan. "Divine Names and Epithets in the Ugaritic Texts." In *Ras Shamra Parallels: The Texts from Ugarit and the Hebrew Bible*, vol. III, AnOr 51, edited by Stan Rummel, 333–469. Rome: Pontificium Insitutum Biblicum, 1981.

Coppens, J. "Les parallèles du Psautier avec les textes de Ras-Shamra-Ougarit." *Le Muséon* 59 (1946) 113–42.

Cornelius, Izak. *The Iconography of the Canaanite Gods Reshef and Baʻal: Late Bronze and Iron Age I Periods (c 1500–1000 BCE)*. OBO 140. Göttingen: Vandenhoeck & Ruprecht, 1994.

Cotton, William R. *Storms*. Geophysical Science Series 1. Fort Collins, CO: ASTeR, 1990.

Craigie, P. C. "The Comparison of Hebrew Poetry: Psalm 104 in the Light of Egyptian and Ugaritic Poetry." *Semitics* 4 (1974) 10–21.

———. "Helel, Athtar and Phaethon (Jes 14 12–15)." *ZAW* 85 (1973) 223–25.

———. *Psalms 1–50*. WBC 19. Waco, TX: Word, 1983.

Cressey, George B. *Crossroads: Land and Life in Southwest Asia*. Chicago: Lippincott, 1960.

Cross, Frank Moore, Jr. *Canaanite Myth and Hebrew Epic: Essays in the History of the Religion of Israel*. Cambridge: Harvard University Press, 1973.

———. "Yahweh and the God of the Patriarchs." *HTR* 55 (1962) 225–60.

Cross, Frank Moore, Jr., and David Noel Freedman, "A Royal Song of Thanksgiving: II Samuel 22= Psalm 18." *JBL* 72 (1953) 15–34.

Crown, Alan D. "Climatic Change, Ecology and Migration." *AJBA* 1 (1971) 3–22.

———. "Toward a Reconstruction of the Climate of Palestine 8000 B.C.–0 B.C." *JNES* 31 (1972) 312–30.

Cullen, H. M., P. B. deMenocal, S. Hemming, G. Hemming, F. H. Brown, T. Guilderson, and F. Sirocko. "Climate Change and the Collapse of the Akkadian Empire: Evidence from the Deep Sea." *Geology* 28 (2000) 379–82.

Curtis, A. H. W. "The 'Subjugation of the Waters' Motif in the Psalms; Imagery or Polemic?" *JSS* 23 (1978) 245–56.

Dahood, Mitchell. "Eblaite *i-du* and Hebrew *ʾēd*, 'Rain Cloud.'" *CBQ* 43 (1981) 534–38.

———. "Hebrew-Ugaritic Lexicography II." *Biblica* 45 (1964) 393–412.

———. "A Note on *ṭôb* 'Rain.'" *Biblica* 54 (1973) 404.

———. *Psalms I, 1–50: A New Translation with Commentary and Notes*. AB 16. Garden City, NY: Doubleday, 1969.

———. *Psalms II, 51–100: A New Translation with Commentary and Notes*. AB 17. Garden City, NY: Doubleday, 1968.

———. *Psalms III, 101–150: Introduction, Translation, and Notes*. AB 17A. Garden City, NY: Doubleday, 1970.

———. "Third Masculine Singular with Preformative *t-* in Northwest Semitic." *Orientalia* 48 (1979) 197–206.

Dalfes, H. Nüzhet, George Kukla, and Harvey Weiss, eds. *Third Millennium BC Climate Change and Old World Collapse*. NATO ASI Series 149. Berlin: Springer-Verlag, 1997.

Dalman, Gustav. *Arbeit und Sitte in Palästina, Band 1 Jahreslauf und Tageslauf*. Schriften des Deutschen Palästina-Instituts 3. Gütersloh: Bertelsmann, 1928.

Danin, Avinoam. "Palaeoclimates in Israel: Evidence from Weathering Patterns of Stones in and Near Archaeological Sites." *BASOR* 259 (1985) 33–43.

———. "Plants as Biblical Metaphors." *BAR* 5.3 (May/June 1979) 20.

Davidson, Robert. *The Vitality of Worship: A Commentary on the Book of Psalms*. Grand Rapids: Eerdmans, 1998.

Day, John. "The Canaanite Inheritance of the Israelite Monarchy." In *King and Messiah in Israel and the Ancient Near East: Proceedings of the Oxford Old Testament Seminar*, JSOTS 270, edited by John Day, 72–90. Sheffield, UK: Sheffield Academic Press, 1998.

———. *God's Conflict with the Dragon and the Sea: Echoes of a Canaanite Myth in the Old Testament*. University of Cambridge Oriental Publications 35. Cambridge: Cambridge University Press, 1985.

———, ed. *King and Messiah in Israel and the Ancient Near East: Proceedings of the Oxford Old Testament Seminar*. JSOTS 270. Sheffield, UK: Sheffield Academic Press, 1998.

Delcor, M. "Les attaches litteraires, l'origine et la signification de l'expression biblique 'prendre a temoin le ceil et la terre.'" *VT* 16 (1966) 8–25.

DeYoung, Donald B. *Weather and the Bible: 100 Questions and Answers*. Grand Rapids: Baker, 1992.

Dietrich, M., and O. Loretz. "Von hebräisch '*m/lpny* (Ps 72:5) zu ugaritisch '*m* 'vor.'" In *Ascribe to the Lord: Biblical and Other Studies in Memory of Peter C. Craigie*, JSOTS 67, edited by Lyle Eslinger and Glen Taylor, 109–16. Sheffield, UK: JSOT, 1988.

Dion, Paul E. "YHWH as Storm-god and Sun-god: The Double Legacy of Egypt and Canaan as Reflected in Psalm 104." *ZAW* 103 (1991) 43–71.

Drews, Robert. *The End of the Bronze Age: Changes in Warfare and the Catastrophe ca. 1200 B.C.* Princeton: Princeton University Press, 1993.

Driel, G. van. "Weather: Between the Natural and Unnatural in First Millennium Cuneiform Inscriptions." In *Natural Phenomena: Their Meaning, Depiction and Description in the Ancient Near East*. Proceedings of the Collquium, Amsterdam, 6–8 July 1989, edited by D. J. W. Meijer, 39–52. Amsterdam: Royal Netherlands Academy of Arts and Sciences, 1992.

Driver, G. R. "Ezekiel's Inaugural Vision." *VT* 1 (1951) 60–62.

———. "Psalm CX: Its Form Meaning and Purpose." In *Studies in the Bible Presented to Professor M. H. Segal by his Colleagues and Students*, Publications of the Israel Society for Biblical Research 17, edited by J. M. Grintz and J. Liver, 17*–31*. Jerusalem: Kiryat Sepher, 1964.

Dumortier, Jean-Bernard. "Un rituel d'intronisation: le ps. LXXXIX 2–38." *VT* 22 (1972) 176–96.

Eichholz, Georg, ed. *Herr, tue meine Lippen auf: Eine Predigthilfe*, vol. 5. 2nd ed. Wuppertal-Barmen: Müller, 1964.

Eisenman, Robert. "Eschatological 'Rain' Imagery in the War Scroll from Qumran and in the Letter of James." *JNES* 49 (1990) 173–84.

Emerton, J. A. "The Etymology of *hištaḥᵃwāh*." *Oudtestamentische Studiën* 20 (197) 41–55.

———. "The 'Mountain of God' in Psalm 68:16." In *History and Traditions of Early Israel: Studies Presented to Eduard Nielsen May 8th 1993*, SVT 50, edited by André Lemaire and Benedikt Otzen, 24–37. Leiden: Brill, 1993.

———. "The Text of Psalm LXVII 11." *VT* 44 (1994) 183–94.

Eslinger, Lyle, and Glen Taylor, eds. *Ascribe to the Lord: Biblical and Other Studies in Memory of Peter C. Craigie*. JSOTS 67. Sheffield, UK: JSOT, 1988.

Études de critique et d'histoire religieuses, Bibliothèque de la faculté catholique de théologie de Lyon 2. Léon Vaganay Festschrift. Lyon: Facultés Cathliques, 1948.
Ewald, G. Heinrich A. *Commentary on the Psalms. Commentary on the Poetical Books of the Old Testament, Division I.* Volume 1. London: Williams and Norgate, 1880.
Fabry, H. J. "רוח rwḥ" *TWAT* 7 (1993) 382–425.
Feigin, Samuel I. "The Heavenly Sieve." *JNES* 9 (1950) 40–43.
Fensham, F. Charles. "Thunder-Stones in Ugaritic." *JNES* 18 (1959) 273–74.
Fenton, T. L. "Comparative Evidence in Textual Study: M. Dahood on 2 Sam. I 21 and CTA 19 (1 Aqht), I, 44–45." *VT* 29 (1979) 162–70.
Fitzgerald, Aloysius. "A Note on Psalm 29." *BASOR* 215 (1974) 61–63.
———. *The Lord of the East Wind*. CBQMS 34. Washington, DC: The Catholic Biblical Association of America, 2002.
Fleming, James Rodger. *Meteorology in America, 1800–1870*. Baltimore: Johns Hopkins University Press, 1990.
Floyd, Michael H. "Psalm LXXXIX: A Prophetic Complaint about the Fulfillment of an Oracle." *VT* 42 (1992) 442–57.
Fokkelman, J. P. "The Structure of Psalm lxvii." In *In Quest of the Past: Studies on Israelite Religion, Literature and Prophetism, Papers Read at the Joint British-Dutch Old Testament Conference, Held at Elspeet, 1988*, OTS 26, edited by A. S. van der Woude, 72–83. Leiden: Brill, 1990.
Foster, Benjamin R. *Before the Muses: An Anthology of Akkadian Literature.* 2 vols. Bethesda, MD: CDL, 1993.
Fox, Everett. *The Five Books of Moses: A New Translation with Introductions, Commentary and Notes*. The Schocken Bible 1. New York: Schocken, 1995.
Freedman, David Noel, and C. Franke Hyland. "Psalm 29: A Structural Analysis." *HTR* 66 (1973) 237–56.
Fretheim, Terence E. "Nature's Praise of God in the Psalms." *Ex Auditu* 3 (1988) 16–30.
Frick, Frank S. "Palestine, Climate of." *ABD* 5:119–26.
———. "Rain." *ABD* 5:612.
Friedman, Irving. "A River Went Out of Eden." *Parabola* 20 (1995) 66–72.
Fulco, W. J. *The Canaanite God Rešep*. AOS 8. New Haven: American Oriental Society, 1976.
Futato, Mark David. "A Meteorological Analysis of Psalms 104, 65, and 29." PhD diss., The Catholic University of America. Ann Arbor, MI: UMI Dissertation Services, 1984.
Gammie, John G. "A New Setting for Psalm 110." *ATR* 51 (1969) 4–17.
Geer, Ira W., ed. *Glossary of Weather and Climate with Related Oceanic and Hydrologic Terms*. Boston: American Meteorological Society, 1996.
Gibson, J. C. L. *Canaanite Myths and Legends*. 2nd ed. Edinburgh: T. & T. Clark, 1977.
———. *Davidson's Introductory Hebrew Grammar: Syntax*. 4th ed. Edinburgh: T. & T. Clark, 1994.
Gilead, M. and N. Rosenan. "Ten Years of Dew Observation in Israel." *IEJ* 4 (1953) 120–23.
Gillingham, Susan E. "The Exodus Tradition and Israelite Psalmody." *SJT* 52 (1999) 19–46.
———. "The Messiah in the Psalms: A Question of Reception History and the Psalter." In *King and Messiah in Israel and the Ancient Near East: Proceedings of the Oxford*

Old Testament Seminar, JSOTS 270, edited by John Day, 209-37. Sheffield, UK: Sheffield Academic Press, 1998.

Gleick, James. *Chaos: Making a New Science.* New York: Penguin, 1987.

Gleßmer, Uwe. "Das Textwachstum von Ps 89 und ein Qumranfragment." *BN* 65 (1992) 55-73.

Golde, R. H., ed. *Lightning, Volume 1: Physics of Lightning.* London: Academic, 1977.

Goodwin, D. W. "A Rare Spelling, or a Rare Root, in Ps. LXVIII 10?" *VT* 14 (1964) 490-91.

Gordon, D. H. "Fire and Sword: The Technique of Destruction." *Antiquity* 27 (1953) 149-52.

Gordon, Robert P. "On BH *ṭôb* 'Rain.'" *Biblica* 57 (1976) 111.

Gosse, Bernard. "Le psaume 83, Isaïe 62,6-7 et la tradition des Oracles contre les Nations des livres d'Isaïe et d'Ezéchiel." *BN* 70 (1993) 9-12.

―――. "Le psaume 147. Le retour des exilés à Jérusalem et l'universalisme de l'action de Yhwh." *ETR* 72 (1997) 597-600.

Goulder, Michael D. *The Prayers of David (Psalms 51-72): Studies in the Psalter, II.* JSOTS 102. Sheffield, UK: JSOT, 1990.

―――. *The Psalms of Asaph and the Pentateuch: Studies in the Psalter, III.* JSOTS 233. Sheffield, UK: Sheffield Academic Press, 1996.

―――. *The Psalms of the Return (Book V, Psalms 107-150): Studies in the Psalter IV.* JSOTS 258. Sheffield, UK: Sheffield Academic Press, 1998.

―――. *The Psalms of the Sons of Korah.* JSOTS 20. Sheffield, UK: JSOT, 1982.

Gray, George Buchanan. *A Critical and Exegetical Commentary on Numbers*, ICC. New York: Scribner's Sons, 1903.

Gray, J. "A Cantata of the Autumn Festival: Psalm LXVIII." *JSS* 22 (1977) 2-26.

Grazulis, Thomas P. *Significant Tornadoes 1680-1991: A Chronology and Analysis of Events.* St. Johnsbury, VT: The Tornado Project, 1993.

Green, Alberto R. W. *The Storm-God in the Ancient Near East.* Biblical and Judaic Studies 8. Winona Lake, IN: Eisenbrauns, 2003.

Greenfield, Jonas C. "Some Glosses on the Keret Epic." *EI* 9, Albright Volume (1969) 60-65.

Greenstein, Edward L. "Mixing Memory and Design: Reading Psalm 78." *Prooftexts* 10 (1990) 197-218.

―――. "Yhwh's Lightning in Psalm 29:7." *Maarav* 8 (1992) 49-57.

Greer, Deon C., ed. *Desertic Terminal Lakes*: Proceedings from the International Conference on Desertic Terminal Lakes held at Weber State College, Ogden, Utah 84408, May 2-5, 1977. Logan, UT: Utah State University, 1977.

Grintz, J. M., and J. Liver, eds. *Studies in the Bible Presented to Professor M. H. Segal by His Colleagues and Students.* Publications of the Israel Society for Biblical Research 17. Jerusalem: Kiryat Sepher, 1964.

Gruber, Mayer I. "Ten Dance-Derived Expressions in the Hebrew Bible." *Biblica* 62 (1981) 328-46.

Habel, Norman C. "'He Who Stretches Out the Heavens.'" *CBQ* 34 (1972) 417-30.

Hackett, John, ed. *Warfare in the Ancient World.* New York: Facts on File, 1989.

Haglund, Erik. *Historical Motifs in the Psalms.* Coniectanea Biblica: Old Testament Series 23. Uppsala: CWK Gleerup, 1984.

Hall, David D., and P. C. F. Smith, eds. *Seventeenth-Century New England: A Conference held by The Colonial Society of Massachusetts June 18 and 19, 1982*. Boston: The Colonial Society of Massachusetts, 1984.

———. "A World of Wonders: The Mentality of the Supernatural in Seventeenth-Century New England." In *Seventeenth-Century New England: A Conference held by The Colonial Society of Massachusetts June 18 and 19, 1982*, edited by D. D. Hall and P. C. F. Smith, 239–74. Boston: The Colonial Society of Massachusetts, 1984.

Hallo, William W. ed. *The Context of Scripture: Volume I, Canonical Compositions from the Biblical World*. Leiden: Brill, 1997.

Halpern, Baruch, and Jon D. Levenson, eds. *Traditions in Transformation: Turning Points in Biblical Faith*. F. M. Cross Festschrift. Winona Lake, IN: Eisenbrauns, 1981.

Hämeen-Anttila, Jaakko. "Arabic *muzn-* and the Common Semitic Root *znm* 'Rain.'" *Acta Orientalia* 48 (1987) 15–17.

Handy, Lowell K., ed. *Psalm 29 through Time and Tradition*. Princeton Theological Monograph Series. Eugene, OR: Wipf and Stock, 2009.

Haran, Menahem. *Temples and Temple-Service in Ancient Israel: An Inquiry into the Character of Cult Phenomena and the Historical Setting of the Priestly School*. Oxford: Clarendon, 1978.

Harding, A. F., ed. *Climate Change in Later Prehistory*. Edinburgh: Edinburgh University Press, 1982.

Harel, M. "Reduced Aridity in Eastern Lower Galilee." *IEJ* 7 (1957) 256–61.

Har-El, Manashe. *Landscape, Nature and Man in the Bible: Sites and Events in the Old Testament*. Jerusalem: Carta, 2003.

Healey, John F. "Ancient Agriculture and the Old Testament." *OTS* 23 (1984) 108–19.

Heim, Knut M. "The (God-)Forsaken King of Psalm 89: A Historical and Intertextual Enquiry." In *King and Messiah in Israel and the Ancient Near East: Proceedings of the Oxford Old Testament Seminar*, JSOTS 270, edited by John Day, 296–322. Sheffield, UK: Sheffield Academic Press, 1998.

Heiser, Michael S. "The Mythological Provenance of Isaiah 14:12–15: A Reconsideration of the Ugaritic Material." *VT* 51 (2001) 354–69.

Henry, Donald O., Priscilla F. Turnbull, Aline Emery-Barbier, and Arlette Leroi-Gourhan. "Archaeological and Faunal Evidence from Natufian and Timnian Sites in Southern Jordan with Notes on Pollen Evidence." *BASOR* 257 (1985) 45–64.

Hiebert, Theodore. *The Yahwist's Landscape: Nature and Religion in Early Israel*. Oxford: Oxford University Press, 1996.

Hill, R. D. "Thunder." In *Lightning, Volume 1: Physics of Lightning*, edited by R. H. Golde, 385–408. London: Academic, 1977.

Hillers, Delbert R. "Amos 7,4 and Ancient Parallels." *CBQ* 26 (1964) 221–25.

———. *Micah*. Hermeneia. Philadelphia: Fortress, 1984.

Holladay, William L. *The Psalms through Three Thousand Years: Prayerbook of a Cloud of Witnesses*. Minneapolis: Fortress, 1993.

Hollyday, Joyce. "Fire, Wind, and Water: A Middle East Reflection." *Sojourners* 26.6 (1997) 28–32.

Horowitz, A. "Climatic and Vegetational Developments in Northeastern Israel during Upper Pleistocene-Holocene Times." *Pollen et Spores* 13 (1971) 255–78.

Hort, Greta. "The Death of Qorah." *Australian Biblical Review* 7 (1959) 2–26.

Houtman, Cornelius. *Der Himmel im Alten Testament: Israels Weltbild und Weltanschauung*, OTS 30. Leiden: Brill, 1993.
Houtsma, M. Th. "Textkritisches." *ZAW* 27 (1907) 57–59.
Hunt, Joseph I. "Translating Psalm 29: Towards a Commentary on the Psalms of the 1979 Book of Common Prayer." *ATR* 67 (1985) 219–27.
Hunter, J. H. "The Literary Composition of Theophany Passages in the Hebrew Psalms." *JNSL* 15 (1989) 97–107.
Ishida, Tomoo. *The Royal Dynasties in Ancient Israel: A Study on the Formation and Development of Royal-Dynastic Ideology*. BZAW 142. Berlin: de Gruyter, 1977.
Issar, Arie S., and Neville Brown, eds. *Water, Environment and Society in Times of Climate Change: Contributions from an International Workshop within the Framework of International Hydrological Program (IHP) UNESCO, held at Ben-Gurion University Sede Boker, Israel from 7–12 July 1996*. Dordrecht: Kluwer Academic, 1998.
Issar, A., H. Tsoar, and D. Levin. "Climatic Changes in Israel during Historical Times and Their Impact on Hydrological, Pedological and Socio-economic Systems." In *Paleoclimatology and Paleometeorology: Modern and Past Patterns of Global Atmospheric Transport*, NATO Advanced Science Institutes Series, Series C: Mathematical and Physical Sciences 282. Proceedings of the NATO Advanced Research Workshop on Paleoclimatology and Paleometeorology, Oracle, AZ, November 17–19, 1987, edited by Leinen, Margaret and Michael Sarnthein, 525–41. Dordrecht: Kluwer Academic, 1987.
Iwry, Samuel. "Notes on Psalm 68." *JBL* 71 (1952) 161–65.
Jaffe, S. "Climate of Israel." In *The Zoogeography of Israel*, edited by Y. Yom-Tov and E. Tchernov, 79–94. Dordrecht: Junk, 1988.
Janecko, Benedict. "Ecology, Nature, Psalms." In *The Psalms and Other Studies on the Old Testament Presented to Joseph I. Hunt*, edited by Jack C. Knight and Lawrence A. Sinclair, 96–108. Cincinnati: Forward Movement, 1990.
Janković, Vladimir. *Reading the Skies: A Cultural History of English Weather, 1650–1820*. Chicago: University of Chicago Press, 2000.
Jaynes, Julian. *The Origin of Consciousness in the Breakdown of the Bicameral Mind*. Boston: Houghton Mifflin, 1976.
Jefferson, Helen Genevieve. "Is Psalm 110 Canaanite?" *JBL* 73 (1954) 152–56.
Jeremias, Jörg. *Das Königtum Gottes in den Psalmen: Israels Begegnung mit dem kanaanäischen Mythos in den Jahwe-König-Psalmen*. Forschung zur Religion und Literatur des Alten und Neuen Testaments 141. Göttingen: Vandenhoeck & Ruprecht, 1987.

———. *Theophanie: Die Geschichte einer alttestamentlichen Gattung*. Wissenschaftliche Monographien zum Alten und Neuen Testament 10. 2nd ed. Neukirchen-Vluyn: Neukirchener Verlag, 1977.
Johnson, Aubrey R. *Sacral Kingship in Ancient Israel*. Cardiff: University of Wales Press, 1955.
Johnson, Elliott E. "Hermeneutical Principles and the Interpretation of Psalm 110." *Bibliotheca Sacra* 149 (1992) 428–37.
Junger, Sebastian. *The Perfect Storm: A True Story of Men against the Sea*. New York: Harper Perennial, 1997.
Keel, Othmar. "Sturmgott—Sonnengott—Einziger: Ein neuer Versuch, die Entstehung des judäischen Monotheismus historisch zu verstehen." *Bibel und Kirche* 49 (1994) 82–92.

———. *The Symbolism of the Biblical World: Ancient Near Eastern Iconography and the Book of Psalms.* New York: Seabury, 1978.

———. *Vögel als Boten: Studien zu Ps 68, 12–14, Gen 8, 6–12, Koh 10,20 und dem Aussenden von Botenvögeln in Ägypten.* OBO 14. Freiburg: Universitätsverlag and Göttingen: Vandenhoeck & Ruprecht, 1977.

Kelly, Sidney. "Psalm 46: A Study in Imagery." *JBL* 89 (1970) 305–12.

Kern-Ulmer, Brigitte (Rivka). "Consistency and Change in Rabbinic Literature as Reflected in the Terms *Rain* and *Dew*." *JSJ* 26 (1995) 55–75.

Kessler, Edwin, ed. *The Thunderstorm in Human Affairs.* Thunderstorms: A Social, Scientific, and Technological Documentary, Volume 1. 2nd ed. Norman, OK: University of Oklahoma Press, 1983.

Kessler, Edwin, and Gilbert F. White. "Thunderstorms in a Social Context." In *The Thunderstorm in Human Affairs.* Thunderstorms: A Social, Scientific, and Technical Documentary Vol. 1, 2nd ed., edited by E. Kessler, 3–18. Norman, OK: University of Oklahoma Press, 1983.

Kilian, Rudolf. "Der 'Tau' in Ps 110,3—ein Mißverständnis?" *ZAW* 102 (1990) 417–19.

Kingsbury, Steward A., Mildred E. Kingsbury, and Wolfgang Mieder, eds. *Weather Wisdom: Proverbs, Superstitions, and Signs.* New York: Lang, 1996.

Kissane, Edward J. *The Book of Psalms: Translated from a Critically Revised Hebrew Text with a Commentary.* Volume 1, Psalms 1–72. Dublin: Browne and Noland, 1953.

———. "The Interpretation of Psalm 110." *The Irish Theological Quarterly* 21 (1954) 103–14.

———. "'Who Maketh Lightnings for the Rain.'" *JTS* 3 (1952) 214–16.

Klingbeil, Martin. *Yahweh Fighting from Heaven: God as Warrior and as God of Heaven in the Hebrew Psalter and Ancient Near Eastern Iconography.* OBO 169. Göttingen: Vandenhoeck & Ruprecht, 1999.

Kloos, Carola. *Yhwh's Combat with the Sea: A Canaanite Tradition in the Religion of Ancient Israel.* Leiden: Brill, 1986.

Knight, Jack C., and Lawrence A. Sinclair, eds. *The Psalms and Other Studies on the Old Testament Presented to Joseph I. Hunt.* Cincinnati: Forward Movement, 1990.

Koch, Klaus. "Šaddaj: Aum Verhältnis zwischen israelitischer Monolatrie und nordwestsemitischen Polytheismus." *VT* 26 (1976) 299–332.

Koehler, Ludwig. "Hebräische Etymologien." *JBL* 59 (1940) 35–40.

———. Walter Baumgartner and Johann Jakob Stamm. *The Hebrew and Aramaic Lexicon of the Old Testament.* 5 vols. Leiden: Brill, 1994, 1995, 1996, 1999, and 2000.

Koopmans, William T. "Psalm 78, Canto D—A Response." *UF* 20 (1988) 121–23.

Korpel, Jarjo Christina Annette. *A Rift in the Clouds: Ugaritic and Hebrew Descriptions of the Divine.* UBL 8. Münster: UGARIT-Verlag, 1990.

Kramer, Samuel Noah. *Sumerian Mythology: A Study of Spiritual and Literary Achievement in the Third Millennium B.C.* Harper Torchbooks: The Academic Library. New York: Harper, 1961.

Kraus, Hans-Joachim. *Psalms 1–59: A Commentary.* Minneapolis: Augsburg, 1988.

Kreuzer, Siegfried. "Zur Bedeutung und Etymologie von *hištaḥªwāh /yštḥwy*." *VT* 35 (1985) 39–60

———. *Psalms 60–150: A Commentary.* Minneapolis: Augsburg, 1989.

Kselman, John S. "Psalm 72: Some Observations on Structure." *BASOR* 220 (1975) 77–81.

———. "Psalm 77 and the Book of Exodus." *JANES* 15 (1983) 51–58.
Kugel, James L. *The Idea of Biblical Poetry: Parallelism and Its History*. New Haven: Yale University Press, 1981.
Kuntz, J. Kenneth. "Psalm 18: A Rhetorical-Critical Analysis." *JSOT* 26 (1983) 3–31.
Lamb, H. H. "Reconstruction of the Course of Postglacial Climate over the World." In *Climate Change in Later Prehistory*, edited by A. F. Harding, 11–32. Edinburgh: Edinburgh University Press, 1982.
Larson, Erik. *Isaac's Storm: A Man, a Time, and the Deadliest Hurricane in History*. New York: Vintage, 1999.
Laskin, David. *Braving the Elements: The Stormy History of American Weather*. New York: Doubleday, 1996.
Lee, Archie C. C. "The Context and Function of the Plagues Tradition in Psalm 78." *JSOT* 48 (1990) 83–89.
Leinen, Margaret, and Michael Sarnthein, eds. *Paleoclimatology and Paleometeorology: Modern and Past Patterns of Global Atmospheric Transport*. NATO Advanced Science Institutes Series, Series C: Mathematical and Physical Sciences 282. Proceedings of the NATO Advanced Research Workshop on Paleoclimatology and Paleometeorology, Oracle, AZ, November 17–19, 1987. Dordrecht: Kluwer Academic, 1987.
Lemaire, André, and Benedikt Otzen, eds. *History and Traditions of Early Israel*. Studies Presented to Eduard Nielsen May 8th 1993. SVT 50. Leiden: Brill, 1993.
LePeau, John Philip. "Psalm 68: An Exegetical and Theological Study." Ph.D. diss., University of Iowa, 1981. Ann Arbor, MI: University Microfilms, 1985.
Levine, Baruch A. *Numbers 1–20: A New Translation with Introduction and Commentary*. AB 4A. New York: Doubleday, 1993.
Lind, Millard C. *Yahweh is a Warrior: The Theology of Warfare in Ancient Israel*. Scottsdale, PA: Herald, 1980.
Lipiński, Édouard. "La colombe du Ps. LXVIII 14." *VT* 23 (1973) 365–68.
———. "Juges 5,4–5 et Psaume 68,8–11." *Biblica* 48 (1967) 185–206.
———. *Le poème royal du psaume LXXXIX 1–5.20–38*. CRB 6. Paris: Gabalda et Cie, 1967.
———. "Shemesh, שמש." In *Dictionary of Deities and Demons in the Bible*, 2nd ed., edited by Karel van der Toorn, Bob Becking, and Pieter W. van der Horst, 764–68. Leiden: Brill, 1999.
Loretz, Oswald. "KTU 1.101.1–3a und 1.2 IV 10 als Parallelen zu Ps 29,10." *ZAW* 99 (1987) 415–21.
———. *Psalm 29: Kanaanäische El- und Baaltraditionen in jüdischer Sicht*, UBL 2. Altenberge: CIS-Verlag, 1984.
———. "Ugaritisch *ṭbn* und hebräisch *ṭwb* 'Regen': Regenrituale beim Neujahrfest in Kanaan und Israel (Ps 85; 126)." *UF* 21 (1989) 247–58.
———. *Ugarit-Texte und Thronbesteigungspsalmen: Die Metamorphose des Regenspenders Baal-Jahwe (Ps 24, 7–10; 29; 47; 93; 95–100 sowie Ps 77, 17–20; 114)*. UBL 7. Munster: UGARIT-Verlag, 1988.
Ludlum, David M. *National Audubon Society Field Guide to American Weather*. New York: Knopf, 1995.
Lugt, Hans. "Wirbelstürme im Alten Testament." *BZ* 19 (1975) 195–204.
Luyster, Robert. "Wind and Water: Cosmogonic Symbolism in the Old Testament." *ZAW* 93 (1981) 1–10.

Macholz, Christian. "Psalm 29 und 1 Kön 19: Jahwes und Baals Theophanie." In *Werden und Wirken des Alten Testaments: Festschrift für Claus Westermann zum 70. Geburtstag*, edited by Rainer Albertz et al., 325–33. Göttingen: Vandenhoeck & Ruprecht, 1980.

Malamat, A. "The Amorite Background of Psalm 29." *ZAW* 100 Supplement (1988) 156–60.

Malchow, Bruce. "Nature from God's Perspective: Job 38–39." *Dialog* 21 (1982) 130–33.

Mané, K. U. "A Severe Rainstorm in the Coastal Plain of Israel." *IEJ* 6 (1956) 115–19.

Mann, Thomas W. "The Pillar of Cloud in the Reed Sea Narrative." *JBL* 90 (1971) 15–30.

Margulis, B. "The Canaanite Origin of Psalm 29 Reconsidered." *Biblica* 51 (1970) 332–48.

Mason, B. J. *Clouds, Rain and Rainmaking*. Cambridge: Cambridge University Press, 1962.

May, Herbert G., ed. *Oxford Bible Atlas*. 3rd ed. New York: Oxford University Press, 1984.

McCown, Chester C. "Climate and Religion in Palestine." *JR* 7 (1927) 520–39.

McKay, J. W. "Helel and the Dawn-Goddess: A Re-examination of the Myth in Isaiah XIV 12–15." *VT* 20 (1970) 451–64.

van der Meer, Willem. "Psalm 77,17–19: Hymnisches Fragment oder Aktualizierung?" *Ephemerides Theologicae Lovanienses* 70 (1994) 105–11.

Meijer, D. J. W., ed. *Natural Phenomena: Their Meaning, Depiction and Description in the Ancient Near East*. Proceedings of the Collquium, Amsterdam, 6–8 July 1989. Amsterdam: Royal Netherlands Academy of Arts and Sciences, 1992.

Melliak, M., J. E. Porada, and T. Özgüç, eds. *Aspects of Art and Iconography: Anatolia and its Neighbors: Studies in Honor of Nimet Özgüç*. Ankara: Türk Tarih Kurumu Basimevi, 1993.

deMenocal, Peter B. "Cultural Responses to Climate Change during the Late Holocene." *Science* 292 (2001) 667–73.

Mettinger, Tryggve N. D. *King and Messiah: The Civil and Sacral Legitimation of the Israelite Kings*. CB Old Testament Series 8. Lund: CWK Gleerup, 1976.

Milgrom, Jacob. *Numbers*. The JPS Torah Commentary. Philadelphia: The Jewish Publication Society, 1990.

Miller, Patrick D., Jr. *The Divine Warrior in Early Israel*. HSM 5. Cambridge: Harvard University Press, 1975.

———. "Fire in the Mythology of Canaan and Israel." *CBQ* 27 (1965) 256–61.

———. "Two Critical Notes on Psalm 68 and Deuteronomy 33." *HTR* 57 (1964) 240–43.

deMoor, Johannes C. *The Seasonal Pattern in the Ugaritic Myth of Ba'lu According to the Version of Ilimilku*. AOAT 16. Neukirchen-Vluyn: Neukirchener Verlag, 1971.

deMoor, Johannes C., and Herman F. de Vries. "Hebrew *hēdād* 'Thunder-storm.'" *UF* 20 (1988) 173–77.

Moore, C. B., and B. Vonnegut. "The Thundercloud." In *Lightning, Volume 1: Physics of Lightning*, edited by R. H. Golde, 51–98. London: Academic Press, 1977.

Mosca, Paul G. "Once Again the Heavenly Witness of Ps 89:38." *JBL* 105 (1986) 27–37.

Moscati, Sabatino. "The Wind in Biblical and Phoenician Cosmogony." *JBL* 66 (1947) 305–10.

Mowinckel, Sigmund. *Der Achtundsechzigste Psalm*. Avhandlinger utgitt av Det Norske Videnskaps-Akademi I Oslo, II. Hist.-Filos. Klasse. No. 1. Oslo: I Kommisjon Hos Jacob Dybwad, 1953.

———. "Drive and/or Ride in O.T." *VT* 12 (1962) 278–99.

———. *Psalmenstudien*, Books I–VI. Amsterdam: Schippers, 1961.

———. *The Psalms in Israel's Worship*. 2 vols. Oxford: Blackwell, 1962.

Mullen, E. Theodore Jr. "The Divine Witness and the Davidic Royal Grant: Ps 89:37–38." *JBL* 102 (1983) 207–18.

Nash, Kathleen Sarah. "The Palestinian Agricultural Year and the Book of Joel." Ph.D. diss., Catholic University of America. Ann Arbor, MI: UMI, 1989.

Nasuti, Harry P. *Tradition History and the Psalms of Asaph*. SBLDS 88. Atlanta: Scholars, 1988.

Neev, David, and John K. Hall. "Climatic Fluctions during the Holocene as Reflected by Dead Sea Levels." In *Desertic Terminal Lakes*: Proceedings from the International Conference on Desertic Terminal Lakes held at Weber State College, Ogden, Utah 84408, May 2–5, 1977, edited by Deon C. Greer, 53–60. Logan, UT: Utah State University, 1977.

Nestle, E. "Miscellen." *ZAW* 25 (1905) 360–67.

Neumann, J. "Evaporation from the Red Sea." *IEJ* 2 (1952) 153–62.

———. "On the Incidence of Dry and Wet Years." *IEJ* 6 (1956) 58–63.

Neumann, J., and S. Parpola. "Climatic Change and the Eleventh-Tenth-Century Eclipse of Assyria and Babylonia." *JNES* 46 (1987) 161–82.

Niemi, Tina M., Zvi Ben-Avraham, and Joel R. Gat, eds. *The Dead Sea: The Lake and Its Setting*. Oxford Monographs on Geology and Geophysics 36. Oxford: Oxford University Press, 1997.

Nir, D. "Whirlwinds in Israel in the Winters 1954/55 and 1955/56." *IEJ* 7 (1957) 109–17.

Noth, Martin. *Exodus: A Commentary*. OTL. Philadelphia: Westminster, 1962.

———. *Numbers: A Commentary*. OTL. Philadelphia: Westminster, 1968.

Nysse, Richard. "Yahweh Is a Warrior." *Word & World* 7 (1987) 192–201.

O'Connell, Kevin G., D. Glenn Rose, and Lawrence E. Toombs. "Tell El-Ḥesi, 1977." *PEQ* 1978, 75–90.

del Olmo Lete, G. *Mitos y leyendas de Canaan segun la tradicion de Ugarit*. Institucion San Jeronimo para la Investigacion Biblica, Fuentes de la Ciencia Biblica 1. Madrid: Ediciones Cristiandad, 1981.

del Olmo Lete, G., and J. Sanmartín. *Diccionario de la lengua ugarítica*, vol. 1, Aula Orientalis-Supplementa 7. Barcelona: Editorial Ausa, 1996.

Orni, Efraim and Elisha Efrat. *Geography of Israel*. 3rd ed. Philadelphia: Jewish Publication Society, 1973.

Otto, Rudolf. *The Idea of the Holy*. Oxford: Oxford University Press, 1958.

Parker, Simon B. "Shahar שחר" *DDD*, 1424–28.

Patai, Raphael. "The 'Control of Rain' in Ancient Palestine: A Study in Comparative Religion." *HUCA* 14 (1939) 251–86.

Paul, Shalom M. "Psalm 72:5—A Traditional Blessing for the Long Life of the King." *JNES* 31 (1972) 351–55.

Pennock, Robert T. *Tower of Babel: The Evidence against the New Creationism*. Cambridge: MIT, 1999.

Plastaras, James. *The God of Exodus: The Theology of the Exodus Narratives*. Milwaukee: Bruce, 1966.

Podechard, E. "Psaume LXVIII." *RB* 54 (1947) 502–20.
———. "Psaume 110." In *Études de critique et d'histoire religieuses*, Bibliothèque de la faculté catholique de théologie de Lyon 2. Léon Vaganay Festschrift, 7–24. Lyon: Facultés Cathliques, 1948.
Pope, Marvin H. *Job: A New Translation with Introduction and Commentary*. AB 15. Garden City, NY: Doubleday, 1986.
Prinz, H. "Lightning in History." In *Lightning, Volume 1: Physics of Lightning*, edited by R. H. Golde, 1–21. London: Academic Press, 1977.
Pritchard, James B., ed. *Ancient Near Eastern Texts Relating to the Old Testament*. 3rd ed. Princeton: Princeton University Press, 1969.
Ptolemy, Claudius. *The Geography*. Edited and translated by Edward Luther Stevenson. New York: Dover, 1991.
von Rad, Gerhard. *Genesis: A Commentary*. OTL. Philadelphia: Westminster, 1972.
Raikes, Robert. *Water, Weather and Prehistory*. New York: Humanities, 1967.
Raphael, C. Nicholas. "Geography and the Bible (Palestine)." *ABD* II, 964–77.
Rendsburg, Gary A. "Hebrew *rḥm* = 'rain.'" *VT* 33 (1983) 357–62.
———. *Linguistic Evidence for the Northern Origin of Selected Psalms*. SBLMS 43. Atlanta: Scholars, 1990.
Reymond, Philippe. *L'eau, sa vie, et as signification dans l'Ancient Testament*. VT Supp 6. Leiden: Brill, 1958.
Rim, M. "Interpretation of Polymorphic Profiles in Soils of the Eastern Mediterranean: An Analysis of the Geophysical Factor in Soil Genesis." *IEJ* 4 (1954) 266–77.
Ritter, Carl. *The Comparative Geography of Palestine and the Sinaitic Peninsula*. 4 vols. New York: Appleton, 1866.
Robinson, Edward. *Biblical Researches in Palestine and the Adjacent Regions: A Journal of Travels in the Years 1838 & 1852*. 3 vols. 3rd ed. London: Murray, 1867.
Rogers, Benjamin Bickley, tr. *Aristophanes I: The Acharnians, The Knights, The Clouds, The Wasps*. The Loeb Classical Library. Cambridge: Harvard University Press, 1967.
Rosenan, N. "One Hundred Years of Rainfall in Jerusalem: A Homotopic Series of Annual Amounts." *IEJ* 5 (1955) 137–53.
Rosenzweig, Cynthia. "Agriculture and Climate." In *Encyclopedia of Climate and Weather*, edited by Stephen H. Schneider, 20–25. 2 vols. Oxford: Oxford University Press, 1996.
Rummel, Stan, ed. *Ras Shamra Parallels: The Texts from Ugarit and the Hebrew Bible*, vol. III. AnOr 51. Rome: Pontificium Insitutum Biblicum, 1981.
Ryan, William, and Walter Pitman. *Noah's Flood: The New Scientific Discoveries about the Event that Changed History*. New York: Simon & Schuster, 1999.
Sabourin, Leopold. "The Biblical Cloud: Terminology and Tradition." *BTB* 4 (1974) 290–311.
Sarna, Nahum M. *Exploring Exodus: The Heritage of Biblical Israel*. New York: Schocken, 1986.
———. *Exodus*. The JPS Torah Commentary. Philadelphia: Jewish Publication Society, 1991.
———. *Genesis*. The JPS Torah Commentary. Philadelphia: Jewish Publication Society, 1989.

———. "Psalm xix and the Near Eastern Sun-God Literature." In *Fourth World Congress of Jewish Studies: Papers*, 171-75. (Jerusalem: World Union of Jewish Studies, 1967).

———. "Psalm 89: A Study in Inner Biblical Exegesis." In *Biblical and Other Studies*, Philip W. Lown Institute of Advanced Judaic Studies Brandeis University, Studies and Texts 1, edited by Alexander Altmann, 29-46. Cambridge: Harvard University Press, 1963.

de Savignac, J. "Theologie pharaonique et messianisme d'Israël." *VT* 7 (1957) 82-90.

Schenker, Adrian. "Gewollt dunkle Wiedergaben in LXX? Am Beispiel von Ps 28 (29), 6." *Biblica* 75 (1994) 546-55.

Schmidt, B. B. "Moon." *DDD*, 1098-1113.

Schmitz, Kenneth L. "World and Word in Theophany." *Faith and Philosophy* 1 (1984) 50-70.

Schneider, Stephen H., ed. *Encyclopedia of Climate and Weather*. 2 vols. Oxford: Oxford University Press, 1996.

Schnider, Franz. "Rettung aus Seenot: Ps 107,23-32 und Mk 4,35-41." In *Freude an der Weisung des Herrn: Beiträge aur Theologie der Psalmen. Festgabe zum 70. Geburtstag von Heinrich Groß*, Stuttgarter Biblische Beiträge 13, 375-93. Stuttgart: Verlag Katholische Bibelwerk GmbH, 1986.

Schnutenhaus, Frank. "Das Kommen und Erscheinen Gottes im Alten Testament." *ZAW* 76 (1964) 1-22.

Schreiner, Stefan. "Psalm CX und die Investitur des Hohenpriesters." *VT* 27 (1977) 216-22.

Schwab, Eckart. "Das Dürremotiv in I Regum 17,8-16." *ZAW* 99 (1987) 329-39.

Scorer, Richard and Arjen Verkaik. *Spacious Skies*. Newton Abbot, UK: David & Charles, 1989.

Scott, R. B. Y. "Dew." *IDB* 1, 839.

———. "Meteorological Phenomena and Terminology in the Old Testament." *ZAW* 64 (1952) 11-25.

———. "Palestine, Climate of." *IDB* 3, 621-26.

Seybold, Klaus. "Die Geschichte des 29. Psalms und ihre theologische Bedeutung." *TZ* 36 (1980) 208-19.

Shalem, N. "Le stabilité du climat en Palestine." *RB* 78 (1951) 54-74.

Shanan, L., M. Evenari, and N. H. Tadmor, "Rainfall Patterns in the Central Negev Desert." *IEJ* 17 (1967) 163-184.

Shoemaker, W. R. "The Use of רוּחַ in the Old Testament, and of πνεῦμα in the New Testament: A Lexicographical Study, Part I." *JBL* 23 (1904) 13-35.

Simpson, Robert H., and Herbert Riehl. *The Hurricane and Its Impact*. Baton Rouge: Louisiana State University Press, 1981.

Skehan, Patrick W. "Strophic Structure in Psalm 72 (71)." *Biblica* 40 (1959) 302-8.

Slayton, Joel C. "Pillar of Fire and Cloud." *ABD* V, 372-73.

Smith, Mark S. "Baal's Cosmic Secret." *UF* 16 (1984) 295-98.

———. "The God Athtar in the Ancient Near East and His Place in KTU 1.6 I." In *Solving Riddles and Untying Knots: Biblical Epigraphic, and Semitic Studies in Honor of Jonas C. Greenfield*, edited by Ziony Zevit, Seymour Gitin, and Michael Sokoloff, 627-40. Winona Lake, IN: Eisenbrauns, 1995.

———. "'Seeing God' in the Psalms: The Background to the Beatific Vision in the Hebrew Bible." *CBQ* 50 (1988) 171-83.

———. *The Ugaritic Baal Cycle: Volume 1. Introduction with Text, Translation and Commentary of KTU 1.1—1.2*. VTS 55. Leiden: Brill, 1994.
Smothers, Edgar R. "The Coverdale Translation of Psalm LXXXIV." *HTR* 38 (1945) 245-69.
Somerville, Richard C. J. "Weather and Climate." In *Encyclopedia of Climate and Weather*, Vol. 1, edited by Stephen H. Schneider, 127-29. Oxford: Oxford University Press, 1996.
Speiser, E. A. *Genesis: A New Translation with Introduction and Commentary*. AB 1. New York: Doubleday, 1962.
Spieckermann, Hermann. "Alttestamentliche 'Hymnen.'" In *Hymnen der Alten Welt im Kulturvergleich*, OBO 131, edited by W. Burkert and F. Stolz, 97-108. Göttingen: Vandenhoeck & Ruprecht, 1994.
———. "'Die ganze Erde ist seiner Herrlichkeit voll': Pantheismus im Alten Testament?" *Zeitschrift für Theologie und Kirche* 87 (1990) 415-36.
Stadelmann, Luis I. J. *The Hebrew Conception of the World: A Philological and Literary Study*. Analecta Biblica 39. Rome: Pontifical Biblical Institute, 1970.
Sterk, Jan P. "An Attempt at Translating a Psalm [110]." *The Bible Translator* 42 (1991) 437-42.
Stevenson, Gregory M. "Communal Imagery and the Individual Lament: Exodus Typology in Psalm 77." *Restoration Quarterly* 39 (1997) 215-29.
Stiebing, William H., Jr. "Did the Weather Make Israel's Emergence Possible?" *BR* 10 (1994) 18-27, 54.
———. *Out of the Desert? Archaeology and the Exodus/Conquest Narratives*. New York: Prometheus, 1989.
Street-Perrott, F. Alayne, and R. Alan Perrott. "Abrupt Climate Fluctuations in the Tropics: The Influence of Atlantic Ocean Circulation." Review article. *Nature* 343 (1990) 607-12.
Strobel, A. "Le psaume LXIV." *RB* 57 (1950) 161-73.
Sukenik, E. L. "The Account of David's Capture of Jerusalem." *JPOS* 8 (1928) 12-16.
Sutcliffe, Edmund F. "The Clouds as Water-Carriers in Hebrew Thought." *VT* 3 (1953) 99-103.
———. "A Note on Psalm CIV 8." *VT* 2 (1952) 177-79.
Tadmor, H., and M. Weinfeld, eds. *History, Historiography and Interpretation: Studies in Biblical and Cuneiform Literatures*. Jerusalem: Magnes, 1984.
Talmon, S. "The Gezer Calendar and the Seasonal Cycle of Ancient Canaan." *JAOS* 83 (1963) 177-87.
Tate, Marvin E. *Psalms 51-100*. WBC 20. Dallas: Word, 1990.
Taylor, J. Glen. *Yahweh and the Sun: Biblical and Archaeological Evidence for Sun Worship in Ancient Israel*. SJOT 111. Sheffield, UK: JSOT, 1993.
Thomson, William M. *The Land and the Book or Biblical Illustrations Drawn from the Manners and Customs, the Scenes and Scenery, of the Holy Land. Volume 1: Southern Palestine and Jerusalem*. New York: Harper, 1880.
Tomback, Richard S. *A Comparative Semitic Lexicon of the Phoenician and Punic Languages*. SBL Dissertation Series 32. Missoula, MT: Scholars, 1978.
van der Toorn, Karel, Bob Becking and Pieter W. van der Horst, eds. *Dictionary of Deities and Demons in the Bible*. 2nd ed. Leiden: Brill, 1999.
Torczyner, H. "The Firmament and the Clouds: *Rāqîaʿ* and *Sheḥāqîm*." *StTh* 1 (1948) 188-96.

Tournay, Raymond Jacques. "Le psaume CXLIV: structure et interprétation." *RB* 91 (1984) 520–30.

———. "Les psaume LXVIII et le livre des Juges." *RB* 66 (1959) 358–68.

———. "Le psaume CX." *RB* 67 (1960) 5–41.

———. *Seeing and Hearing God with the Psalms: The Prophetic Liturgy of the Second Temple in Jerusalem*. JSOTS 118. Sheffield, UK: JSOT, 1991.

Treves, Marco. "Two Acrostic Psalms." *VT* 15 (1965) 81–90.

Tromp, Nicholas J. "Water and Fire on Mount Carmel: A Conciliatory Suggestion." *Biblica* 56 (1975) 480–502.

Tsonis, Anastasios A. "Climate." In *Encyclopedia of Climate and Weather*, Vol. 1, edited by Stephen H. Schneider, 122–26. Oxford: Oxford University Press, 1996.

Ullendorff, Edward. "Ugaritic Studies with Their Semitic and Eastern Mediterranean Setting." *BJRL* 46 (1963) 236–49.

Uman, Martin A. *All About Lightning*. New York: Dover, 1986.

———. *Lightning*. New York: Dover, 1984.

Uval, Beth. "The Dew of Heaven (Gen. 27:28)." *JBQ* 26 (1998) 117–18.

Vawter, Bruce. *On Genesis: A New Reading*. Garden City, NY: Doubleday, 1977.

Veijola, Timo. "Davidverheißung und Staatsvertrag: Beobachtungen zum Einfluß altorientalischer Staatsvertäge auf die biblische Sprache am Beispiel von Psalm 89." *ZAW* 95 (1983) 9–31.

———. *Verheissung in der Krise: Studien zur Literature und Theologie der Exilszeit anhand des 89. Psalms*. Suomalaisen Tiedeakatemian Tiomituksia Annales Academiæ Scientiarum Fennicæ: Sarja-Ser. B Nide-Tom. 220. Helsinki: Suomalainen Tiedeakatemia, 1982.

———. "The Witness in the Clouds: Ps 89:38." *JBL* 107 (1988) 413–17.

Vogt, Ernst. "Die Aufbau von Ps 29." *Biblica* 41 (1960) 17–24.

———. "'Die Himmel troffen' (Ps 68,9)?" *Biblica* 46 (1965) 207–9.

———. "'Regen in Fülle' (Psalm 68,10–11)." *Biblica* 46 (1965) 359–61.

Wagner, Andreas. "Ist Ps 29 die Bearbeitung eines Baal-Hymnus?" *Biblica* 77 (1996) 538–39.

Walter, Irene and Jacob. "Flora." *ABD* 2:803–17.

Waltke, Bruce K., and M. O'Connor. *An Introduction to Biblical Hebrew Syntax*. Winona Lake, IN: Eisenbrauns, 1990.

Ward, James M. "The Literary Form and Liturgical Background of Psalm LXXXIX." *VT* 11 (1961) 321–39.

Watkins, Trevor. "The Beginnings of Warfare." In *Warfare in the Ancient World*, edited by John Hackett, 15–35. New York: Facts on File, 1989.

Watson, Wilfred G. E. *Classical Hebrew Poetry: A Guide to its Techniques*. JSOTS 26. Sheffield, UK: JSOT, 1986.

Weinfeld, Moshe. "Divine Intervention in War in Ancient Israel and in the Ancient Near East." In *History, Historiography and Interpretation: Studies in Biblical and Cuneiform Literatures*, edited by H. Tadmor and M. Weinfeld, 121–47. Jerusalem: Magnes, 1984.

———. "'Rider of the Clouds' and 'Gatherer of the Clouds.'" *JANES* 5, Gaster Festschrift (1973) 421–26.

Weiser, Artur. *The Psalms: A Commentary*. OTL. Philadelphia: Westminster, 1962.

Weiss, Harvey, and Raymond S. Bradley. "What Drives Societal Collapse?" *Science* 291 (2001) 609–10.

Wiggins, Steve A. "Between Heaven and Earth: Absalom's Dilemma." *JNSL* 23 (1997) 73–81.

———. "Pidray, Tallay and Arsay in the Baal Cycle." *JNSL* 29 (2003) 83–101.

———. *A Reassessment of "Asherah": A Study according to the Textual Sources of the First Two Millennia B.C.E.* AOAT 235. Neukirchen-Vluyn: Neukirchener Verlag, 1993.

———. "Tempestuous Wind Doing Yhwh's Will: Perceptions of the Wind in the Psalms." *SJOT* 13 (1999) 3–23.

———. "What's in a Name? Yariḫ at Ugarit." *UF* 30 (1998) 761–79.

———. "Wheel, Tumbleweed or Whirlwind? גַּלְגַּל in the Hebrew Bible." *Maarav* 15.2 (2008) [2010] 175–92.

———. "The Weather under Baal: Meteorology in KTU 1.1–6." *UF* 32 (2000) 577–98.

———. "Yahweh: The God of Sun?" *JSOT* 71 (1996) 89–106.

Wigley, T. M. L., and G. Farmer. "Climate of the Eastern Mediterranean and Near East." In *Palaeoclimates, Palaeoenvironments and Human Communities in the Eastern Mediterranean Region in Later Prehistory*, BAR International Series 133 (i), edited by John L. Bintliff and Willem Van Zeist, 3–37. Oxford: B.A.R., 1982.

Wilk, Stephen R. "The Meaning of the Thunderbolt." *Parabola* 17 (1992) 72–79.

Williams, Jack. *The Weather Book*. New York: Vintage, 1992.

Williams-Forte, Elizabeth. "Symbols of Rain, Lightning, and Thunder in the Art of Anatolia and Syria." In *Aspects of Art and Iconography: Anatolia and Its Neighbors: Studies in Honor of Nimet Özgüç*, edited by M. J. Melliak, E. Porada, and T. Özgüç, 185–90. Ankara: Türk Tarih Kurumu Basimevi, 1993.

Wolff, Hans Walter. "Psalm 110, 1–4." In *Herr, tue meine Lippen auf: Eine Predigthilfe*, vol. 5, 2nd ed., edited by Georg Eichholz, 310–23. Wuppertal-Barmen: Emil Müller Verlag, 1964.

World Meteorological Organization. *International Cloud Atlas*, vol. I. Geneva: World Meteorological Organization, 1956.

———. *International Cloud Atlas*, vol. II. Geneva: World Meteorological Organization, 1987.

van der Woude, A. S., ed. *In Quest of the Past: Studies on Israelite Religion, Literature and Prophetism, Papers Read at the Joint British-Dutch Old Testament Conference, held at Elspeet, 1988*. OTS 26. Leiden: Brill, 1990.

Wyatt, N. "ʿAttar and the Devil." *Transactions of the Glasgow University Oriental Society* 25 (1973–74) 85–97.

———. "Baʿal's Boars." *UF* 19 (1987) 391–98.

———. "The Hollow Crown: Ambivalent Elements in West Semitic Royal Ideology." *UF* 18 (1986) 421–36.

———. "Quaternities in the Mythology of Baʿal." *UF* 21 (1989) 451–59.

———. "The Titles of the Ugaritic Storm-God." *UF* 24 (1992) 403–24.

Yadin, Yigael. *The Art of Warfare in Biblical Lands in the Light of Archaeological Discovery*. London: Weidenfeld and Nicolson, 1963.

Yom-Tov, Y., and E. Tchernov, eds. *The Zoogeography of Israel*. Dordrecht: Junk, 1988.

Young, Serinity. "Religion and Weather." In *Encyclopedia of Climate and Weather*, edited by Stephen H. Schneider, 639–43. Oxford: Oxford University Press, 1996.

Zenger, Erich. *A God of Vengeance? Understanding the Psalms of Divine Wrath*. Louisville: Westminster John Knox, 1994.

Zevit, Ziony, Seymour Gitin, and Michael Sokoloff, eds. *Solving Riddles and Untying Knots: Biblical Epigraphic, and Semitic Studies in Honor of Jonas C. Greenfield.* Winona Lake, IN: Eisenbrauns, 1995.

Zohary, Michael. "Ecological Studies in the Vegetation of the Near Eastern Deserts: I—Environment and Vegetation Classes." *IEJ* 2 (1952) 201–15.

———. *Plants of the Bible: A Complete Handbook to all the Plants.* Cambridge: Cambridge University Press, 1982.

Ancient Document Index

ANCIENT NEAR EASTERN DOCUMENTS—UGARITIC

KTU 1.2 i 32	44, 74
KTU 1.2 iv 8	118n134
KTU 1.2 iv 29	118n134
KTU 1.3 i 24–25	138n84
KTU 1.3 ii 40	118n134
KTU 1.3 iii 7	138n84
KTU 1.3 iii 38	118n134
KTU 1.3 iv 4	118n134
KTU 1.3 iv 6	118n134
KTU 1.3 iv 51	138n84
KTU 1.3 v 42	138n84
KTU 1.4 iii 11	118n134
KTU 1.4 iii 18	118n134
KTU 1.4 v 60	118n134
KTU 1.5 ii 7	118n134
KTU 1.10 I 7	118n134
KTU 1.10 iii 36	118n134
KTU 1.14 iii 7	68
KTU 1.19 i 44	118n134
KTU 1.23	137
KTU 1.92 37	118n134
KTU 1.92 40	118n134

HEBREW BIBLE

Genesis

1	72, 74, 40
19:24	40
31:36	37
31:40	132, 133, 134

Exodus

9	123
9:13–35	96
9:18–26	122
9:22–26	44
9:23–24	122, 124
9:23b–24	45
9:24	45, 48
13:21	46, 112
14:19	113
14:21	33
15	33, 122n11
16:13–14	109
16:14	123
17:1–7	55
33:19	53

Leviticus

26:36	63n2

Numbers

11:8	143, 143n7
11:31–35	79

Deuteronomy

28:12	75
28:22	37
33:26	118

Joshua

10:11	121

Judges

4–5	78
5:4–5	93n40, 94, 94n46
9:48	126

1 Samuel

17:53	37

2 Samuel

5:8	51n79
17:12	86
22	32, 42n54, 65
22:11	64
22:12	105
22:14	42n54, 50n77
22:16	65
22:43	66

2 Kings

2:21	133n56
4:41	133n56
6:11	23

Isaiah

5:11	37
17:13	70, 70n30, 70n35, 71, 80
19:7	63n2
41:2	63n2

Jeremiah

10:13	75, 115n117
36:30	132, 133, 134
51:16	75, 115n117

Lamentations

4:19	37
5:10	64

Ezekiel

1:22	132
24:10	37
43:24	133n56
47:19	94n43
48:28	94n43

Hosea

8:7	71

Joel

2:23	98
2:24	89n20
3–4	15n13
4:13	89n20
4:14b–16	15n13

Obadiah

18	37

Jonah

1:4	23

Micah

5:6 [7]	86

Job

6:16	132, 133
13:25	63n2
32:13	63n2
37:10	132, 133
38:22	75, 109n97
38:22–24	56
38:25	90
38:28	137
38:29	132, 134
39:1	61

Psalms

1	152n4
1:3	148, 150
1:4	63, 66, 81
2:7	136
4:7 [6]	141
5:10 [9]	29

7	152n4	35:5	63, 66, 73, 81
7:13 [12]	36	36	152n4
7:14 [13]	36, 37, 38, 49	36:6 [5]	101, 105, 107, 108, 111, 119
8:9 [8]	39	36:10 [9]	140
8:13 [12]	39	37:2	148, 150
8:14 [13]	39	37:6	141
10:2	37n40	38	152n4
11	152n4	38:3 [2]	36, 38, 49
11:6	39, 49, 63, 81, 83, 101	38:4–9 [3–8]	38
17:15	141	38:13 [12]	29
18	5, 8, 40, 42n54, 51, 65, 102, 106, 114, 152n4	39:4 [3]	141
		42	52, 152n4
18:8 [7]	41	42:2	52
8–16 [7–15]	32	42:3 [2]	141
18:9 [8]	39, 40, 49, 60	42:7 [6]	53
18:10 [9]	101, 114, 119	42:8 [7]	51–54, 59, 61
18:11 [10]	63, 64, 72, 73, 81	42:9 [8]	53
18:12 [11]	105	43:3	140
18:13 [12]	102, 119	44:4 [3]	141
18:13–14 [12–13]	41, 47, 49, 121, 124	46	8
		46:7 [6]	141
18:14 [13]	50, 61	48	152n4
18:15 [14]	31, 32, 33, 35, 36, 38, 49	48:8 [7]	63, 67, 75, 79, 81
		50	142, 144, 152n4
18:16 [15]	65, 81	50:1–3	141, 144
18:29 [28]	140	50:3	24, 30, 39, 42, 49
18:43 [42]	66, 81	51	152n4
18:44 [43]	32	51:9 [7]	125, 131
18:51 [50]	32	52:4 [2]	29
19	152n4	52:9 [7]	29
19:2–7 [1–6]	142	52:11	29
19:5–7 [4–6]	140	55	152n4
19:7 [6]	142, 145, 149	55:3 [2]	25
21	8	55:9 [8]	24, 26, 28, 30, 63, 68, 81
21:10 [9]	141	55:10 [9]	25
27:1	140	55:12 [11]	29
29	7, 8, 11n3, 12, 51, 57, 58n99, 152n4, 160	57	152n4
		57:2 [1]	29, 29n16, 30
29:3	51, 61	57:11 [10]	101, 105, 107, 111, 119
29:5	58		
29:7	47	58	152n4
29:8	60	58:10 [9]	24, 25, 30
29:9	60	65	7, 8, 11n3, 12, 88, 95, 95n55, 152n4
31:17 [16]	141		
32	152n4	65:10 [9]	91
32:4	143, 145, 149	65:10–11 [9–10]	83, 88, 100
33:7	75	65:12 [11]	99n67
35	152n4	67:2 [1]	141

Psalms (continued)

68	xii, 8, 54, 94, 118, 152n4
68:3	63n2
68:5 [4]	54, 101, 117, 119
68:8 [7]	94, 95
68:8–9 [7–8]	94, 100
68:8–10 [7–9]	83, 93
68:9 [8]	95
68:9–10 [8–9]	100
68:10 [9]	95, 100
68:11 [10]	99n67n68
68:15 [14]	125, 126, 131
68:33 [32]	54
68:33–36 [32–35]	54
68:34 [33]	54, 61, 118
68:34–35 [33–34]	54
68:35 [34]	54, 101, 105, 108, 119
69:25 [24]	141
72	152n4
72:4	85
72:4–14	86
72:5	84, 141
72:5–7	84
72:6	83, 84, 85, 91, 101
72:8	85
72:14	85
72:15	85
72:17	141
74:16	140
74:17	146, 150
77	33, 106, 152n4
77:17 [16]	33, 39, 92, 106
77:17–21 [16–20]	80
77:18 [17]	36, 38, 55, 83, 92, 95, 100, 101, 105, 106, 119
77:18–19 [17–18]	49, 54, 60, 61
77:19 [18]	28, 31, 32, 36, 55, 70, 71, 79, 81
77:21 [20]	80
78	79, 122, 152n4
78:8–53	79
78:14	101, 112, 113, 119
78:23	101, 105
78:23–24	108, 119
78:24	83, 86, 101, 109
78:26	79, 81
78:26–27	79
78:27	87, 101
78:32	81
78:39	63, 69, 76, 81
78:44–53	122
78:47	122
78:47–48	48, 121, 122, 124
78:48	48, 49, 122
79:5	141
80:4 [3]	141
80:8 [7]	141
80:20 [19]	141
81	55, 152n4
81:6 [5]	55
81:8 [7]	55, 61
83	8, 26, 152n4
83:14 [13]	28, 63, 69, 71, 79, 80, 81
83:16 [15]	24, 26, 28, 30, 77, 78, 81
84	152n4
84:7 [6]	83, 97, 100
84:12 [11]	142, 145
85	152n4
85:4 [3]	141
85:13 [12]	99
89	152n4
89:7 [6]	101, 105, 109, 119
89:16 [15]	141
89:37 [36]	141
89:37–38 [36–37]	110
89:38 [37]	119
89:47 [46]	141
90:6	148, 150
90:8	141
91:3	29
91:5	36
94:1	140
94:20	29
97	152n4
97:2	112, 114, 119
97:3	39, 43, 49
97:2–5	114
97:4	31, 33, 42, 47, 49
97:5	141, 147
99	152n4
99:7	101, 112, 119
103	152n4
103:15	72

103:16	63, 72, 81	133	152n4
104	7, 11n3, 12, 56, 67, 72, 103, 119, 152n4	133:3	135, 138, 139
		135	152n4
104:2–4	103	135:4	34
104:3	44, 64, 65, 72, 73, 74, 81, 100, 101, 103, 118, 119	135:5–7	34
		135:7	31, 34, 42, 47, 49, 56, 63, 75, 81, 83, 87, 100, 101, 115, 119
104:4	39, 43, 49, 66, 73, 74, 81	135:8–12	34
104:6	56	136:7–8	140
104:6–9	44, 72	140	152n4
104:7	56, 61	140:11 [10]	39, 46
104:10–12	97	144	8, 152n4
104:12	96	144:5	35, 141
104:13	72, 83, 96, 103	144:6	31, 35, 36, 38, 49
104:19	140	144:7	35
104:22	140	146	152n4
104:30	74, 76	146:4	63, 76, 81
105	44, 46, 152n4	147	88, 152n4
105:32	39, 44, 45, 48, 49, 83, 96, 101	147:8	83, 88, 100, 101, 104, 119
		147:9	88, 104
105:32–33	121, 123, 124	147:16	125, 129, 130, 131, 145
105:39	46, 113, 119	147:16–18	130, 131
107	27, 152n4	147:16–17	130, 146
107:25	24, 27, 28, 30, 63, 74, 81	147:17	76, 145, 147, 149
107:27	27	147:18	63, 76, 81, 130, 132, 147, 150
107:28	27		
107:29	27, 30	148	124, 152n4
108	152n4	148:3	141
108:5 [4]	101, 105, 111, 119	148:8	24, 28, 30, 39, 47, 49, 63, 77, 81, 101, 116, 121, 124, 125, 130, 131
110	152n4		
110:3	135, 139		
113:3	140		
118:27	140	**Proverbs**	
119:53	64, 141		
119:135	141	7:17	93n42
121:6	149	21:6	63n2
124:4	94n43	25:14	115n117
		26:23	37n40

Ancient Document Index 187

www.ingramcontent.com/pod-product-compliance
Lightning Source LLC
Chambersburg PA
CBHW031429150426
43191CB00006B/464